INTRODUCTION
TO THE
STUDY and PRACTICE OF LAW
IN A NUTSHELL
FIFTH EDITION

By
KENNEY F. HEGLAND
James E. Rogers Professor of Law
University of Arizona

THOMSON
— ★ — ™
WEST

Mat #40745000

Nutshell Series, In a Nutshell, the Nutshell Logo and West Group are trademarks registered in the U.S. Patent and Trademark Office.

COPYRIGHT © 1983, 1995 WEST PUBLISHING CO.
© West, a Thomson business, 2000, 2003
© 2008 Thomson/West
        610 Opperman Drive
        St. Paul, MN 55123
        1–800–313–9378

Printed in the United States of America

ISBN: 978–0–314–19415–2

TEXT IS PRINTED ON 10% POST CONSUMER RECYCLED PAPER

Lawyers—

In good times, jokes
In bad, friends.

*

A NOTE ON THE FIFTH EDITION

Working on a prior edition, I gave my student editor the umpteenth draft of the chapter on legal writing. "I think you need something on how to stop rewriting."

I failed. I have *extensively* rewritten. Some of the changes are cosmetic but others are substantive. The chapters on *study skills, exams*, and *legal argument, writtten and oral*, are much improved. It is not that I have changed my mind about things. It is just that, reviewing what I have previously written, I have seen new relationships, had new insights, and thought of better explanations. And there are always new jokes.

As to my student editor, she had asked the impossible: there is *no* magic moment when all is said and done. You will find this true studying law. Every time you go back to review you will have new insights; you will see nuances where once was only black and white; and you will deepen your understanding of law. Hopefully, along the way, you'll come up with some good jokes. But be forwarned:

Writing law, analyzing law, studying law, you are <u>never</u> done; you simply run out of time.

*

PREFACE

I started with a girl with some flowers in her hand walking in a room in a country house. Sentences simply grew into paragraphs, and paragraphs became a chapter. I knew I had started a novel but I didn't know what novel it was.

—Ian McEwan, on writing *Atonement*

In three years, give or take, you will be walking across a stage with a diploma in your hand. Weeks will grow into months and months will become a year. You will know you have started a career but you won't know what career it will be.

I am absolutely delighted to be with you. Over the years this book, now in its fifth edition, has introduced thousands of law students to the mysteries and joys of law school. It has made them better students and hence, down the road, better lawyers. I'm thrilled and, frankly, I'm humbled.

Now it's your turn. About to embark, you'll have fears, hopes, and dreams.

"Will I flunk out? Will I make a difference? Will my life be full and happy? Do I have to read the *whole* book?"

Alas, no matter how lofty our dreams, no matter how deep our fears, we live in the present moment.

No, you *don't* have to read the whole book, at least not now. A crib sheet follows.

That said, don't expect to kick back, underline, and nod off. *You'll throw pots*: you'll analyze judicial opinions, brief cases, take exams, practice writing, and critique legal memos. You'll be tempted to skip these exercises. *Resist.* Law school is famous for the *lack of feedback*; perhaps the first thing you'll turn in is the final exam (and the only feedback you will get is a grade). Do the exercises, then read my discussion of common mistakes and my suggestions for improvement. This may be the *only* feedback you'll get.

A quick word to *non-law student* readers. If someone close to you is a law student, you will get a good sense of what they are going through and may be a tad more tolerant of their grumbling. You will learn how the law works—not of the stuff of law (legal doctrines such as Free Speech or Equal Protection) but rather the *life* of law. You will see how judges make decisions, how lawyers plan lawsuits, and how they struggle with ethical issues. I'll even take you through a trial, not as exciting as *Law and Order*, but more real and almost.

Not bad read, that.

Here's the crib sheet.

The *Prologue* and *Parts One* (Legal Analysis) and *Two* (Study Skills) are *essential*. Read them *now*, *before* you start law school or in the first week or two. *Reread* them again during your first semester and things will become even clearer. *Part Three* focuses on exams and is obviously first semester reading. *Part Four* begins with a discussion as to how judges decide cases and then turns to legal writing and oral argument. These chapters can wait but not for long; you probably will be doing some writing and oral argument in the first months of law school. *Part Five* walks you through a jury trial and will help you understand how legal doctrines play out in the heat of battle; and, perhaps more to the point, help you understand your Civil Procedure course. *Part Six* deals with your second and third years in law school and with the kinds of legal careers that will open for you. It can wait.

Here now the more detailed overview.

Prologue: The best of schools, the worst of schools

Is there a method to the madness? Do our educational methods prepare you for the practice of law? Generations of law students have graduated without a clue.

Part One: Legal Analysis Made Simple

This is the heart of the entire matter. Working on your very first case, you will learn how our *common law* system works, and the promises and discontents of the doctrine of precedent. We'll look at statutory interpretation, meet standard arguments like "slippery slope," and grapple with some ethical issues that lawyers face. Work hard on this section and, perhaps without knowing it, you will begin "thinking like a lawyer."

Part Two: Study Skills

Legal study is unlike what you are used to. It stresses *application* over memorization. You will learn how to read appellate cases, how to brief them, and how to make the most of your classes. Of course, law school is stressful. This part closes with a chapter on *"Fear and Loathing in the First Year."* (You are not alone.)

Part Three: Exams

The first chapter is titled *Writing Law School Exams: The Only Skill Worth Having*. Not so. No matter your grades, never forget all you have accomplished. I'll give you some law and an exam to take. Then I'll walk you through a couple of answers so you can get a sense of what is expected. We'll also look at *multiple choice* exams.

Part Four: Written Legal Analysis and Oral Advocacy

Lawyers write. Lawyers argue. The chapters can supplement your writing course and help you through the scary time of Moot Court. There is a chapter "How Judges Decide" where one of the most closely guarded secrets of our profession is exposed: arguing before the United States Supreme Court is basically the same as arguing spilt milk in the kitchen. (*Never* concede this to your overly impressed relatives and friends).

Part Five: Litigation

Finally something to kick back and read. You'll walk through a typical lawsuit, from late-night television advertising to closing argument. You'll see a Complaint, read a deposition, hear jury instructions, and finally visualize yourself waxing poetic, bringing tears from the jurors and a knowing nod from the judge. And, as an extra, we solve the problem of the tree falling in the forest.

Part Six: Finishing School and Beginning a Career

Many have no idea what they will do after graduation. That is probably a good thing: even the best of plans change. The last two chapters of this book, which should be read sometime during your first year, will introduce you to the vast range of available options and give you some ideas on things to do during law school to see which might be right for you. One chapter describes the options in terms of variables, such as working with people versus working with ideas, contentiousness and *esprit de corps*. The next is a series of short pieces by lawyers doing various kinds of law jobs. Of course, before you begin your career, you will need to get by the last two years of law school. The first chapter of this part tells you how to get the most out of those years and includes a short history of American legal education.

ACKNOWLEDGMENTS

Over the years this book has gone through count-less drafts, edits, and discussions. I have been lucky enough to know so many insightful people who have generously shared their time, their questions, and their good ideas.

First my students, at Arizona, Harvard and U.C.L.A. Their insightful questions (and blank stares) have forced me time and again to think more deeply about matters I thought I understood.

For this edition I want to particularly thank Anthony King and Brooke Mickelson for their won-derful edit, and Barbara Lopez for catching all of the mistakes they missed. Paula Nailon and Lee Tucker reviewed several chapters and made valuable sug-gestions.

Other folks helped on this or previous editions: Jamie Ratner, Charles Ares, Stanley Feldman, Anna Medico-Stevens, Eric Bean, Amy Wilkens, Laura McKinny, Mohyeddin Abdulaziz, Barbara Atwood, Bill Boyd, Dan Dobbs, Carol Eliot, Toni Massaro, Suzanne Rabe, Andy Silverman, Karen Waterman, David Wexler and Winton Woods. At one point, Kay Kavanagh read the entire manuscript, made great suggestions and was marvelously supportive. (Struggling authors, send her your stuff.)

My sister, Sherina Cadmun, as always, played the tough, constructive critic. My parents, Edwina Kenney and "Heg", taught me so much about writing that, even though they are now gone, I know what they would say. I want to also thank my mentor George Gross, who not only helped with this draft but taught me, long ago, the joys of writing (but not, alas, the difference between "that" and "which). My sons, Robert, Alex, Caleb and Ben have all helped at various times and in various ways. Finally, Barbara, who always helps and always encourages

As to copyright permissions, I thank Scott Turow, *One L.* Excerpts reprinted with permission of G. G. Putman's Sons.

Finally, my two dear friends at U.C.L.A., Professors David Binder and Paul Bergman. In their numerous excellent books, they have always acknowledged the considerable intellectual debts they owe me. Most gracious. For example, in their recent *Lawyers as Counselors*, they basically admitted that my insightful suggestions were the core of the book's Chapter 23. The book runs twenty-two chapters. As Jack Benny once responded to such devastating wit:

"You would never get away with that if my writers were here."

OUTLINE

Page

Preface -- VII

Prologue -- 1

> The best of schools,
> the worst of schools.

Part One: Legal Analysis Made Simple

Overview -- 11

Chapter

1. The Second–Case in-the-World ------------------- 13

> Analyzing and distinguishing cases, deal-
> ing with cases of first impression and
> an opportunity for you to practice
> lawyering.

2. Case Analysis -------------------------------------- 24

> Legal argument as ping pong; on overrul-
> ing of prior cases and the appearance of
> permanence; and two more opportuni-
> ties for you to practice.

3. Case Synthesis -------------------------------------- 38

> Looking for underlying principles to
> explain the bloomin' confusion of case
> law: making law respectable by calling
> it a "science." And yet another oppor-
> tunity to practice.

Chapter   **Page**

4. Cases of First Impression --------------------------   50

How to argue social policy and defeat stock legal arguments; how to use hypotheticals and analogies; and how to trust, but challenge, your intuitions.

5. Statutory Interpretation ----------------------------   60

Interpreting statutes and avoiding arguments that eat Pittsburgh.

6. Some Questions of Jurisprudence ---------------   70

The promise of *stare decisis* (efficiency, predictability, equality) and its costs; some current jurisprudential debates— formalists, realists, law and economics, and CRITS.

7. Some Questions of Ethics --------------------------   86

Hired guns, moral actors, and some tips on how to resolve the difficult ethical issues that will surely come.

Part Two: Study Skills

Overview --   91

8. Studying Law: Application, not Memorization   94
What's your goal?

9. Reading Cases---   98

Tips on how to read cases and your first cadaver.

10. Briefing Cases --   111

Tips on how to "brief" cases and yet another cadaver.

Chapter   **Page**

11. Being There: Class --------------------------------- 129
      The pre and post game show, note-taking
        and raising your hand.

12. Study Aids, Study Groups, Outlining and Messy
      Casebooks --------------------------------------- 138
      Resisting the siren song of commercial
        outlines; the importance of writing;
        study groups; journals; and solving the
        forest/tree problem.

13. Fear and Loathing in the First Year ----------- 147
      On being the dumbest person in your
        class (everyone is).

Part Three: Exams

Overview -- 161

14. Writing Law School Exams: The Only Skill
      Worth Having --------------------------------- 163
      Goals, techniques, and the famous, infa-
        mous (?) *IRAC.*

15. Practice Test --- 175
      A typical law school exam question to
        answer.

16. The Tale of Two Answers ------------------------- 183
      Two answers to compare.

17. Multiple Choice Exams ---------------------------- 198
      All that glistens is not gold: how they are
        designed to fool you.

Chapter	**Page**

18. Zen and the Art of Exams ------------------------ 205
    Forget chapters 14, 15, 16, and 17. Be
    with the exam. Oooommmm.

Part Four: Legal Writing and Oral Advocacy

Overview -- 209

19. Spilt Milk: How Moms, and Judges, Decide   211
    Facts, policy, and staying consistent.

*20. Written Legal Analysis: Goals, Getting Bet-
    ter, and Getting Started* -------------------- 230
    Good legal writing is alike; bad legal writ-
    ing is bad in its own way. Some tips
    from novelists on how to start and how
    to get better.

21. Writing Tips ------------------------------------ 238

22. Murder Your Darlings -------------------------- 247

23. Writing Exercises ------------------------------ 253

24. Oral Argument ---------------------------------- 262
    Your goal—to help the court (really)—and
    how to achieve it, without passing out.

25. Oral Argument: An Example -------------------- 278

Part Five: Litigation

Overview -- 283

*26. Case Planning: The Interplay of Law and
    Fact—Backwards* ----------------------------- 285
    How lawyers plan cases; how they get
    paid; and the politics of jury instruc-
    tions.

Chapter

27. *Complaints, Answers, Pretrial Motions a* *Discovery* ------------------------------------
The paperwork of litigation (complaints, answers and motions) and pretrial discovery.

28. *Trials* --- 311
An overview of the trial process, from jury *voir dire* to closing argument. And the definitive answer to the question concerning the tree falling in a forest when no one is there to hear (or, if someone is there, is napping).

29. *K v. Landlord, Greatest Hits* --------------------- 324
The dynamics of trial—expert testimony, hearsay objections, cross-examination, and a plethora of lawyer scheming.

Part Six: Finishing School and Beginning a Career

Overview --- 343

30. *The Second and Third Years* -------------------- 345
Courses to take, activities to pursue, and a short history of legal education.

31. *Career Choices* -------------------------------------- 362
Opportunities, things to think about, and getting more information.

32. *Lawyers on Lawyering* ----------------------------- 379
Lawyers from various kinds of practices discuss what they do and what they like and don't like about the practice.

*

INTRODUCTION

TO THE

STUDY and PRACTICE OF LAW

IN A NUTSHELL

FIFTH EDITION

*

PROLOGUE

THE BEST OF SCHOOLS, THE WORST OF SCHOOLS

It won't be the same old stuff.

As an undergraduate you sat, taking notes; the professor lectured. You left, often inspired, occasionally depressed, but feeling that your life had *advanced*, you had learned new things:

"Sartre believed that essence precedes existence" (or vice versa—I'll look it up for the final).

"The Second Law of Thermodynamics suggests that entropy (a measure of disorder) will continue to increase until the universe becomes a mush of completely undifferentiated chaos."

"Sartre, had he known of the Second Law of Thermodynamics, would have been even more depressed."

Naturally, when you get to law school, you expect to go to class, sit back and *learn* the law.

"Murder is the unlawful killing of a human being."

"Minors don't have contractual capacity."

"Torts are not English muffins."

1

It is not to be. Law professors seldom lecture, rehashing last night's Chapter 22. In law school you won't read chapters at all; you'll read "judicial opinions," in law school vernacular, *"cases."*

After a trial, the loser appeals, raising legal points as to why the judgment was wrong. The appellate judges decide and write an *opinion* justifying their decision. Opinions recite the facts and then discuss, and resolve, the legal issues raised by those facts. These judicial opinions are the *cases* you will read to learn the law.

When you get to class, professors assume you understand the cases; their job is to put you to work. You won't passively take notes; you'll actively analyze the cases, testing their coherence, exposing their assumptions, and pondering their implications: "Let's change the facts of the case and see if it comes out the same way."

Classes are never boring; good ones are exhausting and confusing.

You'll leave class convinced that you lost ground: "Before class, I worked hard and finally figured what 'murder' is. I felt good about myself. Had a spring in my step. Then came class—people to the left of me, people to the right of me ... getting called on ... and questions, questions, questions. Never any answers! When the person next to me answered, was she right or wrong? The professor didn't say, only turned and called on someone else. What was the professor getting at? I no longer know what murder is.... Frankly, I don't think I even know what a human being is, much less an English muffin.''

Preparing for class isn't a cakewalk either. You don't skim text looking for central ideas; you'll struggle trying to figure out what the judges were saying—how did they get from A to C without mentioning B? Expect to be whipped by a two-page case. Partly it's the language. Much of the first year is *vocabulary building*, just like grade school:

''Marie, stand up and spell 'assumpsit.' ''

''Good, now, Jamie, use 'assumpsit' in a sentence.''

Bewildered, don't lament. You're not dumb; you speak the wrong language. Picture yourself in Greece, in a crowded restaurant. People are talking, apparently about events of great moment, and you don't understand a word.

''Oh, no ... I'm an idiot. I should never have come. I'm going to flunk Greece.''

Law exams are different, too. You won't be asked to regurgitate what you have learned (''Define murder.'') nor will you be given broad essay questions such as, ''Is Law Just?'' Law exams will require you to apply the law you have learned to new situations. You will be given little short stories filled with the stuff of human drama: neighbors arguing over the location of a fence, business people arguing over the meaning a contract, and criminal defendants claiming ''The Devil made me do it.'' It will be your job to ''discuss'' the case. What legal issues does it raise? What factors might a court use to resolve them? This is, by the way, exactly what lawyers do, day in, day out.

Law exams are great fun to *take,* and you will be surprised at how much you have learned and how competent you are becoming. (Law exams are *not* great fun to *worry* about.)

You will learn to *read carefully*—more carefully than ever before. Often you will have to reread a paragraph or sentence several times before you realize what that you thought was a discussion about D was really about B. You will become sensitive to the ambiguities of language (to the point of losing old friends, friends who prefer their familiar sloth, *"Can* you pass the salt?" to your newly minted precision, *"Will* you pass the salt *to me?"*) You will come to suspect the rush to judgment (it seems there is nothing so sweet to us humans as condemning others on the basis of third-hand gossip, partially overheard in noisy lunch rooms). You will come to appreciate that even the most despised among us have things that can be said on their behalf. In fact, you will get so good at seeing the other side that eventually you'll have a hard time getting mad at the plumber.

What's this about *"thinking like a lawyer?"* No one can really define it but that doesn't mean it's hype. Thomas Kuhn, in *The Structure of Scientific Revolutions*, describes the training of scientists. They repeat the grand experiments of the past, not to learn what those experiments disclosed, that's in the textbook, but to learn how to do science. At graduation, ask them, "What is good science?" They will smile meekly and shrug their shoulders; they can't define it *but they can recognize it and they can do it!*

Reading and struggling with opinions and statutes, you too are repeating the grand experiments of the past. At your graduation, if asked, "What is thinking like a lawyer?" you'll smile meekly and shrug: but you will be able to recognize it, and you'll do it.

One aspect of "thinking like a lawyer" can be defined. Paul Freund, the legendary Constitutional Law scholar at Harvard, called it *"Yes, but...."* reasoning. It contrasts sharply with our traditional mode of analysis, perfected on the playgrounds of our youth:

"Is so!"

"Is not!"

"Is so!"

"Is not, and I'm telling!"

Lawyers make difficult decisions. All have *costs.* Rather than denying them *(Not so! Not so!),* learn to acknowledge them: *"Yes,* that decision will lead to those negative consequences, *but* there are other considerations."

If you like grappling with the Big Questions, you'll love the law: free will and autonomy; the quest to predict and control the future (the stuff of Greek tragedy); the nature of knowledge and the

precision of language; the deep human need to have
rules and with the deep human need to be free of
rules; questions of justice and fairness and economic efficiency. Perhaps you considered all of these as
an undergraduate but, at the end of the day, you
went to the movies. Here, at the end of the day, we
must answer the question which triggers all the
others: what should we *do* in this particular case?
Will *this* accident victim recover? Will *this* contract
be enforced? Will *this* defendant walk free? Deciding, not merely discussing, makes all the difference.

Best of all, your classmates. From different col-
leges, of different ages, of different cultures, all
resulting in a marvelous mix of different insights
into the law and into the human condition. You will
learn so much from them. Each and every one,
smart. *Celebrate your classmates*. Don't hang back.
Before class, talk Property, debate abortion, complain about the profs. Recluses miss half their education.

All good law schools are alike. Go to Tennessee
Valley Night Law School and, once inside, you could
be at Harvard. Same cases, same books, same Nutshells (thankfully) and the same professional strut.
If you didn't get into your first choice, take comfort;
if you did, be humble.

All good law schools use "Socratic method." Under the professor's questioning, students extract
from judicial opinions the relevant rules of law.
This is a very cumbersome. It be a whole lot easier
to assign a text that simply comes out and tells you

what you need to know, that torts are not English muffins. *What does the Socratic method have to do with the practice of law*?

Everything!

Day in, day out, trying murder cases, negotiating widget contracts, and counseling divorce clients, lawyers focus on the *interplay of law and fact*. Legal rules gain meaning *only* in relation to specific factual patterns. Conversely, the facts of a given dispute are *only* relevant to the degree that they trigger the application of specific legal rules. Staying up late struggling to understand the assigned cases, being battered around in the class with new fact patterns and competing legal rules, you are focusing on the interplay of law and fact, learning how to apply legal principles to the new situations and how to evaluate the legal significance of various real life events. You're lawyering.

All of this will be strange and threatening; unchartered waters. You will be very uneasy. "Look, all of that stuff you've been writing is fine, but, at the end of the day, I gotta know whether a tort is an English muffin—not all the policies and arguments why it should be, not all the practicalities why it shouldn't be. I'm off to buy a study aid. I'll cram! Just like the good old days!".

William James, a founder of modern psychology, teaches that memory involves both retention and retrieval and that retrieval is improved as more paths leading to it are created. In his *Psychology: The Basic Course,* he warms of cramming:

> *Speedy oblivion is the almost inevitable fate of all that is committed to memory in this simple way. Whereas, on the contrary, the same materials taken in gradually, day after day, recurring in different contexts, considered in various relations, associated with other external incidents, and repeatedly reflected on, grow into such a system, form such connections with the rest of the mind's fabric, lie open to so many paths of approach, that they remain permanent possessions. This is the intellectual reason why habits of continuous application should be enforced in educational establishments.*

Think of the Socratic Method as *continuous application*. You will learn torts at a level that will be with you when you need it, in perhaps twenty or thirty years, long after your understanding of Sarte has itself fallen victim to the Second Law of Thermodynamics.

The uniformity of legal education means something else as well. All lawyers have gone through what you are about to. I don't care if your hero is Earl Warren, Anthony Scalia, Thurgood Marshall, or Sandra Day O'Connor; I don't care if your hero prosecutes vicious criminals or defends the downtrodden; I don't care if your hero advises the President or advertises on the Late Show. All of them once sat where you will sit; all of them read many of the cases you will read; all of them cursed the profs; all of them longed for clear rules; and, ultimately, all of them realized, "By Jove, I think I've got it . . . really got it!"

And so, dear friend, will you.

You are now part of a great tradition. Despite the jokes, it is a great tradition: that our country is as free and open as it is reflects, in significant part, the hard and often gutsy work of lawyers. Don't forget it! Don't forget to *do* it.

Don't forget one other thing. You have come to law school to become a *lawyer*, to use your knowledge and smarts to help others. In the hurly-burly of law school, you might forget this and come to believe what matters most is being a successful *law student*. If you don't get the grades you wished for, you might be tempted to "drop out in place" and get through the rest of school with minimum effort. Don't. You are here to become a great lawyer, not to be a great law student. Even if you get straight C's, you can still accomplish your goal, *but only* if you continue to push yourself.

Time to put away childish things. From now on, it's not about you; it's about your clients.

PART ONE

LEGAL ANALYSIS MADE SIMPLE

"Professors hide the ball!" A common first-year lament.

Here *is* the ball. Legal analysis.

Chapter 1 puts you in the position of a lawyer and gives you your first case. Working through it, you will consider the three questions that lie at the heart of our common law system: Should judges follow the rules announced in prior cases? Assuming they should, how does the system work? Finally, if there are no prior cases, how do judges decide?

Chapter 2 shows you how "cases" come to be and describes how judicial opinions are written. This will help you read cases for class. You will have the opportunity to practice an important lawyering skill: *arguing* and *distinguishing* cases. You will do a lot of this in your classes.

Chapter 3 describes the mechanics of *stare decisis* (the fancy name for following precedent). We will also look at *case synthesis*. While *case analysis* takes cases apart, *case synthesis* is the process of taking two or more cases and trying to find a rule that explains what at first may look like inconsistent results. We'll see how this works and note that it responds to the deep human need to impose order on an unruly universe.

Chapter 4 looks at "cases of first impression" (those where there is no controlling prior authority). Chapter 5 discusses a key lawyering skill, interpreting language, here in the context of statutory construction. Does "No Vehicles in the Park" include Big Wheels?

Chapter 6 extends our discussion of precedent. I'll briefly introduce some competing schools of legal thought: legal formalism, legal realism, critical legal studies and the law and economics movement. These great debates inform how law is taught. I'll also discuss a central problem in law: the general and the specific.

We'll end this Part with some ethical questions.

Read this part now. It may not be as simple as advertised, law isn't. But it will be quite helpful in the storms that surely shall come.

CHAPTER 1

THE SECOND–CASE-IN-THE-WORLD

There is only one game worth playing: the *"Second–Case-in-the-World Game."* It is the *key* to your entire legal education.

(There you have it. You have learned something *profound* in the very first paragraph! You're going to love this book.)

"Is it enough for us to know that the Second–Case-in-the-World *is* the only game worth playing or must we know *why* it is the only game worth playing?" Alas, a typical student question.

Alas, a typical professorial response:

"Knowing *why* is knowing *what.*"

("Wow, an incomprehensible, *Zen-like* sentence on the first page! This is gonna be great!")

The *what* of your legal education is the "law," such as the rule that minors don't have contractual capacity. *Why* don't they? Grappling with *why* the law is as it is, you will learn it (the *what*) at a much deeper level. Knowing *why* is knowing *what.*

I'll stress the *why* of things throughout the book. But it's time to meet your first client.

13

Ms. K. sustained grave personal injuries when she tripped on a common stairway in her apartment house. Inspection showed that the stairway was negligently maintained by her landlord: a step was defective.

This looks pretty good: you came to law school to help injured clients be compensated for injuries suffered at the hands of negligent landlords. But wait, there is an *egads*! In the lease Ms. K signed, you find:

Tenant agrees that Tenant shall not bring any action against Landlord for negligently maintaining any common areas of the apartment house, including common stairs.

This is known as an "exculpatory clause" and, unless you can get the judge to throw it out, Ms. K loses. You will want to make this argument:

"Your Honor, you should not enforce this clause because the law should not allow landlords to avoid liability for negligently harming tenants by inserting such clauses in the lease. They violate public policy and shouldn't be enforced."

Preparing your case, and doing some legal research, you run into yet another *egads*, the first case in the world:

Globe v. Credit Bureau

Scrooge, Chief Justice. *Plaintiff Globe hired defendant Credit Bureau to run a credit check on Paul Jones who wished to borrow money from plaintiff. Due to defendant's neglect, it failed to find a mort-*

gage that was on Jones' property; it reported that Jones had good credit. Had it found the outstanding mortgage, it would have labeled Jones a bad credit risk. Based on this favorable yet erroneous report, plaintiff lent Jones money that was not repaid.

Plaintiff sued defendant for negligence, arguing, "If it weren't for your negligence, I would not have lent the money, and thus, I would not have lost the money."

Defendant moved to dismiss plaintiff's case based on a clause in the contract between plaintiff and defendant wherein plaintiff agreed not to sue defendant for negligence. In response, plaintiff argued that the agreement not to sue should not be enforced by a court because it would violate public policy to do so.

We reject that argument. We do not believe that exculpatory clauses offend public policy and hence they will be enforced. We stress the importance of freedom of contract. If parties who make contracts cannot agree to limit the extent of liability, it is difficult to see where such a ruling would lead.

Judgment for the defendant.

Your life has just become much more complicated. If you argue "exculpatory clauses violate public policy," the judge will, gruffly, interrupt:

"Sorry, Counselor, Justice Scrooge has said that they don't and that's that!"

Back to the wall (when most creative lawyering gets done), you would first look at the relationship

between the first case (Globe) and the second case
(Ms. K's). Because K's is the second case, that
relationship has yet to be established. One possibility, and the one you would favor, is that there is *no*
relationship at all: what Justice Scrooge ruled has
no bearing on your case, it's pretty much like what
your Aunt Margaret had to say on the subject.

> *"Your Honor, what Justice Scrooge has to say
> doesn't matter at all. You should decide the matter
> anew."*

Landlord will argue the opposite: what Scrooge
said is the "law" and the judge in the next case, Ms.
K, must follow it. If you lose that argument, all is
not lost. You would argue that it is the "law" only
in situations like those presented in the *Globe* and
that the situation with Ms. K is very different.

> *"If what Scrooge said does matter, the case he was
> considering was so different than that of Ms. K
> that what he said doesn't apply to Ms. K. You
> should decide the matter anew.*

The *doctrine of precedent* and the *art of distinguishing cases* are basic to your legal education.
Let's take a quick look at them, beginning with the
question: *Why* should current judges pay attention
to what prior judges have ruled? Under our system,
they are committed to do so.

Precedent

At the core of our jurisprudence is the concept of
precedent or *stare decisis*. The root idea is that, in
reaching decisions, courts should follow the rules

laid down by judges in prior cases. If the first judge ruled, "Negligent drivers should pay, in addition to their victim's medical bills, compensation for their pain and suffering," then the second judge, when faced with a case of a negligent driver, should apply the same rule and allow compensation for pain and suffering. It would be improper for the judge to say, "Well, I don't think victims should get compensated for pain and suffering, and I'm going to do it my way!"

Let's back up and consider the matter anew. I want you to argue that the doctrine of precedent should *not* be followed. This gets to the *why*.

The matter is already decided so won't that be a waste of time to argue about it? *Never, not once, assume that the status quo makes sense*, that a group of wise folks sat down and planned things out and that they had "their reasons" and that we live in the best of all possible worlds. A lot of what we live is simply historical accident. Is law school three years because once a lot of professors and lawyers got together and after much study and debate decided three years was the time needed to educate a lawyer properly? No! Law schools are three years because the first law school was three years. That's the long and short of it.

It is only by questioning the "wise lessons of the past" that we can either embrace them or reject them. Learning today's Wisdom, don't just accept it, *challenge* it.

One way to challenge the status quo is to envision a different system and then compare. We could have a system where, when folks got into a dispute, they'd go to the designated Wise One and tell their stories. The Wise One would decide, free from the obligation to decide as did other Wise Ones.

What are the costs and benefits of requiring the Wise One to decide cases the same way prior Wise Ones have?

What are the costs and benefits of allowing the Wise One to decide cases without reference to prior decisions?

These questions might seem a tad abstract. Bring them down to your own experiences. Following past decisions is a familiar concept, no doubt employed by your parents ... *sometimes* ... and no doubt employed by yourself ... *sometimes*. Take an example from your past. "Last week, faced with the same situation, I did X. Should I do X now, merely because I did X last week?"

Take a few minutes and write out your answers to my questions. Writing is a marvelous way of learning. I will repeat this again and again and again, and some of you might actually try it once, probably sometime in November. I am a man of few illusions. But I know this because I live this: *Writing out your thoughts slows the mind, highlights gaps and inconsistencies, and deepens analysis.*

Of course, you can keep on reading, confident in the knowledge that eventually I will discuss the issue. When I do, you will learn something ... but knowledge you get from others is a tad lifeless and dead, something to be memorized and forgotten. The knowledge you develop yourself is, well, a triumph.

Jotting in the margin is not only permitted but encouraged, not only for your development as a law student, but also to shut down the second-hand market.

———————

If you can convince your judge to ignore Scrooge on the basis that precedent should not be followed, then you can jump ahead and try to convince the judge that exculpatory clauses violate public policy. But what if you lose your first move? "Nope, I am committed to the doctrine of precedent and Justice Scrooge has said '*We do not believe that exculpatory clauses offend public policy and hence they will be enforced.*'"

Is your goose cooked? Think. How might you respond?

Analyzing and Distinguishing Cases

Assume that we decide, as we have, that courts should follow prior cases. Assume now that we have two cases. In Case One, the judge announced Rule X. Under the doctrine of precedent, the judge in Case Two must apply Rule X but *only if* Case Two is sufficiently *like* Case One such that it would make sense to follow the rule of Case One.

As lawyers state the question, "Does Case One (and the rule of law it laid down) *control* Case Two?" This question introduces the art of legal analysis and legal argument. Its importance cannot be overstated; you will spend much of your first year perfecting this skill.

To say a case is *distinguishable* is like saying someone is quoting something out of context: "A table for one" has a different meaning if uttered in a restaurant as opposed to a morgue.

Take a close look at the *facts* of *Globe* and compare them with the facts of Ms. K. Based on these factual differences, you are to argue:

Your Honor, the rule laid down by Scrooge, that exculpatory clauses do not violate public policy, should not apply in this case because Globe is distinguishable in that . . . .

How are the cases factually different? (If you refuse to write, at least pause and think. Here is an opportunity to be right!)

To flesh out your argument you must not only point to factual differences but also indicate *why* they would matter. For example, the fact that the plaintiff names are different in the two cases would not alone justify a different outcome.

Why would it matter that we are dealing with a personal injury rather than a financial loss?

Why would it matter that we are dealing with a tenant and not a business?

Even if you convince the judge that *Globe* is *distinguishable*, all that means is that the judge *need not* follow the rule of that case: the judge can consider the matter anew. At least you are back to where we started:

> *"Your Honor, you should not enforce this clause because the law should not allow landlords to avoid liability for negligently harming tenants by inserting such clauses in the lease. They violate public policy and shouldn't be enforced."*

Cases of First Impression

Sometimes a judge is faced with a case where there is *no* controlling law and thus must decide it as a matter of *first impression*. This can happen if there have been *no* prior cases ruling on the issue or, if there have been, they are all *distinguishable* and thus do not *control*. (This also assumes that there are no controlling statutes on the subject, but we haven't gotten to statutes yet.)

What kinds of arguments should a judge consider in deciding a matter of first impression? Of course, a judge will want to do *justice between the parties*. While most would assume that justice is on the side of Ms. K, what would the landlord say? Put yourself in his shoes. Most people think they are in the right. Why does he?

Another concern of the judge would be to *create good law*. That is because whatever she decides will become a precedent and must be followed by future judges. Why would it be a good rule to strike exculpatory clauses in apartment house leases? *Flesh out the argument. Yes, but* what will the landlord say in response?

On the Need to See the Relationship Between Arguments

We have been considering three separate arguments on behalf of Ms. K.

1. That courts should *not* follow precedent; what Scrooge had to say is no more relevant than what your second cousin, once removed, has to say.

2. That *Globe* is distinguishable.

3. That the exculpatory clause in Ms. K's lease violates public policy and should not be enforced.

You must understand not only the various points but also the relationship between them. Legal arguments get complicated. A lawyer may make four basic points. Does the lawyer need to win all four points to win the case? Or will one victorious point carry the day? To raise your math anxiety, there are several possibilities:

$1+2+3+4$ = VICTORY

> Here the lawyer must prevail on all four points in order to win; lose one and it's back to late-night advertising.

$(1+2)$ or $(3+4)$ = VICTORY

> Here the lawyer doesn't have to win all the points, only either (1 and 2) *or* (3 and 4).

1 or 2 or 3 or 4 = VICTORY

Here, Hog Heaven.

There are several other combinations, such as $(1+2+3)$ or 4 = VICTORY. In our case, Ms. K makes three points:

1. Precedent shouldn't matter.

2. *Globe* is distinguishable.

3. As a matter of public policy, agreements not to sue should be rejected.

For her to win, fill in the blanks:

1 __ 2 __ 3 = VICTORY

At this point, **STOP!!!** Fill in the blanks and take this last opportunity to write your thoughts on the three topics. In the next chapters, I give you mine.

CHAPTER 2

CASE ANALYSIS

Judicial argument is quite somber and grown-up: the judges fearsome in black, the audience nervous with anticipation, a lawyer opening with "May it please the Court" and, sitting in the corner, a little old bailiff, whispering "Hush."

I like to think of it as *ping pong*.

One lawyer serves what he thinks will be a winner but his opponent fends it off, returning a crushing forehand which she believes will end the matter; but, with a quick turn of phrase, the first returns a deep one to her backhand; and on and on it goes until finally the judges yell, "Hold, enough!" and then scurry off to discuss and decide the case.

Let's do a play-by-play of the case we considered in the first chapter, *K v. Landlord*:

Landlord: You can't sue me because, in the lease you signed, you promised not to sue me.

Tenant: *Yes,* I made that promise, *but* it should not be enforced because it violates public policy.

Landlord: *Yes,* it might seem to, *but* the court rejected that argument in *Globe*.

Tenant: *Yes,* the court held that such clauses do not violate public policy, *but* the case is distinguishable because it involved a financial loss and not a personal injury. Second, *Globe* involved a contract signed by two business people, while our case involves a landlord and a tenant.

Landlord: *Granted,* there are factual differences between the two cases; *nonetheless,* the rule of *Globe* should apply, no matter the kind of injuries or the kind of contract, because the *rationale* of the case applies. It stands for the proposition that parties have freedom of contract and can make whatever agreements they please. The court in *Globe* stated, "The parties must be free to make their own contracts, and once the courts start rewriting them, there will be no end in sight."

Tenant: *Yes,* the Court said that, *but* those words were used in a particular factual context. The kinds of injuries do matter. It is one thing to agree not to sue for financial harm, but quite another to agree not to sue for doctors' bills and lost earnings. *True,* there is a great public interest in freedom of contract, *yet* there is also a great public interest in preventing physical injury. Allowing landlords to exempt themselves from liability will encourage them to be negligent, thus leading to more injuries.

Landlord: You would deny freedom of contract.

Tenant: *We agree* that freedom of contract is important; *however,* freedom of contract is premised on the notion of *equal bargaining* power, which assures both sides are making free choices. Who the parties are *does* matter. It is one thing to say that parties of equal bargaining power, as the two business people in Globe were, should be allowed to agree to what they will; it is quite another to allow a strong party to force a weak party into accepting his terms. And that's what we have in this case. Enforcing this term against Ms. K will *violate* her freedom of contract.

Judge Flintstone: (in desperation) *Hold, enough!*

Now, when lawyers actually argue a case, they don't go back and forth like this. One gets up and makes his argument, then the other gets up and makes hers, with the lawyer going first having a short time for rebuttal. Not to worry—there is a chapter on Legal Argument later. However, it is extremely helpful to think of legal argument as ping-pong because it helps you understand who is making what argument for what purpose.

So what happens after argument? The judges leave, discuss the case, and, eventually issue a written opinion.

K v. Landlord

Flintstone, J. *This case involves the validity of an exculpatory clause in an apartment lease where the tenant is suing for personal injuries caused by the alleged neglect of the landlord.* **While it is true** *that this court, in* **Globe,** *upheld an exculpatory clause, we note that was in the context of a commercial contract and involved only financial loss.* **Even though** *we quite properly give contracting parties* *great freedom to fashion their own agreements, and* **despite the fact** *that we are fearful of where voiding such agreements will lead us, we feel we must invalidate this agreement. We note that there is inherent unequal bargaining strength between landlords and tenants and that, in this case, the tenant is seeking recovery for personal injuries. A landlord, under traditional doctrine, has a duty to take reasonable steps to keep common areas safe; if we allow landlords to escape this duty by the simple expedient of a standard lease term, physical injuries that could be avoided will not be.*

Note that legal writing is marked by *words of contrast* which you should begin using:

> *On the one hand . . . .*
>
> *Although this is so, that is so.*
>
> *Even though . . . .*
>
> *However . . . .*
>
> *While X is true, so is*

Judges *write down the middle* by collapsing the competing arguments. They do not, for example, list all of Ms. K's points in one paragraph and then all of Landlord's in the next. That would be very awkward. It is much better to bring the competing contentions, point by point, together. This is very helpful and, as I will stress throughout this book, when contention meets counter-contention, one's analysis simply gets better: how can I resolve this conflict? Note that the court could have identified who was making which argument:

Landlord *argues that Globe upheld an exculpatory clause, and* **Ms. K** *responds that was in the context of a commercial contract and involved only financial loss.*

This gets awkward. To avoid this, don't label:

While it is true *that this court, in Globe, upheld an exculpatory clause, we note that was in the context of a commercial contract and involved only financial loss.*

Writing down the middle is the way to go: rub contention and counter-contention together and force your analysis deeper. In a sense you are restaging the ping-pong game. Note, however, that you don't have to identify the players.

A funny thing happens when the judges don't identify the players. The case reads as if the judges made it all up themselves. They didn't. Judges are like Gilbert and Sullivan's Ruler of the Queen's Navy: *"And I never thought of thinking for myself at all."*

Every case judges cite, every point judges make, they stole from one of the lawyers!

That judges never think of thinking for themselves at all is actually a virtue. Under our adversary system, all positions should be considered in the heat of battle.

Assume that K's lawyer argued only the personal injury aspect and did *not* bring up unequal bargaining. If Flintstone, on her own, decided the case on that issue, it would not be fair to the landlord. The landlord would not have had the opportunity to argue against it. Without his argument, the decision might be bad because, without being tested in adversarial fires, Judge Flintstone doesn't know how good the point is.

Yes, *but* if judges rely *only* on the arguments developed by counsel, injustice can result. What if Ms. K hired a dullard as a lawyer who overlooks key arguments? Should she lose a substantial case simply because she hired an incompetent?

Tough call. Respected judges go both ways on it.

Returning to ping-pong, a great device to help you understand a court decision is to *restage the game*. Figure out which party raised which point and why. To get a feel for this, recall that Judge Flintstone mentioned three points in the opinion:

Globe

commercial loss

freedom of contract

Which side brought up *Globe* and *why*? Which side brought up "commercial loss" and why? Which side argued "freedom of contract" and why? Jot! You have room.

Beginners answer only the "who brought it up?" question and not the "why?" question. Yes, Ms. K did bring up the matter of "commercial loss." But why?

Was she bringing it up as a knockout blow, one designed to convince the court to hold that the clause should not be enforced? Or was it merely a

counter-punch, one to ward off landlord's contention that the Court should follow the *Globe* case?

Cases get complicated:

I. Plaintiff's main contention.

    *A. Defendant's response to defeat that conten-
tion.*

    *1. Plaintiff's response to defendant's attack,
arguing that defendant's attack in fact falls
short.*

    *a. Defendant's response to plaintiff's re-
sponse, which, if correct, would defeat it.*

Often the judges, in their opinion, will focus solely
on the issue raised in (a) and go on at great lengths.
Understanding that the judges have decided that
the defendant wins point (a), without ping-ponging,
will not help you understand how this impacts the
ultimate outcome: "If the defendant wins (a), then
plaintiff's argument in (1) fails, which means that
defendant's argument in (A) is valid, and thus
plaintiff's main contention fails."

Admittedly, seldom will a professor ask, "Which
side raised that point? Cited that case? And for
what purpose?" So what's the value of replaying the
game? Understanding.

Returning to the case of *K v. Landlord*, note that
Judge Flintstone *distinguished* the case of *Globe*;
she did not *overrule* it. Judges can do this. Flintstone could have said:

"The case of *Globe* is simply not well thought-out. It is overruled. All exculpatory clauses are invalid as being against public policy."

That Flintstone chose not to do this tells us a lot about our case system.

On Overruling and the Appearance of Permanence

Sometimes courts *overrule* prior cases by admitting that they (or, more likely, their *predecessors*) got it wrong. The most famous overruling was in *Brown v. Board of Education,* which overruled the "separate but equal" doctrine of *Plessy v. Ferguson* and held segregated schools to be unconstitutional.

Once a case is overruled, it can't even come to the party. *Plessy v. Ferguson* is no longer good law: it has been overruled. Lawyers cannot use that case in their legal arguments. Had Flintstone overruled *Globe*, the next case would be resolved by looking only at *K v. Landlord*, with no reference to *Globe*.

Courts are very reluctant to overrule prior decisions. It presents a major theoretical problem. Judges, in reaching their decisions, are supposed to follow the law. If law comes from prior cases, where do they get the law to overturn a case? In addition, overruling threatens the notion of predictability. How can you ever rely on a case if a later court can overrule it? Take *Globe*. Even if the second case was on all fours, indeed involved the same parties and the same contract, a lawyer couldn't confidently advise, "The exculpatory clause will be enforced." The next judge might simply overrule *Globe*.

For these reasons, courts prefer to "distinguish" prior cases.

This preference has an interesting side effect. *Law appears to be above history, standing separate from the chaotic changes in cultures and beliefs.* Had Flintstone overruled *Globe*, we could see that things had changed. The world of *Globe* was likely a world where giants walked the earth and stern judges (Justice Scrooge, pre-ghost) let the chips fall where they might. The world of *K* and Flintstone is likely the world of judges committed less to freedom of contract and more to judicial intervention in the name of fairness. These are radically different worlds, but to read the opinion in *K*, which merely distinguished *Globe*, no one would know it. The *seamless web* of distinguished cases conceals the fact that judges and law respond to the great changes in society: *law is part of our culture, not something brooding in the corner.*

Change, of course, is inevitable, except from a vending machine.

Now, because Flintstone distinguished *Globe* rather than overruled it, both cases are still "good" law (when lawyers say something is "good" law they mean the case has not been reversed or, in the case of statutes, repealed; they do not mean they would necessarily take it home for dinner.) So let's take two cases and apply *Globe* and *K*.

An Opportunity to Practice:
Cases Three and Four

Case Three

Assume a statute provides that tenants must be given a 30–day notice before they can be evicted. Joe, a single father earning a low wage, moved into an apartment house with his two children. He signed a lease waiving his right to a 30–day notice. The landlord has brought an eviction action which could not be brought under the statute. The landlord asserts that the protection was waived.

Discuss. *(The most dreaded word in the English language.)*

Case Four

At a Tyrannosaurus riding stable (this gets boring for me, too), a rider (a lawyer) is eaten (alas, bringing audience to its feet). The lawyer's heirs bring suit based on the owners' negligence (they forgot to feed it). Needless to say, as part of the riding agreement the lawyer signed on that fateful day, there was a clause providing, "Riders cannot sue for negligence."

Discuss.

Discussion of Cases

Hopefully, with pencil in hand or with computer running, you took advantage of the two problems to begin to develop your skills in case analysis. If not, it's still not too late.

Both cases raise basically the same issue: will the court enforce the exculpatory clause? Both also raise the issue of whether, to avoid the clause, you need *both* unequal bargaining power and personal injury (as you had in *K v. Landlord*) *or* whether it is enough if you have only one of the two?

Hopefully, when you read the problems and began to think about them, these issues more or less *jumped* out at you. This illustrates the first of several points I want to make about the exercise.

You learn the law by struggling with it, not by closing your eyes and memorizing it. As you worked your way through *Globe* and *K v. Landlord* you were not trying to learn contract law; you were struggling to understand the cases and why they were decided the way they were. Your knowledge of contract law and your ability to spot contract issues came as *a byproduct of that struggle.*

Of course, you can avoid that struggle and the late nights by leaving the driving to someone else. You can buy study aids that tell you such things as:

Exculpatory clauses are enforced in commercial contexts but have been held unenforceable in apartment house leases.

I don't care how many times you underlined that, copied it on flash cards, or put it to music, it would not have helped you when it mattered, when you had to answer the questions.

The second point is the need to focus on the *relationship* between elements. Is the relationship between unequal bargaining and personal injury an *"and"* relationship or is it an *"or"* relationship? In other words, must there be both unequal bargaining power *and* personal injury before the court will throw out the exculpatory clause, or is one enough? If it is an *"and"* relationship, then both Joe and the lawyer's heirs would be out of luck. While Joe did not have equal bargaining power, there was no personal injury; while the lawyer suffered personal injury, she had oodles of bargaining power. (Not only was she a lawyer, but, unlike a tenant who needs a place to live, she did not need to go riding and could therefore easily walk away if she didn't like the contract.)

To figure out the relationship, review what Judge Flintstone wrote:

We note that there is inherent unequal bargaining strength between landlords and tenants and that, in this case, the tenant is seeking recovery for personal injuries. A landlord, under traditional doctrine, has a duty to take reasonable steps to keep common areas safe; if we allow landlords to escape this duty by the simple expedient of a standard lease term, physical injuries that could be avoided will not be.

This raises my third point. Judges often take the easy way out. In *K v. Landlord,* we had both elements and Judge Flintstone did not have to decide if one of them would be enough. She does not tell us the relationship between them; she just mentions them and then decides. It will be up to the judges deciding the next cases, like those of Joe and the lawyer's heirs, to decide the issue.

Rather than being faulted for "taking the easy way out," Judge Flintstone should be praised for following the judicial tradition of deciding *only* the case before the court. Because the case had both elements, Judge Flintstone did not have to decide whether one would be enough. We follow prior decisions because we believe that the prior judges thought deeply about them before coming to their decision. Because Judge Flintstone did not *have to* decide the issue in *K v. Landlord*, she would not have thought deeply about the issue. Therefore, it was better for her to just keep quiet.

My final point is that legal analysis is more than simply spotting the issues. Issues give you a *framework* for analysis; they are not the analysis. To illustrate this, in Joe's case, one might write:

> *While Joe lacked equal bargaining power, there was no personal injury.* While it is true *that courts have refused to enforce exculpatory clauses if they deny recovery for personal injury, and this is not the case here,* a case might be made *that the requirement to give a 30–day notice before eviction also protects public safety in that it allows individuals like Joe to find a new place to move his family before he is thrown out in the street.*

Always remember *"yes, but." Yes,* there are no personal injuries here, *but* maybe I can equate the possible harm to Joe with personal injury.

Don't be upset if you didn't "get" this point in your answer. You probably got some that I didn't. In any event, I will have more to say on this subject in later chapters. You will be given another opportunity to practice, and then I will give you model answers to work with.

This has been a long chapter.

Goodnight. Whisper hush.

CHAPTER 3

CASE SYNTHESIS

In our prior chapter, we tore apart *Globe* and *K v. Landlord*. This is known as *case analysis*. The process of putting two or more cases together is known as *case synthesis*. Expect to do a lot of it during your first year. A casebook will have a couple of cases, usually from different jurisdictions, which face the same general issue but which come to apparently different results.

"Consistent or inconsistent?" puffs the prof.

You will long to make them consistent. There is a deep human need to reduce the "bloomin' confusion" of our world to patterns that we can understand and, eventually, control. We need to understand the apparent randomness of things. If every event in our lives were a specific instance reflecting no underlying cause or theme, we could never learn from our experiences, for there would be nothing to learn. If sickness, floods, and famines had no causes we could understand, we would huddle in our caves fearing vicious and irrational gods (which are an explanation in their own right but not much of one).

William James wrote of "our pleasure at finding that a chaos of facts is the expression of a single underlying fact" and that, in our chaotic world, "each item is the same old friend with a slightly altered dress." He continued:

Who does not feel the charm of thinking that the moon and the apple are, as far as their relation to the earth goes, identical; of knowing respiration and combustion to be one; of understanding that the balloon rises by the same law whereby the stone sinks?

How does a scientist reduce the world's complexity? By finding a "law" that explains apparently different phenomena. An apple falls and the moon circles the earth: at first blush, these seem to be very different kinds of phenomena, but wait, both are but different manifestations of the law of gravity. How do lawyers reduce complexity? By stating a rule of law that explains what appear to be inconsistent cases.

That science and law are similar is not a fanciful suggestion. In fact, the father of modern American legal education and, in 1870, the first dean of the Harvard Law School, Christopher Columbus Langdell, claimed that law *is* a science. Just as botanists go to botanical gardens to study plants in order to discover the laws of nature, lawyers and law students go to the law library to study judicial opinions to discover the basic principles underlying law. According to the law-as-science thesis, while there may be a great number of cases, careful analysis of them will lead to the realization that they are really specific manifestations of a relatively small number of basic legal principles, with each case then becoming the same old friend, in a slightly altered dress. Once we understand these principles we can predict with great confidence the outcome of cases yet to be conceived.

Let me show you how this works. You will learn in your first-year Contracts class that gift promises are unenforceable. Say I promise to give you $50 tomorrow. If I do, fine, but if I don't, the courts will not enforce my promise. To explain this result, the courts came up with the doctrine of consideration: to be enforceable the person making the promise must "get something" for the promise. For example, if a father asks a stranger to care for his sick adult son and promises to compensate the stranger for his expenses, then the father's promise would be enforceable: he "got something" for it, the care of his son.

But what happens if the father's promise comes *after* the stranger cared for his son? Then the father *"got nothing"* for his promise (the care had already been given) and hence his promise would be unenforceable. This is the case *Mills v. Wyman*, a case you're likely to read in your Contracts class. Wyman, the father, heard that Mills had played the part of a Good Samaritan in caring for his son during his last illness. He wrote Mills, promising to pay his expenses but thereafter refused to do so. Mills filed suit.

"My promise," argued the father, "is not enforceable because I got nothing for it. When I made it, Mills had already cared for my son."

At this point, Mills, the Good Samaritan, brought to the court's attention a series of cases where the courts enforced promises even though, like the father, those making the promises had "gotten nothing" for them. The cases were of two types:

Bankruptcy Cases.

1.   A owes B $1000 pursuant to a previous transaction.

2.   A goes to bankruptcy court and has his debt to B discharged; he is now under no *legal* obligation to pay B.

3.   Thereafter, A promises to pay B $1000.

In this kind of case, the courts had enforced A's promise even though he didn't seem to get anything for it (anything that he didn't already have).

Statute of Limitations Cases.

1.   A owes B $1000 pursuant to a previous transaction.

2.   Under the *Statute of Limitations,* B has only four years in which to file suit on the debt. Thereafter it is barred.

3.   B allows the four years to pass without filing suit; A is now under no *legal* obligation to pay B.

4.   Thereafter, A promises to pay B $1000.

In this kind of case, the courts had enforced A's promise even though he didn't get anything for it (anything he didn't already have).

Of course, *neither* of these kinds of cases involved fathers promising to pay for past care of their children. But the theory is that these specific instances (bankruptcy and statute of limitation cases) are simply manifestations of an underlying legal principle, much like the specific instances of the orbit of the moon and the fall of an apple are manifestations of the underlying law of gravity. To decide whether to enforce the father's promise, the judge simply finds the underlying legal principle and applies it.

The judge puts on a white coat, assumes a somewhat crazed look, and weird background music comes up: what is the underlying legal principle that explains the Bankruptcy and Statute of Limitations cases? The judge studies the cases and notes that, in both kinds of cases, the person making the promise to pay the debt *once* had a legal obligation to pay it. *Eureka*! The underlying legal principle:

Even if the promisor did not get something for the promise, the promise is enforceable if the promisor had a prior legal obligation to pay.

This principle neatly explains the prior cases: in each the promisor had the required prior legal obligation. Now, if we were to apply this newly discovered legal principle to the case at hand, the father's promise would *not* be enforced because he did not have a prior legal obligation to pay the Good Samaritan.

But not so fast there! Are we sure we got it right? The ancient Greeks had a different explanation of why apples fell and it seemed to work: apples fell because they wanted to get to the ground. Maybe there is a different legal principle to explain the Bankruptcy and Statute of Limitations cases. Studying those cases, we could conclude that in all of them the promisor had a *moral obligation* to pay the debt. We could come up with an alternative explanatory legal principle:

Even if the promisor did not get something for the promise, the promise is enforceable if the promisor has a moral obligation *to keep it.*

If this is the correct explanation, then the father's promise *would* be enforced because he has a moral obligation to pay the expenses. Obviously, a great deal is at stake in deciding what theory to adopt.

How is the judge to choose? Sometimes there will be language in the prior cases that points the way. Judges often include such language to help future judges who will be applying their decision as precedent. For example, in the bankruptcy cases, the judges could have written:

We note that the person who made the promise to pay had a prior legal obligation to do so, and this is critical.

Or they might have written:

We note that the person who made the promise to pay had a prior legal obligation to do so, but we do not think this is critical; it is more important that he had a moral obligation to pay.

If there is no such language, what's a poor judge to do? In the next chapter I will review some *good* arguments that can be used, but here, however, is the essential point: the result is *not* dictated by the "science of law" because the science of law has produced two equally logical explanations of the prior cases. As Oliver Wendell Holmes once wrote:

> *The life of the law has not been logic: it has been experience. The felt necessities of the time, the prevalent moral and political theories, intuitions of public policy, avowed or unconscious, even the prejudices which judges share with their fellow men, have had a good deal more to do than the syllogism in determining the rules by which men should be governed.*

For a fascinating look at how scientists decide between competing scientific theories, see Kuhn's *The Structure of Scientific Revolutions*. His basic argument is that the choice is *not* a scientific one, in that the competing theories usually come out pretty much the same in terms of explaining (and in failing to explain) the observed data. He argues that the choice is often based on aesthetics: on which theory is more elegant and which presents more exciting research possibilities.

Today no one believes law is a science in the sense that all of the cases can be explained by a series of underlying basic principles. Langdell himself might have had his doubts: when he came across a case that he couldn't fit into his scheme, one he couldn't make consistent with other cases, he would simply label that case as "wrong" and move on. (A scientist can't make this move: "This tree isn't growing the way my theory says it should.

This tree is wrong." She can, however, fail to see the nonconforming tree, but that's another book.)

There are inconsistent cases out there. They raise a host of theoretical problems: just what *is* the law if it can be "X" in California but "Not X" in Arizona? Lawyers, bless them, have a short fuse for theoretical problems. When they come across inconsistent cases, they label "X" the *majority rule* and "Not X" the *minority rule* and then go out for coffee.

In any event, a lot of good lawyering goes into trying to make cases consistent by discovering underlying legal principles, and a lot of good lawyering goes into arguing why one explanatory principle is better than another. It is great intellectual training to try to make cases consistent; work hard at it in your studies. But don't get comatose if you can't. Here is an opportunity to practice.

Let's return to a problem considered in the last chapter. You must decide whether to enforce a term in a residential lease that waives the statutory requirement of 30–day notice before eviction. There are two prior cases:

Globe: enforcing a contract term that prevented a party from being sued for negligence resulting in financial loss.

K v. Landlord: refusing to enforce a contract term that prevented a party from being sued for negligence resulting in personal injury.

On its face *Globe* (exculpatory clauses are *valid*) is inconsistent with *K* (exculpatory clauses are *invalid*). One's an apple falling to earth, the other's the moon orbiting the earth. Take a few moments to try to articulate a legal doctrine that makes them consistent. "*Globe* and *K* seem to be inconsistent with one another, but really they are just different manifestations of one underlying rule, which is . . . ."

I'll give you my answer in a minute. This will be more helpful to you if you stop reading now and try to come up with your own. Jot!

Two alternative theories come to mind that make *Globe* and *K* consistent:

*Exculpatory clauses are **valid** unless they relieve liability for physical injury.*

or

*Exculpatory clauses are **invalid** unless they relieve liability for financial loss.*

Neat. *Globe* and *K* are no longer specific instances; just as the falling apple and the circling moon are different manifestations of the same underlying physical law, these two cases are different manifestations of the same underlying rule of law. We have explained both cases in that we were able to fashion rules that explain both. Good for us.

Note that, although both rules explain both decisions, they point to radically different outcomes downstream. Under the first rule, most waivers of exculpatory clauses would be valid, and, by analogy, so too would a term waiving statutory notice requirements because they do not trigger physical injury. Under the second, most exculpatory clauses would be invalid, and, by analogy, so would the waiver of the right to receive adequate notice before eviction because it does not involve financial loss. Which is the correct reading of the cases? Again, we leave logic and turn to "felt necessities."

Controlling Authorities

Let's clear up some technical matters concerning what we mean by such terms as "controlling authority" and "primary authority."

Several years ago, a juvenile court judge in Florida was asked to decide the right of a surrogate mother to retain custody of her child. Paid to carry the father's baby to term, the surrogate mother changed her mind and wished to keep the child. The father filed an action to gain custody based on her promise to give the child to him and on the fact that he was the biological father. It was the first such case ever, the ultimate case of first impression.

The press wrote as if the trial judge's decision would conclusively establish the respective rights of surrogate mothers nationally and for all time.

Not so.

Under the doctrine of *stare decisis*, courts are *obligated* to follow *only* the law set down by higher courts in their *own* state and those of the United States Supreme Court. These cases are known as "*controlling authority*." Trial courts in, say, Iowa *must* follow the law laid down by the Iowa Supreme Court; they are not obligated to follow the law as laid down by the California Supreme Court or any other state courts. Note that, even in Florida, the judge in the next courtroom could ignore his neighbor's surrogate decision. He would be bound only by the decision of a higher court, a Florida appellate court.

This does not mean the Florida decision would have no impact elsewhere. If a judge were faced with a similar case in Montana, the Florida decision could be cited as "*persuasive*" (as opposed to "*controlling*") authority. It is significant, but not conclusive, that a judge in Florida came to a particular decision: he spent a lot of time thinking about the issue and what he decided is probably right. There are several sources of "persuasive authority" (things that lawyers can cite to judges in support of their positions). They include decisions from other states, statutes from other states, Restatements, law review articles, and state bar journal articles.

There are two other terms you will come across that may cause confusion: *primary authority* and *secondary authority*. Primary authorities are the cases and statutes themselves; secondary authority is what commentators say about them, perhaps in law reviews or legal reference books.

Finally, in terms of definitions, be aware that lawyers use the word "control" in two different senses, a *status sense* and an *application sense*. If we are in a Missouri trial courtroom, all Missouri State Supreme Court decisions "control" legal controversies in that courtroom in the status sense of that word. The trial court judge must follow them if they apply to the case before him. Cases from the Supreme Court of, say, Maine, do not "control" in this status sense; the Missouri trial court judge can ignore them even though they address the exact same issue that he must decide.

All of this is straightforward enough, but lawyers muddy the waters by arguing that a case that clearly controls in the status sense, say, a case from the Missouri Supreme Court, does not "control" the particular decision the trial judge must make if that case is "distinguishable." So in our little corner of the world, you can have a "controlling" case which doesn't "control."

But what if there is no controlling authority, no persuasive authority, no secondary authority? In the case of first impression, the judge stands alone on the desolate shore. Is "freedom" just another word for nowhere else to look?

CHAPTER 4

CASES OF FIRST IMPRESSION

Thus far we have looked at how judges analyze and synthesize prior appellate cases in order to guide their decisions. But what if there are no prior decisions? Indeed, how was the *first* case decided? This presents something of a chicken and egg problem, which, of course, we'll solve.

In practice, most appealed cases are of "first impression" in the sense that there is no prior controlling case (or statute) clearly deciding the matter. If one clearly did, then the only argument the losing party would have is that the *case* should be *overruled* or *statute* found *unconstitutional*.

Most of the cases you will read are something of a mixed bag, with lawyers distinguishing cases and, in addition, making the kinds of arguments we will review in this chapter.

Remember Ms. K:

"Your Honor, the case of Globe is distinguishable and its holding, that exculpatory terms are enforceable, should not apply."

If she wins this argument, she hasn't won. She still must convince the judge to throw out the term; in a sense, overcoming prior cases, Ms. K has made hers a case of *first impression*. Here are some of the arguments she might use:

Arguments based on hypotheticals and analogies.

Policy arguments.

Slippery slope arguments.

We'll see how these work and look at typical responses.

Hypotheticals and Analogies

Hypotheticals are quite popular in legal analysis and argument. Assume that no court has *ever* refused to enforce a contract clause. Ms. K's lawyer, asking the court to refuse to enforce a clause, would think of a hypothetical case where a court would do just that. The argument becomes:

"Your Honor, in the situation I am about to describe, I am sure you will agree that no court would enforce the contract. Well, enforcing the exculpatory clause in this case would be basically the same thing."

Think of a contract term that a court would *obviously* not enforce? Take your time.

————————

My case of non-enforcement: A six-year-old promises to give his allowance, every week, to his big brother. No court is going to enforce that deal.

Of course, the attorney arguing for enforcement of the term will make up her own hypothetical case,

one in which a court would surely enforce the
contract, perhaps one signed by two major corporations after months of negotiation by competent lawyers.

Now we have two cases, neither of which happened, but so what? The next step is to decide
whether our case, the one involving the exculpatory
clause, looks more like the kid's contract or more
like that of the corporations.

> *"Your Honor, this is basically like a case where a
> six-year-old agrees to give up his allowance; that
> agreement would not be enforced and neither
> should this one."*

> *"No, Your Honor," replies the other side. "It's
> more like an agreement between two corporations,
> one we would surely enforce. You should enforce
> this one as well."*

How do we decide which it is more like? By
articulating *why* the hypothetical cases are easy
ones. Why, exactly, is the six-year-old case an easy
case? Once we understand that, then we can look
and see if those reasons (policies) apply to the case
at issue.

> *"We don't enforce kids' contracts because we don't
> think they know what they are agreeing to. Ms. K
> didn't know what she was agreeing to because the
> clause was buried in the lease."*

> *"No," replies the other side. "We don't enforce
> kids' contracts because we feel that they are not
> capable of understanding what they are agreeing*

to. Ms. K, as an adult, surely is capable of know-ing what she agreed to; if she didn't take the trouble, that's not our concern."

What we have done is make up easy cases and, by asking ourselves why they are easy, we have, in effect, written the supporting opinion. We have created two new first cases, along with their sup-porting rationale. Presto! What was the first case now becomes the third, and we land safely on familiar ground.

Neat trick!

As to the chicken/egg quandary, easy. The egg came first and, to explain its existence, created a hypothetical parent, the chicken, and the rest is history. Okay, sure, it might have been the other way around, with the chicken coming first and then creating a hypothetical egg to explain itself. Maybe we still don't know which came first, but at least now we know how they pulled it off.

An Aside On Intuition ("Free Radicals")

It is often thought that legal analysis and argu-ment are matters of logic but intuition plays a huge role. It is the engine that starts the whole process.

Split-brain research suggests that the two sides of the human brain have different roles. The right side is the intuitive side; it sees relationships, pictures, and sings. Unfortunately, it has grunts for words. The left side is organized, logical, and has a brilliant vocabulary; alas, it has nothing interesting to say, pretty much limited to such things as "Pass the salt."

Split-brain research helps us to understand how we think. Prize both your logic and your intuitions. Facing a new problem, your mind might throw out, "Gee, Ms. K's problem strikes me as the same as that of a six-year-old giving away his allowance." This is the brain's right side, grunting. I call these grunts *free radicals*.

While most of us have only the vaguest idea what "free radicals" are, we do know they are bad. Real bad. In law, free radicals are free-standing "good points" tied to no proposition of law. Without the link, they aren't good. I knew a very talented lawyer who did prison reform work. After several years, she quit. "I am sick of trying to make filthy and dangerous jail conditions into 'cruel and unusual punishments.'" But courts have no power to do anything about filthy and dangerous conditions; they can only act to prevent "cruel and unusual punishments." Filthy and dangerous conditions are free radicals; they must be tied to legal requirements.

Free radicals are the product of the right side of our brain. They are often brilliant. Beginners don't know how to handle them. Some just write them down in briefs or on exams: *"This case is like a six-year-old kid's signing away his allowance."* Standing alone, free radicals don't make sense.

Other students, realizing that they don't make sense, run away from them and never mention them. *Both* approaches are wrong. Your right brain is generally pretty insightful. Neither simply record the grunts nor run away from them: use the left side of your brain to tie your intuitions to legal principles. When you are thinking about a legal problem, things will pop into your mind: *What's my right brain telling me now? What relationship does it see?*

Intuition is not the solution: it is an *invitation* to the hard analysis needed to get to a solution.

Policy Arguments

As a first-year law student, one of my biggest shocks came when I was talking with a second-year student about his Moot Court and he mentioned he was going to make some policy arguments.

"Policy arguments? You can *do* that?" In my first several months of law school I had somehow picked up the notion that law was pretty mechanical: find the law and apply it. But policy considerations are of critical importance in judicial decisions; those decisions create law and in turn become precedent. *Looking ahead, will the decision be good law?*

In the chapters on legal argument, I will go into policy arguments in greater detail: where do you find policies and how do you support them? Here I just want to give you a sense of the arguments.

In the case of Ms. K, the landlord's attorney would no doubt argue for a rule that promises should be enforced because that furthers the policy of freedom of contract. "Ms. K agreed to the term;

if you allow her to get out of her agreement, you have reduced her to a child, someone whose decisions we ignore."

There are two ways to meet policy arguments. The first is to come up with your own.

Yes, there is a great public interest in freedom of contract, but there is also a great public interest in preventing physical injury. Allowing landlords to exempt themselves from liability will encourage them to be negligent, thus leading to more injuries.

There is no established pecking order that ranks policies, such as:

Freedom of contract trumps public safety, or

Public safety trumps freedom of contract.

When conflict emerges, the judge will simply have to choose. This is very much like the judicial choice between two competing explanations of a series of prior cases and, indeed, very much like the judicial choice involved in determining whether a prior case controls or is distinguishable.

The second response to a policy argument, and one that is great fun if you can pull it off, is to steal your opponent's argument and turn it around:

Yes, freedom of contract is important, but freedom of contract is premised on the notion of equal bargaining power, which assures both sides are making free choices. To allow a strong party to force a weak party into accepting his terms denies the weaker party freedom of contract.

Note that these arguments have focused on the policy implications of the decision at issue. Another kind of policy argument focuses not so much on the decision itself but on where it might lead. These arguments go by "Slippery Slope," "Opening Floodgates," or, for some reason, "Allowing the Camel's Nose in the Tent." They are so common that they deserve special treatment.

Slippery Slopes, Floodgates, and The Collapse of Western Civilization

"Your Honor, if you do what my opponent wants you to do, X, which may be a very sensible thing to do, then in the next case the judge will have to do Y, which we all agree would be a bad thing to do, so don't do X."

We saw a slippery slope argument in *Globe*: "If we void this term, then we don't know where we would stop rewriting contracts". There are *three* responses to slippery slope arguments.

1. Pre-distinguish.

Once you step onto the slope, you need not tumble to the bottom because there are things to grab on your way down. "Your Honor, if you void the exculpatory clause, this will not mean that in the next case you will have to rewrite a *rent term*, as there are obvious distinctions between the two. Exculpatory clauses affect public safety; rent terms do not." What you are doing is inviting the judge to "pre-distinguish" the opinion, thus effectively slamming the door on those poor fools who are paying too much rent.

> *"We note that our decision merely goes to the narrow issue involving physical injury and would not apply to lease terms not involving such injury."*

2.   Tumble all the way.

Another response to the slippery slope argument is that falling all the way down might not be such a bad idea. "Hey, that's not a bad idea. Given that many landlords take advantage of their tenants, courts should rewrite unfair leases."

3.   Reverse the slope.

The final possible response to a slippery slope argument is to counter with your own. Whenever a judge is asked to make a decision, he stands on a sharp pinnacle with slippery slopes falling sharply on all sides. *All slippery slope arguments are reversible.*

> *Your Honor, if you enforce this clause because you don't want to get involved in rewriting contracts, then in the next case you will have to <u>enforce</u> a clause which requires the tenant, if one day late, to forfeit her first born.*

Meet slippery slopes with your own slippery slopes.

The *floodgate* argument is essentially a slippery slope argument.

> *"Your Honor, if you do justice in this case, all manner of ragamuffins will be pounding down*

your door asking for justice. You might as well
kiss your golf game goodbye."

This argument, although quite popular, has always struck me as curious. One response is that
justice isn't such a bad idea. The other, more solici-
tous to the golf industry, is to suggest to the court
that the rule could be drawn quite narrowly so that
ragamuffins stay where they belong.

CHAPTER 5

STATUTORY INTERPRETATION

A city ordinance makes it a misdemeanor to "operate a vehicle in a public park." Ben, driving his Big Wheel, which is a fancy tricycle, is busted in the park. Is he guilty?

If you said no, YOU ARE WRONG.

Perhaps you assumed that Ben is probably a toddler and, as such, can't be guilty of a crime. But you must read more closely: Ben's age is not mentioned. More significantly, you probably just assumed a definition of "vehicle," one which included large oil tankers but excluded children's toys. *Never assume definitions! Never!*

If there is one quote I want you to remember—indeed, if there is one *thing* I want you to remember—it comes from Robert Bolt's wonderful play, *A Man for All Seasons*. It deals with personal integrity and the importance of law. Why not cut down the laws to get the Devil?

"And when the last law was down, and the Devil turned round on you—where would you hide, the laws all being flat? ... d'you think you could stand upright in the winds that would blow then?"

Recall this when friends start attacking your career choice and the "technicalities" of the law. What winds would blow. As good as that quote is, however, it is not the one I want to stress.

To set the scene, King Henry VIII has broken with the Pope in order to marry Anne Boleyn. He demands, upon the penalty of treason, that all of his subjects take an oath approving of the marriage. Sir Thomas More, a Catholic, disapproves of the marriage. When he first hears of the oath, as a careful lawyer, he entertains the possibility that he can sign it and remain faithful to his beliefs.

More: What is the oath?

Roper: It's about the marriage, sir.

More: But what is the wording?

Roper: We don't need to know the wording—we know what it will mean.

More: It will mean what the words say.

Read closely. You need to know the *words*; don't breeze by, catching their drift, knowing what they will mean. "Wait a minute, maybe 'Vehicle' can include Big Wheels."

Thus far we have been dealing with judicial opinions. Statutes are another source of law:

1. Which trumps?

2. If a statute is ambiguous, how do we figure out what it means?

On Statutes and Cases

Both statutes and case law are law—judges *must* follow controlling statutes and controlling cases. Generally statutes trump. Legislatures can overrule judicial opinions by simply passing a statute, *unless* the judicial opinion rested on the United States Constitution, which trumps everything, or on the state constitution, which trumps state statutes. Judges can throw out statutes *only* if they contravene the Constitution.

To illustrate, if a court said, "Exculpatory clauses in leases are valid," the legislature could change that result by simply passing a statute saying they were void. On the other hand, if the legislature passed a statute saying, "Exculpatory clauses in leases are valid," a court *could not* change that rule unless it found it to be unconstitutional.

Bottom line; if you want to change the world, become a legislator, not a judge. (This sentence entirely ignores the Civil Rights Movement and other great moments in our legal history, but Nutshell Writers have to make tough choices.)

On Statutory Construction

Statutory interpretation is a variation of the Second Case in the World (*everything* is).

Assume: "No Vehicles in the Park." Ben, now four, rides in on his Big Wheel. Has he violated the statute? The answer turns on the meaning of "vehicle."

Much of your legal education (and much of your legal practice) will deal with the interpretation of language. You will interpret contracts, statutes, judicial opinions, regulations, and even confessions. The question is always one of *intent*: when the person or parties used the word, what did they intend?

Often you don't have to go any further than the word itself. For example, if Ben's big brother, Caleb, was driving a large gasoline transport truck in the park, there is little doubt that he was running afoul of our rule about "vehicles" in the park. Unfortunately, few of your cases will be that easy. Those cases are never litigated. However, every day you will meet cases like Ben's, where it is unclear what language was intended to cover.

Unless the language has a plain meaning (Caleb's gasoline truck), the first move in interpreting language is to put it in *context*. If "No Vehicles in the Park" had been announced in a judicial opinion, we would have the *facts* of the case to help guide us. Did the judges, in using the word "vehicle," intend to cover such things as Big Wheels? If the rule had been announced in the context of a dispute over heavy trucks in the park, then we might conclude that the court, in using the word "vehicle," meant things of that ilk—things that could run people over and things that pollute the air and things that make loud noises. Ben's Big Wheel does none of these things, and hence, the word "vehicle" should not be interpreted to include it.

Note that this is similar to distinguishing cases: "Yes, the Court said 'No vehicles in the park,' but that was in the context of discussing heavy trucks. Surely that rule should not be applied to a case involving a Big Wheel; the case is distinguishable."

Further, if the rule "No Vehicles in the Park" had been announced in a judicial opinion, we would have the court's *rationale or justification* to help us. Assume the judges said:

> *"Public safety, noise abatement, and pollution control all require us to prohibit vehicles in the park."*

We would then have some sense of how the judge was using the word "vehicle" and whether it would include Big Wheels.

Again, the first move is to look to the *context* in which the language was used. Occasionally this is possible with a statute.

1. Sometimes there will be *legislative history* in which the legislature writes out what it has in mind.

2. Sometimes what appears to be an isolated statute was, in fact, a part of a larger legislative package. Perhaps "No Vehicles in the Park" was part of a "Clean Air Act." If it was, one could argue that, in using "vehicles," the legislature intended only those vehicles that pollute the air.

3. Sometimes statutes amend prior statutes. If the old statute read "No cars or trucks in the

park," one could argue that, in substituting the word "vehicle," the legislature intended an inclusive definition.

In your Legal Research class, you will learn how to check out all of these possibilities. (It's never fun but we never promised you a rose garden—whatever we mean by that.)

Unfortunately, most statutes are simple declaratory sentences, with no description of the kinds of situations the legislators had in mind in passing the statute (the "facts" in a case) and with no statement of why they adopted the statute. Like the ghost of Hamlet's father, most statutes simply appear and announce "pity me not, but lend thy serious hearing to what I shall unfold."

Seriously listening, all we hear is "No Vehicles in the Park" and the rest is silence. Still, we have to decide the matter of the Big Wheel. How?

We assume that the legislature must have had its reasons in passing such a law, and then we ask ourselves what that reason might have been. Once we have decided upon that reason, we have a context in which to interpret the language.

"Your Honor, the legislature must have intended not only to abate noise and pollution in the park, but also to prevent clutter and to protect public safety. A park filled with Big Wheels is not a pleasant place for adults to be, and Big Wheels do in fact present a risk of injury."

Of course, the opposing lawyer would posit different legislative purposes.

Here, too, lawyers put forth *hypotheticals* and *draw analogies*. Let's see how this works. The lawyer would first make up two easy cases: a gasoline transport truck would surely be a "vehicle" within the meaning of the statute, while a child's toy model truck would surely not be. Then the argument would be by analogy:

> *"Your Honor, a Big Wheel is more like a gasoline transport truck than a toy model car for the following reasons . . . ."*

To make these arguments by analogy, we are forced to tease out why our easy cases are, in fact, easy cases. Why is the gasoline transport case an easy one? Does that reasoning apply to Big Wheels?

Perhaps this entire discussion is simply an instance of bad legislative drafting. Let's say the legislature envisioned the problem and passed a statute reading:

> *No Vehicles in the Park, and this includes Big Wheels!*

Have we, and the legislature, finally ended this ridiculous illustration?

> *"My Big Wheel was <u>on the road</u>, not <u>in the park</u>. The purpose of the rule is to prevent damage to grass and flowers. The rule reads 'in the park' and not 'on the road.' The very precision of the rule shows that the legislature was drafting very carefully. Besides, I had only one Big Wheel. The*

*rule specifically says 'Big Wheels.' Probably the
rule was aimed against vendors or people putting
on races. So there!"*

Let the legislature throw some more words at the
problem; soon we will have an Internal Revenue
Code, much too big to fit on a Yellow Sign. Back to
the wall, defeated by a four-year-old, the legislators
will throw up their hands and install a new sign:

Warning: Certain rules may or may not apply.

An Aside on Drafting with Precision

In practice you will draft contracts and, perhaps,
even statutes. In the next three years of law school,
you will be preached: "Precision!" But there are
costs.

*Early statutes defined "theft" as a "felonious tak-
ing." What did that mean? Reformers were uncomfortable (they always are). Redrafted, theft became "to take an object of value from another with
the intent to deprive said owner of said object
permanently." In the old days, mothers, who stole
food for starving babies, walked free: whatever a
"felonious taking" was, that wasn't it. But it was
permanently depriving said owner, with intent no
less!*

One problem with precision is that it is verbose.
Compare "felonious taking" with the mouthful that
came after. Verbose means boring, pedantic, and,
worst of all, costly.

Precision controls discretion. It controls discretion yet therein lies a problem. It is folly to believe

that we can anticipate the future with such clarity that we know exactly what should be done in all situations. Yet the advocates of precision insist we try. Mothers go to jail.

Finally, precision may be the enemy of compromise. In China, around the time of Confucius, there was a debate about whether the laws should be written down. The argument *against* this was that once the law was written, people would insist upon their rights, whereas in a just society people compromise.

Vagueness encourages compromise and vagueness allows for flexibility.

I am not advocating sloppiness (tenure might not even protect me). But realize the costs of lengthy documents, drafted with precision. Perhaps you better serve your client with a (cheap) short and vague memorandum of understanding that will allow for compromise down the road.

Aside: Why Do Judges Write Opinions

Turning briefly to a question of political science, it tells us a lot about courts and legislatures that courts must publicly justify their decisions while legislatures just vote. Judges have to write opinions, justifying the rules of law they lay down. This is because judges have limited power. Very few are elected. Their decisions should rest on reason, and that reasoning should be made public in order to prevent possible abuses. Legislators are elected, and if they misuse their power, they can be thrown out of office. Further, political decisions can be irrational as long as they are those of the majority.

Arguments That Eat Pittsburgh

Sometimes a word in a statute will be interpreted in such a fashion that it turns and devours the statute itself. Let's assume a burglary statute that requires, among others things, a "forced entry." Let's further assume a fact pattern where the culprit walked into the house though an open door.

If we were to interpret "forced entry" to include walking into a house, because walking requires "force," we have effectively defined that provision of the statute out of the statute. All entries are now "forced entries," and the requirement vanishes. The response is, "That cannot be a proper interpretation because the legislature, in requiring a forced entry, must have wanted to distinguish some kinds of entries from others".

Be sensitive to these kinds of arguments. Would the proposed definition turn upon and consume the rule? We will see illustrations of this throughout the book.

I call these "arguments that eat Pittsburgh." Why? Once a poet was asked the meaning of one of his abstract poems. "When I wrote it, God and I both knew. Now only He does."

CHAPTER 6

SOME QUESTIONS OF JURISPRUDENCE

My first job was with a legal services program, California Rural Legal Assistance, and one of my first clients was a farm worker whose family was cut off welfare because he refused to work raking leaves in a local park. The welfare law provided that recipients could be terminated if they refused to engage in "work-training programs." My theory was that raking leaves was not such a training program. My client knew how to work and worked long and hard when he did; however, the season was over, and there was simply no work for him. His family needed food. I appealed his termination and discovered, talking with another lawyer in another poverty law office, that the hearing officer who was to hear my case had heard an identical case of hers. She had written an opinion upholding my contention.

Hog Heaven! "Send me a copy."

Several weeks later, near the end of our hearing, I opened my closing argument by reading from her opinion. It was elegant. I sensed, however, that she was getting restless: "Where did you get that? Give me that. What I wrote in *that* case was for the

70

parties to understand my reasoning. It has nothing to do with *this* case!"

Apparently decisions of welfare hearing officers aren't precedent. Oh well, you can't learn *everything* in law school.

Fast forward to the International Court of Justice, where the governing statute seems to reject the notion of precedent: "The decision of the Court has no binding force except between the parties and in respect to that particular case."

Following precedent is *not* inevitable, but we do. Why revisit it?

Because it quickly takes us to the heart of our legal system, for the lack of a simpler word, to jurisprudence, the philosophy of law. We'll look at the law's central dilemma (the *general* versus the *specific*), introduce some important concepts, such as the differences between *rules* and *standards*, and meet some interesting people along the way: the *Crits,* the *formalists,* the *realists,* and the *law and econ* guys, those with the slide rules and pocket protectors. We'll also take a quick look at a significant debate: the degree to which law actually controls judges, which, at bottom, is whether there is any law at all.

Following precedent has its costs. First, the lawyer becomes King. If prior decisions didn't matter, folks would simply go to a judge, cite the controlling law ("Work Training Programs can be required") and make their arguments ("Raking leaves isn't a work training program."). There would be little need for lawyers, and no need for the specialized knowledge on how to find and analyze the "prior cases." (There goes Westlaw!)

Second, cases can be *wrong*. Early Supreme Court decisions upheld segregation. If judges were not obligated to follow prior decisions, errors could be *ignored*; under a doctrine of precedent, they must be *corrected*. One of the joys of your first year is to watch the common law correct errors, by creating new duties, new defenses, and by distinguishing bad cases into oblivion. Rarely do they overrule them, as in the case of *Brown v. Board of Education*. However, before these bright shining moments, the errors were still *good* law and, in our celebration of the common law's "working itself pure," we should pause to consider all who suffered due to previous errors, faithfully followed.

Third, to work at all, precedent must work at a *general* level even though justice, like the Devil, may reside in the details. We'll come back to this point, but let's now turn to the justifications *for* the doctrine of precedent.

1. *Predictability*. For people to plan their lives and for lawyers to advise their clients, it is important to know, once and for all, whether Park Cleaning Projects are proper "Work Training Programs."

2. *Control of judicial whim*. Judges have power. Any system that vests power in officials must have devices to control that power. By forcing judges to rule in accord with prior decisions

makes it much less likely that they will be able to abuse their discretion by favoring certain parties or interests.

3. *Universalization.* The doctrine of precedent forces judges to look back *and* to look into the future. This too helps filter out personal bias. Immanuel Kant advised us to universalize our decisions: we should do only that which we would have everyone, in a similar situation, do. The doctrine of precedent forces judges to universalize, to decide not only for the current litigants, but for all similar litigants.

4. *Correctness.* Although discredited today, in olden days prior decisions were followed because they were *right*. Cases could be right in one of two senses. First, the law in some sense exists "out there" and can be "discovered" (the early common law was very much about discovering law). Second, even if law doesn't exist out there, human reasoning is such that it would lead, after much hard work, to the same conclusion. If either of these possibilities is correct, then it would be a waste of time to re-litigate issues because the outcome would be the same.

Let's take a closer look at these justifications.

Predictability and Control of Judicial Whim

Precedent promises both predictability and control of judicial abuse. Once the first judge rules

"Park Cleaning Projects are not legitimate," people can plan their lives without worrying that a future judge, perhaps out of racial animus, would rule that they are. Two questions come to mind:

1. If there was no doctrine of precedent, would judges be all over the lot?

2. Assuming they would be, does precedent deliver on its promise of predictability and control?

"If there were no laws, what would happen?" Young children, asked that question, predict doom: "There would be all kinds of murders and stuff." This can be either Early Hobbesianism or self-fulfilling prophecy. Children believe in grown-ups. Why would they have laws unless, without them, there would be all kinds of murders? Why would we have a doctrine of precedent unless, without it, judges would be all over the lot?

Say we have ten judges and no doctrine of precedent. If five were to rule that Park Cleaning Projects weren't valid, while five would rule that they were, life becomes something of a crap-shoot. However, if the tally was nine to one, then we would have a fairly predictable system and people could plan their lives around it. Of course, the doctrine of precedent does not deliver 100% predictability because cases can be distinguished or overruled. The question is whether precedent delivers *more* predictability than would a system where judges decided on their own. Again, merely because we have a system of precedent, don't just assume that it is the more predictable.

The more common critique is that precedent doesn't *deliver*. Cases can be *distinguished* and statutes *interpreted*. Perhaps there is so much play in the system that doesn't control judges at all, that they can always make it come out the way they want to? If so, then the whole house of cards comes crashing down: *stare decisis* cannot deliver on its promise of predictability or on its promise to control arbitrary decision-making by judges.

Law professors in the "Critical Studies Legal Movement," known more affectionately as *Crits* (not to be confused with the street gang), write law review articles asserting that judicial rules are a sham. Take the Constitutional requirement that the President must be at least 35 years old, a clear rule if there ever was one. Not so, claim the Crits.

To validate the election of a teenager, a judge could rely on the well-known theory of statutory interpretation: statutes should be interpreted in light of their purpose. The purpose of the age requirement, the judge would opine, was to ensure the President was well-educated and mature, and this teen candidate is both. As to plain language in the Constitution, the judge could turn to the theory of literary interpretation known as *deconstructionism,* which suggests that the meaning of a text resides in the reader and that all readings are equally valid. Great news if you can read a book any way you want. You need only one, sometimes read-

ing it as *Huck Finn*, and other times reading it as
Cases and Materials on Civil Procedure.

As a quick aside, the substantive argument of the
Crits is that law oppresses minorities and women
and that it justifies illegitimate hierarchies. While
Crits long for the 1960s, the other major intellectual
movement pines for the 1870s. The "Law and Economics Movement" looks at the effect of legal rules
on the market and tries to figure out what rules are
most efficient. (It would simply be too wonderful if
these profs were known as the "Bloods," but the
universe is not that kind.) You will get caught up in
these debates whether you know it or not: your
professors are involved and that will affect how they
teach the law.

You may become a Closet Crit yourself: "Now
that I understand law, it's a sham; judges do what
they want." Three things to consider: First, casebooks have only close, difficult cases, those which
are bound to be the most uncertain. Second, the
judges tell me that they feel bound to decide matters in ways they don't necessarily want to. Third,
the debate assumes that judges have overriding
political or moral values that they are just itching to
impose on us. More likely, they just want to go
home to dinner. Few legal contests are about
whether to care for one's aging mother or leave her
alone to go fight the Nazis. Most legal contests are
about rather mundane disputes, such as which side
of the road to drive on. Judges will turn to prior
cases to decide them and then go home. They will
not stay up all night figuring out how to attack

those cases, writing tenure pieces on how recent advances in relativity theory have rendered the notion of "the right side of the road" meaningless.

But let's assume that there *is* a lot of play in the system; that does *not* make it a sham.

Legal Realism, a movement started in the 1920s, argued that there was vastly more to judicial decisions than simply logic. It was a reaction to the conservative bent of the then-prevailing view of law, *Legal Formalism*. Formalists contended that prior cases logically compelled certain outcomes (usually conservative ones). A typical legal realist law review article would line up cases pointing in different directions and thus conclude that there was more to judging than logically applying prior cases. Professor Llwellyn, whom you will probably meet in your first-year readings, was a leading realist. His take on precedent is worth noting. Even though a prior case was not determinative, it can contain "good and shrewd judicial discussion of useful criteria to use—persuasive, too, I suggest, to any court to which it might be quoted—*because it helps*."

Legal uncertainty is a problem. Here a quick aside on how the law has attempted to deal with it.

An Aside on Legal Uncertainty: Restatements and Bright Lines

To decide a legal controversy correctly, one must first find the right *rule* to apply and then to *apply* it correctly. Uncertainty infects both steps.

As to the first, when the common law system was young, there weren't that many cases, and thus it was easy to find the correct rule to apply. When you have thousands, the system breaks down. A diligent researcher could find, somewhere, a case standing for about any possible proposition. To help solve that problem, the *Restatement Movement* was started. Groups of law professors and leading practitioners would sit down to distill the common law rules, add their own thinking, and, when common law rules clashed, pick the one that made the most sense. Alas, old habits die hard. Now, like barnacles, scores and scores of judicial opinions hang on the Restatements "interpreting" them. Now, with computer-retrieval systems, research becomes cheap and easy. Lawyers used to look for cases in their own state; it was just too hard to search nationally. Now, however, lawyers in San Diego can quickly access cases from Boston; the flood of relevant authority has expanded vastly. Who knows what eventual effect this will have on our system?

The *bright line rule* is a device to reduce uncertainty at the level of *application*. Assume a judge writes:

> *"Programs offering little in the way of teaching new work skills are not legitimate 'Work Training Programs' for individuals who have a proven work record."*

This rule makes it difficult to plan your life or advise your client. Does a specific program offer "new work skills" and does a given individual have a "proven work record?" A *bright line* rule would be "*A program offering only manual labor is not a legitimate Work Training Program.*" It is easy to apply but there are costs.

Let's stop to introduce some important concepts: "*rules v. standards*" and "*over-and under-inclusive.*" Wanting to improve highway safety, you could have a *rule* ("Don't go over 65") or a *standard* ("Drive at a safe speed"). Rules are *easy to administer* (did they or didn't they?), but are often both *under-inclusive* not including cases they should (unsafe slow driving) and *over-inclusive,* including cases they should not (safe fast driving). To solve these problems, you could have a *standards*: ("Drive at a safe speed.") Standards, at least in theory, avoid both the over-and under-inclusive problems: you can target unsafe drivers every time, whether they are going too fast or too slow. However, standards are very hard to administer because they require individual assessment.

The more bright-line the rule, the more it will act as a rule; the more fuzzy it is, the more it will act as a standard. This is a fundamental legal quandary, one which will haunt you, or entertain you, from here on out. How about an example. A building contractor builds a house but fails to do it exactly as the contract required. Should he be able to collect on the contract? The law could have a bright line rule ("Nope") or it could have a standard ("He can collect if he substantially performed"). Of course, what is "substantial performance" must be a case by case decision. Justice Cardozo, in *Jacob & Young v. Kent,* faced this dilemma and ruled in favor of the substantial performance standard in order to be fair to the contractor who had done his best and came close. He stated the issue in his wonderful prose:

> *Those who think more of symmetry and logic in the development of legal rules than of practical adaption to the attainment of a just result will be troubled by a classification where the lines of division are so wavering and blurred. Something, doubtless, may be said on the score of consistency and certainty in favor of a stricter standard. The courts have balanced such consideration against those of equity and fairness, and found the latter to be weightier.*

Others have taken a different view. For example, years later another Justice on the New York Court of Appeals, Justice Jasen, wrote:

> *As in every situation where the law must draw a line between liability and nonliability, between responsibility and nonresponsibility, there will be borderline cases, and injustices may occur by deciding erroneously that an individual belongs on one side of the line or the other. To minimize the chances of such injustice occurring, the line should be drawn as clearly as possible.*

There is a lot to consider. Let me add to the mix two things that might not jump quickly to mind.

First, it is all well and good to decide matters on the basis of "equity and fairness" as long as you are the one making the decision. However, what if you are asserting unpopular positions or are simply unpopular? It can be argued that your only chance would be in a very formalistic system, one with very clear rules, one where the judges could not take away your rights to achieve their concept of equity and fairness.

Second, and on the other hand, something can be said for "wavering and blurred" lines, even without the claim that they can produce more justice. "Negotiating in the shadow of the law" suggests that one look at not only how law plays in the courtroom but also how it plays in the street. When the law is uncertain, there is an incentive for the parties to compromise their dispute. If both the plaintiff's lawyer and the defendant's lawyer are telling their clients the same thing ("Gee, I don't really know if we will win or lose if we go to court"), cooler heads are more likely to prevail, triggering serious negotiations. It can be argued that the more certain the law is, the more pig-headed people can become: ("I want it all! I don't have to compromise. I gotcha!")

How we come out on the issue may be less a product of intellectual assessment and more a product of our psychological bents. Cardozo seems to suggest this: some people seem instinctively to lean towards "symmetry and logic" and seek "consistency and certainty," while others lean towards "equity and fairness" and embrace "wavering and blurred" lines. Maybe our deepest jurisprudential beliefs stem from a Series of Unpleasant Events suffered on school playgrounds.

Universalization

The doctrine of precedent forces judges to universalize their decisions. It raises their gaze from the specifics of the case toward long-term goals and reduces the opportunity to decide on improper, case-specific grounds. (Other checks on judicial abuse include the requirements that judges follow prior decisions and justify and publish their decisions; as we will see elsewhere in this book, another check on judicial abuse can be law students analyzing judicial opinions in law reviews.)

The problem with universalization is that it may blur significant details. Take another problem researchers give children:

Carl's wife is dying. The druggist has a drug that will save her life but costs $1000. Carl doesn't have the money. One night he breaks into the drugstore and steals the medicine. He gives it to his wife, and she gets well. Did Carl do the right thing?

Graduate students will answer at the level of "property rights" versus "human rights." But maybe this is wrong-headed. Young kids want more details:

Does Carl love his wife? Did he try real hard to get the money? What's the druggist like? Does he kick puppies who accidentally wander into his store?

Laugh as you will, but when you actually make decisions (as opposed to discussing them in class), you probably consider any manner of specific details. Maybe there are no two cases that are really "alike" and it is simply a mistake to believe that they are.

The conflict between the general and specific is endemic to law. You cannot have a rule of law that reads:

It is okay to steal medicine, at least up to $1000 worth, if it is needed to save the life of your wife, as long as you love her and as long as you tried really hard to get the money and provided further that the druggist is a bad guy who kicks puppies for no good reason.

Such a law does not work; it is too specific. Lawyers could not rely upon it to make predictions; judges could not rely on it to make decisions. Our dilemma is this: legal rules must be somewhat general, or they won't work at all; if they are somewhat general, they may be suppressing specific facts that should matter.

The last justification for our doctrine of precedent is one you seldom hear of: the first judge got it right. The problem with this justification is that it suggests natural law, partisan religion, and weird stuff.

Natural Law, Right Answers

Stories are found things, like fossils in the ground.... Stories are relics, part of an undiscovered pre-existing world. The writer's job is to use the tools to get as much of each one out of the ground intact as possible.

So says Stephen King in his book, *On Writing*. To suggest, however, that judges find the law would be laughable in today's law school; so too the suggestion that human reason will lead us to correct solutions. We all know that judges create law, not find it, and that human reason is but the facile servant of political or psychological dictates.

Ours is a world of relative value and power politics. We rejoice in debunking ideas and authorities and love to point to political or psychological factors as the "real" reasons behind decisions. As undergraduates, we analyzed Marx in terms of Freud and Freud in terms of Marx. It is difficult for us to believe that judicial decisions are "right" in any strong sense of the word. But others have so believed.

Once people believed in "natural law," that law somehow exists "out there," independent of us. Under this view, judges don't make law; they discover it. Scientists, after all, did not *invent* gravity. We don't buy natural law anymore. We believe that judges are not *discovering* the law; they are *creating* it. But if that is so, how can we say any law or practice is unjust? Slavery? Dictatorship? Cruel and unusual punishment? Are these just matters of convention, or individual opinion, or whim?

I can understand why those who thought they were discovering the law believed that they were; thinking hard on a subject and writing on a subject feels a lot more like discovery than invention. Sitting here, watching the cursor blink, I get stuck. I begin to rethink my life, and then, suddenly, something will pop into my mind. That seems like discovery. Of course, it is easy to discount how things seem. Richard Pryor, caught in the act with another woman, yells at his wife, "Things are not as they seem. I am not having an affair; do you believe me or do you believe your lyin' eyes?"

CHAPTER 7

SOME QUESTIONS OF ETHICS

A cartoon shows a middle-aged couple in shock and surprise: "Oh, no! We forgot to have children!"

To conclude our discussion of legal analysis with some thoughts on legal ethics smacks of "Oh, no! I forgot ethics!" Well, perhaps. But you will be shocked when you are a lawyer just how often difficult ethical dilemmas arise. Daily. In practice you will specialize in a few areas of the law, such as criminal law, security law, elder law, or entertainment law. You will quickly learn the substantive doctrines in those areas; so substantive law, the stuff of law school, won't be much of an issue.

The hard parts of legal practice are dealing with people (and I can't help you there; novels might) and resolving the tough ethical issues. To get you thinking about such issues, consider the following problems that could arise in your first case, that of Ms. K and her landlord.

1. If a landlord comes and asks you to draft a form lease, do you automatically include an exculpatory clause (assuming they are legal in your jurisdiction)? Should you discuss the issue with the landlord, expressing your feelings about the propriety of the clauses?

2.   Assuming exculpatory clauses have been held unenforceable in your state, what if the landlord says, "Draft one anyway. Maybe the courts will change their minds; in any event, most of my tenants don't know the law and won't sue."

3.   Assume that exculpatory clauses are valid in your state. A landlord who has been quite negligent and whose negligence has seriously injured a tenant seeks your representation. Reviewing the store-bought lease, you find an exculpatory clause buried on the second page. Would it be proper for you not to raise the defense? If you do raise it, should you tell your not-too-bright opponent that similar clauses have been found invalid in other states?

4.   Should you decide these issues yourself or should you do whatever the official ethics code dictates?

All states have adopted ethical codes for lawyers to follow. Often they don't answer the questions you will face. How do you decide? Surely you start with the controlling rules, and surely you will want to talk to others, both lawyers and non-lawyers. Here are some other ideas.

"Act only on that maxim by which you can at the same time will that it should become a universal law." So advised Kant. Let's say I am tempted to cheat on my taxes. If I do, must the maxim I thereby endorse be very abstract ("Everyone can cheat") or can I put in some needed qualifications ("Minor cheating is OK as long as you are a nice person who has earned a piddling amount from Nutshell royalties")?

Along these lines it might be well to write a rule that would either allow you to do what you are considering or prohibit you from doing what you do not wish to do. In discussions of ethical matters, law students are often rather quick with the approval or condemnation of certain activities lawyers engage in. Pressed to write a rule governing such conduct often helps them think thorough their positions.

Another method is so simple it sounds ridiculous: think of a person you respect and ask yourself what he or she would do.

One final matter concerns the debate you will no doubt engage in time and again. As a lawyer, should you be a "hired gun" and do whatever your client wants, so long as it is legal?

Professor Thomas Shaffer has a brilliant analogy. You are a druggist and someone comes in to buy a hypodermic needle. You believe he is a heroin addict. One choice is to sell him the needle; what he does with it is his business. This is the "hired gun" response. Another choice would be to refuse to sell it to him because you don't want to facilitate such behavior. The problem with both approaches is that they are settled by power: in the first, the buyer has it; in the second, the druggist does. Shaffer gives us a way out. The druggist should begin a conversation: "I think you are going to use this to shoot heroin, and I believe it is wrong to be an addict." The important aspect of this solution is that the druggist must be open to being convinced by the buyer, must be open to the possibility of agreeing that it is fine for this person to be an addict. Otherwise, it will be a feigned discussion, one we are likely to engage in with our young children: "You think it is fine to stay up all night watching *South Park*. O.K. Let's talk about it."

This doesn't mean that you check your common sense and your ethical sense at the door. As Elihu Root once said, "about half the practice of a decent lawyer consists in telling would-be clients that they are damned fools and should stop."

PART TWO
STUDY SKILLS

Expect a bewildering set of materials: "cases" from different states and from different times, Restatements, law reviews, Uniform Codes, state and federal statutes and maybe even snippets of the United Nations Charter. What's going on? What are you to make of this mess? Should you memorize case names? Dates? The language of the Restatements? How a state statute differs from a Uniform Code provision?

Let's back up and ask, "What do lawyers do?" Clients come, seeking help. When they explain their situation, their lawyers will spot the legal problems that must be resolved. Based on their training, these lawyers will know the law's general solutions to these problems; and, based on that knowledge, will ask their clients to amplify certain portions of their stories in order to determine how the law's general solutions would play out in the clients' situations.

In law school, you are learning how to be a lawyer. You are learning:

1. To spot legal issues (problems) lurking in life's encounters;

2. To know the general solutions the law has adopted to solve these problems; and

3. To apply these solutions to the case at hand.

This is the essential format you will follow in your various tasks, from writing memos to taking exams. Law students, when I tell them that, have a hard time believing it. "Yeah, well, that's cool, but do I have to memorize dates?" Hopefully, as you work your way through this Part, you will get a hands-on sense of what I mean. Knowing what you are trying to learn will inform your understanding of how to learn it.

In Chapter 8, I expand on your educational goals and relate them to educational methods.

Most of your time will be spent reading and briefing cases. Chapter 9 gives you some tips on how to read cases and gives you one to work on. Chapter 10 goes into the matter of case-briefing, and it, too, gives you a case to work on. Do the work. Not only will you understand the general advice better, but you will also be getting a head start on your Contracts class; the two cases I use are classic first-semester fare.

Chapter 11 offers advice on how to get the most out of your classes, and Chapter 12 discusses the use and abuse of study aids, and "outlining" your courses (a grand law school tradition).

The last chapter in this Part, "Fear and Loathing in the First Year," is basically therapy. Read it when you suddenly realize that you are the dumbest person in law school. Because this insight strikes different students at different times, there is no set time for that chapter.

CHAPTER 8

STUDYING LAW: APPLICATION, NOT MEMORIZATION

The mind that is not baffled is not employed.
Poet Wendell Berry

Law is not something we know, but something we do. Like baseball.

Professor Grant Gilmore

What should you be doing? "Learning the law."

Wrong.

Over the years many students have come to me with: "I thought I would have done better in your class. I really *know* Contracts."

That might have been their problem. Having taught the course for decades, I still don't *know* contracts.

If knowledge be your quest, bad things happen. First, you will be tempted to close your eyes and *memorize* battery's four elements (or were there five?). To quote, again, the philosopher and psychologist William James:

"Speedy oblivion is the almost inevitable fate of all that is committed to memory in this simple way. Whereas, on the contrary, the same materials recurring in different contexts, and repeatedly reflected up, grow into such a system that they remain permanent possessions."

For James, the key is *continuous application*.

If you're after knowledge, you will protect your hard-won insights: ("OK, *finally* I figured out that battery consists of *four* elements. Enough already!") Fearing that the center will not hold and things will fly apart, you will not challenge your knowledge ("How is element two different from element four? Wait! Oh, no, maybe there are only three elements, or maybe four is really two elements which makes, what, five? Help!").

Challenge your understandings. Relish your ignorance. *Baffle your mind*.

The quest for knowledge quickly becomes the search for "right answers." Of course, those who write study aids know the right answers; you scurry to the bookstore. You lose confidence when you make a mistake ("There are *five* elements to battery—why did I ever come here?"). Classroom encounters become, not an opportunity to try out your ideas, but a forum to expose your stupidity.

I don't know Contracts; you won't either. Hopefully, by the end of the semester, you'll be able to *do* Contracts. Grant Gilmore, a giant among law professors, told us: *Law is not something we know, but something we do.*

How do you *do* law? Get in the trenches. Relish ambiguities and ask difficult questions. Refuse to be satisfied with easy understandings. Give up the quest for clarity: *law is fuzzy*. (It's not you, it's the law.) Never walk away smug, simply run out of time.

In earlier editions I called this chapter "Study Skills." As a great believer in the power of language, I now realize that "study skills" is a downer, calling up images from Edgar Allan Poe:

Once upon a midnight dreary,
  While I pondered, weak and weary,

Over a quaint and forgotten case,
  While I'd nodded, nearly napping,

Turning the page, nary a picture,
  Nothing but small font, evermore!

"Doing law" is more descriptive but it too suggests a certain heaviness, a certain seriousness. Professor Gilmore told us that doing law is like playing baseball—something that we get better at with practice. So let's use a lighter, happier expression to get us through those long dreary nights: *practicing law*. As the midnight hour approaches, don't greet the next case with, "Oh, no, another ten pages!" but rather with, "Great, another opportunity to practice!"

"All that sounds like fun, but I still have to know the elements of battery!"

Indeed you do. But, having practiced with them, having applied them to various situations, and having challenged them, they will not be on their way to "speedy oblivion" but rather will be your "permanent possessions."

Finally, just like practicing baseball, or the piano, or a foreign language, *expect* to make mistakes. You *will* misunderstand cases, garble statutes, and curse long professorial rants. *Don't fear mistakes, relish them;* often you learn more from them than from your insights. As Roosevelt said, "the only thing we have to fear is fear itself." Fast forward to our own time and another of my heroes, Ms. Fizzle of *The Magic School Bus*. As are you, her preschoolers embark on wonderful educational experiences. As they set off, she shouts,

Remember! Take chances! Make mistakes!

CHAPTER 9

READING CASES

"Who's on first?"

"No. Respondent's on first."

"Who's she?"

"The appellee."

The staple of the first-year diet is the appellate case. Something happens (usually bad), and a lawsuit is filed; at the trial court, someone loses, perhaps the plaintiff, perhaps the defendant. The loser, filing an appeal, now becomes the "appellant" while the other side is called the "respondent," or, sometimes, the "appellee." To make matters worse, occasionally the appellant will win at the first appellate court and his adversary appeals and now the appellant becomes the respondent. Whatever.

In this chapter, I'll ask you to do some work. You can skim though it but that would be foolish.

Reading cases is hard. As a first cut, consider four simple questions:

1. Who are the parties?

2. What is the argument (in legal jargon, the "issue" the court must decide)?

3.   Who wins and what happens next? (Is there to be a new trial?)

4.   What should I get from this case?

Given these questions, read my slightly altered version of a famous case, that of *Walker–Thomas.* Underline parts you feel are important. Write in the margins. Don't just read the case; go after it.

WILLIAMS v. WALKER–THOMAS FURNITURE CO.

U.S. Court of Appeals, District of Columbia Cir., 1965.

J. Skelly Wright, Circuit Judge. *Walker–Thomas Furniture Company operates a retail furniture store in the District of Columbia. During the period of 1957 to 1962, Ms. Williams purchased a number of household items from Walker–Thomas, for which payment was to be made in installments. The terms of each purchase were contained in a printed form contract which provided that, in the event of a default in the payment of any monthly installment, Walker–Thomas could repossess the item.*

The contract further provided that "the amount of each periodical installment payment ... shall be credited pro rata on all outstanding bills...." The effect of this rather obscure provision, known as a cross-collateral clause, was to keep a balance due on every item purchased until the balance due on all items, whenever purchased, was paid. As a result, the debt incurred at the time of purchase of each item was secured by the right to repossess all the items previously purchased by the same purchaser.

On April 17, 1962, Ms. Williams bought a stereo set of stated value of $514.95. At that time, she had an outstanding balance of previous purchases of $164. The total of all of the purchases she had made at the store over the years came to $1,800. Over the years she had paid $1,400. At the time of this purchase, Walker–Thomas was aware of Ms. William's financial position. The reverse side of the stereo contract listed the name of her social worker and her $218 monthly stipend from the government. Nevertheless, with full knowledge that Ms. Williams had to feed, clothe, and support both herself and seven children on this amount, Walker–Thomas sold her a $514 stereo set.

Shortly after purchasing the stereo, Ms. Williams failed to make her payments, and Walker–Thomas brought this action to repossess every item she had purchased at its store over the years. The court below found that, under the contract, Walker–Thomas had the right to do so and granted judgment for it. Ms. Williams appeals that decision to this court.

Ms. Williams' principal contention, rejected by the trial court, is that cross-collateral clauses are unconscionable and, hence, not enforceable. The trial court explained its rejection of this contention as follows:

"I cannot condemn too strongly appellee's conduct. It raises serious questions of sharp practice and irresponsible business dealings. A review of the legislation in the District of Columbia affect-

ing retail sales and the pertinent decisions of the highest court in this jurisdiction disclose, however, no ground upon which this court can declare the contracts in question contrary to public policy. I think Congress should consider corrective legislation to protect the public from such exploitative contracts as were utilized in the case at bar."

We do not agree that the court lacked the power to refuse enforcement to contracts found to be unconscionable. In other jurisdictions, it has been held as a matter of common law that unconscionable contracts are not enforceable. While no decision of this court so holding has been found, the notion that an unconscionable bargain should not be given full enforcement is by no means novel. In Scott v. United States (1870), the Supreme Court stated:

"If a contract be unreasonable and unconscionable, but not void for fraud, a court of law will give to the party who sues for its breach damages, not according to its letter, but only such as he is equitably entitled to."

Since we have never adopted or rejected such a rule, the question here presented is actually one of first impression.

Congress has recently enacted the Uniform Commercial Code, which specifically provides that the court may refuse to enforce a contract which it finds to be unconscionable at the time it was made. The enactment of this section, which occurred subsequent to the contracts here in suit, does not mean that the common law of the District of Columbia was other-

wise at the time of enactment nor does it preclude the court from adopting a similar rule in the exercise of its powers to develop the common law for the District of Columbia. In fact, in view of the absence of prior authority on the point, we consider the Congressional adoption of that section persuasive authority for following the rationale of the cases from which the section is explicitly derived. Accordingly, we hold that where the element of unconscionability is present at the time a contract is made, the contract should not be enforced.

Unconscionability has generally been recognized to include an absence of meaningful choice on the part of one of the parties together with contract terms which are unreasonably favorable to the other party. Whether a meaningful choice is present in a particular case can only be determined by consideration of all the circumstances surrounding the transaction. In many cases, the meaningfulness of the choice is negated by a gross inequality of bargaining power. The manner in which the contract was entered is also relevant to this consideration. Did each party to the contract, considering his obvious education or lack of it, have a reasonable opportunity to understand the terms of the contract, or were the important terms hidden in a maze of fine print and minimized by deceptive sales practices? Ordinarily, one who signs an agreement without full knowledge of its terms might be held to assume the risk that he has entered a one-sided bargain. But when a party of little bargaining power, and hence little real choice, signs a commercially unreasonable contract with little or no knowledge of its terms, it is hardly likely that his consent, or even an objective manifestation of his consent, was ever given to all the terms. In such a case the usual rule that the terms of the agreement are not to be questioned should be abandoned, and the court should consider whether the terms of the contract are so unfair that enforcement should be withheld.

In determining reasonableness or fairness, the primary concern must be with the terms of the contract considered in light of the circumstances existing when the contract was made. The test is not simple, nor can it be mechanically applied. The terms are to be considered "in the light of the general commercial background and the commercial needs of the particular trade or case." Professor Corbin, a leading expert in the field, suggests the test as being whether the terms are "so extreme as to appear unconscionable according to the mores and business practices of the time and place." We think this formulation correctly states the test to be applied in those cases where no meaningful choice was exercised upon entering the contract.

Because the trial court did not feel that enforcement could be refused, no findings were made on the possible unconscionability of the contracts in these cases. Since the record is not sufficient for our deciding the issue as a matter of law, the cases must be remanded to the trial court for further proceedings.

So ordered.

Take a few minutes to jot down what you learned from this case.

Discussion

No doubt you read carefully but not as carefully as you will. Can you answer these questions?

1. What was the precise issue before this court? How was it resolved?

2. Remembering that judges are like the Ruler of the Queen's Navy, and never think of thinking for themselves, which side called the judge's attention to *Scott v. United States*? What argument was made based upon that case?

3. Why didn't the court simply apply the UCC to this case? Congress had passed it and made it the law.

4. What argument did the store make based upon the fact that Congress passed the UCC?

5. Two elements of unconscionability are discussed. What are they? And what is the relationship between them? For a term to be found unconscionable must both elements be found or only one?

To answer these questions, you will have to *reread* the opinion. Get used to rereading opinions.

They're not *War and Peace*. Once you have, take a stab at the questions. Write your answers. Then we can compare notes.

———————

Don't panic: you are not expected to *know* which party cited what authority or which party made what argument. I am not talking about what you want to take away from a case; that is the subject of the next chapter on case briefing. What I am talking about is the intensity with which you read cases; better yet, *dissect* cases.

Recall my comparison of legal argument and ping-pong. It is extremely useful to restage the game: as to each argument and as to each case, which side was relying on it? For what purpose? A careful reader would know, as she read along or with a moment's reflection, which side cited *Scott* and for what purpose; a careful reader would not, however, try to "learn it." Who cited *Scott* in terms of legal doctrine doesn't matter.

My answers:

1. The precise issue was whether the courts of D.C. have the *power* to refuse to enforce parts of contracts if they are *unconscionable*. The court below didn't think it had the power. This case does *not* decide whether the particular clause was unconscionable; the case is sent back to the lower court to make that determination.

This raises an interesting point. The case appears in Contract books, not to teach you anything about the power of the D.C. courts, but rather to teach you something about unconscionability. Hence what you are supposed to get from a case may not be what the case was technically about.

"What happens next?" is an essential question. In a torts case, say, a defendant might raise a defense and the issue before the appellate court is, *if* the defendant can establish the facts underlying the defense, would it defeat the plaintiff's case. If the answer is yes, then the matter will be remanded to the trial court to see if the defendant, as a factual matter, can prove the needed facts.

2.   The customers brought up *Scott* in support of their argument that the courts have an inherent power to refuse to enforce contracts, at least not to their "letter," if they are "unconscionable."

A somewhat plausible "wrong answer" would be that the store cited *Scott* for the proposition that the courts enforce, even if not to their "letter," unconscionable contracts. The problem with this answer is that the store, given the tenor of trial court opinion, knows that the "letter" the court would refuse to enforce would be the cross-collateral clause.

3.   The court couldn't just apply the UCC to the case because the contracts in question were signed *before* the UCC was passed. Statutes, generally, cannot have *retroactive* effect.

This raises a fascinating jurisprudential issue. Assume, when the contract was signed, unconscionable contracts were enforceable. *Congress* can't retroactively change the rule ("unconscionable contracts will *not* be enforced") because that would be unfair to Walker–Thomas. But apparently there is nothing wrong with the *courts* changing the rules ("unconscionable contracts will *not* be enforced"). Of course it can be argued that the court *really* wasn't changing the rules at all; that in some sense the common law in D.C. always had a doctrine of unconscionability; it's just that no one realized it before Judge Wright came along and told us.

But what happens when a court *overrules* prior decisions? Aren't they changing the rules, upsetting apple carts, retroactively? Ask your profs.

4.　What argument the store made based on Congress's passage of the UCC is a difficult question, as you must *infer* what the argument was. The argument is that, prior to the passage of the UCC, the courts of D.C. could not refuse to enforce contracts on the basis of unconscionability: if they already *had* that power, why would Congress pass the UCC *giving* them that power?

Note here the reversibility of many legal arguments. The court, adopting something of an "in your face" style, writes:

"The enactment of the UCC does not mean that the common law of the District of Columbia was otherwise at the time of enactment. In fact ... we consider the congressional adoption persuasive

authority for following the rationale of the cases from which the section is explicitly derived."

5.　To show a contract provision unconscionable, the customer must show *both* lack of meaningful choice *and* terms unreasonably favorable to the other party.

*"Unconscionability has generally been recognized to include an absence of meaningful choice on the part of one of the parties **together with** contract terms which are unreasonably favorable to the other party."*

It is critical that you focus on the *relationship* between elements. In our prior math notation, here we find a 1 + 2 = VICTORY equation, not a 1 **or** 2 = VICTORY one.

A Few Tricks to Reading Closely

1.　First, what is the *issue*: what legal point must the court decide in order to resolve the case?

2.　Second, be clear on the basics:

What happened in the court below?

Who is appealing?

On what theory?

Who wins and why?

What happens next? Is the case over or is it sent back for a new trial?

3. Third, be clear about the *relationship* between arguments and between elements. If the court is making two points, the relationship can be:

1 + 2 = VICTORY

   or

1 **or** 2 = VICTORY

Again, to prevail on unconscionability, the customer must show "lack of meaningful choice" **and** "unreasonable terms"; one is not enough.

Before you move on to the next case you must read, be sure you can answer all three of the above questions. Use it as crib sheet.

If you have time, and occasionally you should have, take your analysis deeper by considering two other questions:

4. As to each argument the judges make, *ask*, "Who did they steal that one from?"

5. Play loser. Pretend you are the lawyer representing the losing side in the case and that the court's opinion is simply your opponent's argument. How will you respond to it? Often, opinions seem so clearly right that we ask ourselves, "Why did the losing side even bother?" Always remember that the losing side thought that it would win! Judicial opinions are "winners' history."

———————

This has been a lot of work. What have you learned? Contracts can be denied enforcement if

they are found to be unconscionable and unconscionability consists of two elements. Why didn't we
just tell you and save the muddle?

To give you practice, not only analyzing cases, but
also in struggling though tough material. You are
now better prepared to tackle all the other cases
you will read as a student and as a lawyer.

And you are a tad smarter—hard mental work
does that to you.

CHAPTER 10

BRIEFING CASES

Briefing is a brilliant educational device. I will begin by asking you to brief a case.

"You can't do that. You haven't told us *how* to brief a case!" A better point: I haven't told you *why* you should brief.

One reason is for review; you don't want to have to reread all those cases reviewing for finals. The real worth of briefing, and why you must do your own, is that it forces you to grapple with the cases and to reduce them to their core. *Brevity is a virtue in both regards.*

An appellate opinion is a *rule of law* announced in a specific *factual context* and justified by a particular *rationale*. The *traditional briefing format* uses these categories of analysis:

1. Facts

2. Issue/Holding ("Rule of Law")

3. Rationale

If you are called on in class to recite a case, you will say something like, "The facts of the case are ... and the issue before the court was ... and the court held that ... for the following reasons...." (assuming that you don't just freeze up and die).

The "issue" is the legal question the court must decide. In *Walker–Thomas*, the case you read in the last chapter, the issue was whether the court has the power under common law to void unconscionable contracts. Recall, in *Globe*, our old favorite, the issue was whether exculpatory clauses violated public policy.

The "holding" of the case is how the court resolved the "issue." It becomes the "rule of law" for which the case stands. These terms can be hopelessly muddled.

Issue: Does the court have the power to void unconscionable contracts?

Holding: The court has the power to void unconscionable contracts.

Rule of Law: The court has the power to void unconscionable contracts.

. . . . .

Issue: How to define unconscionability?

Holding: Unconscionability involves two elements
. . . . .

Rule of Law: Unconscionability involves two elements . . . . .

The essential thing is not the label but the learning; you must be able to state the legal *question* the court had to decide, the *law* it used to decide it, and *how* it decided it.

You are about to meet two extraordinary people, Justice Cardozo (a true common law giant) and Lucy, Lady Duff–Gordon (who is seen, alas, not at her finest—in law, people are seldom seen at their finest). Lucy was a well known designer of women's clothes and, leading the way for today's superstars, was one of the first celebrities to endorse products. Whether she was a role model is lost in the historical record. She did, however, survive the *Titanic*.

But we are not here to gossip.

To help you brief the case, there is a contract doctrine called "mutuality of obligation." Unless both sides are bound to do something under the contract, neither is. In this case Lucy, the defendant, promised Wood, a marketing agent, the exclusive right to market her endorsement. Lucy cheated by making some deals on the side! When Wood sued, she defended on the basis of "mutuality of obligation."

> *"Sure, I made a promise to Wood, but Wood never actually promised to do anything for me. He could walk away from the contract any time he wanted to. Because he didn't have any promises to live up to, under the doctrine of mutuality, I don't have to live up to mine."*

Your brief shouldn't be more than a page and should follow the traditional format: facts, issue, and rationale. Before you can begin a brief, you must read the entire case, maybe more than once. However, as you read it, underline what you think is important and, yes, jot ideas in the margins. The basic questions you will have to answer are: What was the question the court had to decide? What were the important facts in the case? Why did the court decide as it did?

WOOD v. LUCY, LADY DUFF–GORDON

New York Court of Appeals, 1917.

Cardozo J. *The defendant styles herself "a creator of fashions." Her favor helps a sale. Manufacturers of dresses, millinery, and like articles are glad to pay for a certificate of her approval. The things which she designs, fabrics, parasols, and what not, have a new value in the public mind when issued in her name. She employed the plaintiff to help her to turn this vogue into money. He was to have the exclusive rights, subject always to her approval, to place her indorsement on the designs of others. He was also to have the exclusive right to place her own designs on sale, or to license others to market them. In return she was to have one-half of "all profits and revenues" derived from any contracts he might make. The exclusive right was to last at least one year from April 1, 1915, and thereafter from year to year unless terminated by notice of 90 days. The plaintiff says that he kept the contract on his part, and that the defendant broke it. She placed her indorsement on fabrics, dresses, and millinery without his knowledge, and withheld the profits. He sues her for the damages, and the case comes here on demurrer.*

The agreement of employment is signed by both parties. It has a wealth of recitals. The defendant insists, however, that it lacks the elements of a contract. She says that the plaintiff does not bind himself to anything. It is true that he does not promise in so many words that he will use reason-

able efforts to place the defendant's indorsement and market her designs. We think, however, that such a promise is fairly to be implied. The law has outgrown its primitive stage of formalism when the precise word was the sovereign talisman, and every slip was fatal. It takes a broader view today. A promise may be lacking, and yet the whole writing may be "instinct with an obligation," imperfectly expressed (Scott, J., in McCall Co. v. Wright, 133 App. Div. 62, 117 N.Y.S. 775). If that is so, there is a contract.

The implication of a promise here finds support in many circumstances. The defendant gave an exclusive privilege. She was to have no right for at least a year to place her own indorsement or market her own designs except through the agency of the plaintiff. The acceptance of the exclusive agency was an assumption of its duties. Many other terms of the agreement point the same way. We are told at the outset by way of recital that:

"The said Otis F. Wood possesses a business organization adapted to the placing of such indorsement as the said Lucy, Lady Duff–Gordon, has approved."

The implication is that the plaintiff's business organization will be used for the purpose for which it is adapted. But the terms of the defendant's compensation are even more significant. Her sole compensation for the grant of an exclusive agency is to be one-half of all the profits resulting from the plaintiff's efforts. Unless he gave his efforts, she

*could never get anything. Without an implied prom-
ise, the transaction cannot have such business "effi-
cacy, as both parties must have intended that at all
events it should have." Bowen, L.J., in the Moor-
cock, 14 P.D. 64, 68. But the contract does not stop
there. The plaintiff goes on to promise that he will
account monthly for all moneys received by him, and
that he will take out all such patents and copyrights
and trademarks as may in his judgment be necessary to protect the rights and articles affected by the
agreement. It is true, of course, as the Appellate
Division has said, that if he was under no duty to
try to market designs or to place certificates of
indorsement, his promise to account for profits or
take out copyrights would be valueless. But in determining the intention of the parties the promise has a
value. It helps to enforce the conclusion that the
plaintiff had some duties. His promise to pay the
defendant one-half of the profits and revenues resulting from the exclusive agency and to render accounts
monthly was a promise to use reasonable efforts to
bring profits and revenues into existence. For this
conclusion the authorities are ample.*

*The judgment of the Appellate Division should be
reversed . . . .*

Try your hand at briefing the case; then we'll
discuss it.

Issue/Holding/Rule

Stating the issue is a matter of art and, occasionally, contention. Sometimes courts come right out
and tell you "The issue we have to resolve is . . . ."

or "We therefore hold that . . . ." When they do, hog heaven. But generally they don't; you have to root around some. (Sorry for the imagery.)

In *Lucy,* you had to root around. How did you state your issue? Consider two possibilities:

Issue: Will the contract be enforced?

Issue: Will the court imply a promise on the part of an agent to use reasonable efforts to market endorsements of a famous woman where both sides signed the contract and where they agreed to split the profits and he agreed to account for them.

What do you make of these statements of the issue? Jot!

The first is wildly too broad: it's always the issue (except in Torts, where it's "Was it a tort?"). State the issue so that it can be turned into a useful rule of law: "Contracts can be enforced" isn't one.

The second rendition illustrates the frying pan: being too specific. It can become a rule of law, but not much of one.

Rule of law: The court will imply a promise on the part of an agent to use reasonable efforts to market endorsements of a famous woman where both sides signed the contract and where they agreed to split the profits and he agreed to account for them.

As a rule of law, this wouldn't do much work in future cases because it seems to encompass very specific facts. What if Lucy wasn't famous? What if he hadn't agreed to account for the profits? You must strive for a statement of the issue that, when answered, can become a useful rule of law, neither too broad nor too specific.

Issue: Will the court imply a promise to use reasonable efforts on the part of an agent who has been given an exclusive contract?

Lawyers can argue as to the precise issue. Some might include, for example, additional matters:

Issue: Will the court imply a promise to use reasonable efforts on the part of an agent who has been given an exclusive contract *and who has made some promises in the contract*?

The question is whether the case stands for a broad or narrow proposition of law. Will it apply only in cases where the agent has made "some promises" or in all cases where he has an "exclusive"? There are no right answers, only good arguments.

Facts

Include only *operative facts,* those that make a difference in the court's decision. The others, let's call *tidbits*. Tidbits are easy to recognize. In *Lucy,* some of the tidbits were that Lucy designed parasols, that the contract was dated a certain date, and, alas, that her favor helps a sale.

Reread your statement of facts: have you included tidbits, facts that played no part in the court's decision? *Including tidbits is a "no-no."* They make your brief longer, and hence less helpful when it comes time to review. More importantly, including tidbits may indicate that you are "looking busy" and sticking things in without forcing yourself to consider their relevance.

What were the *operative facts*? Some are clear, such as the fact that Wood did not, in so many words, promise to undertake any work for Lucy. Your brief should have included that. Reasonable minds can differ on some of the facts at the margin. Is Wood's promise to "account monthly" an operative fact, or is it a tidbit? Another way of asking that question is, "If he hadn't made that promise, would the court refuse to imply the promise of *reasonable efforts*?" I don't think so. As I don't think the court's decision would have been different, I don't think "monthly accounting" was an operative fact. But who am I to say? Perhaps, down the road, a court might distinguish *Lucy* on that very basis:

> *"In the case before us, we are asked to imply a promise as was done in* Wood v. Lucy. *However, in that case the agent had made some express promises, including to account monthly to his principal. Given the fact the agent made some express promises, it is easy to imply others. In the case before us, the agent made no express promises at all, and hence we refuse to follow* Wood v. Lucy *and will not imply a promise to use reasonable efforts."*

This illustrates a central point: what is, and what isn't, an operative fact is very much at issue in applying and distinguishing cases. Recall our discussion in Chapter 2 of whether *Globe* controlled *K v. Landlord* or whether the cases were distinguishable based on the factual differences.

Given uncertainty as to centrality, there may be a tendency to err on the side of inclusion. "Well, I'm not sure if that fact matters, so I'll put it in." Bad idea. Best to do your work *now*, before you think of another excuse later: "Is this fact important or isn't it?"

Warning. You will work hard on a brief and, at class, discover that others (alas, perhaps including the Prof) saw things differently, saw your tidbits as pivotal, and your operative facts as beneath mention. Don't get depressed. You brief cases, *not* to get them right, but to get into the thick of things. It's OK to be wrong as long as you're muddy.

Rationale

Restate the court's reasoning in *your own words* (or, if you prefer, those of Chaucer). Copying what the court said is tedious and mindless.

The law has outgrown its primitive stage of formalism when the precise word was the sovereign talisman, and every slip was fatal. It takes a broader view today. A promise may be lacking, and yet the whole writing may be "instinct with an obligation," imperfectly expressed.

I don't care how many times you copy that over. To understand it, you simply must try to express it in your own words. What does it mean? Talk about "imperfectly expressed"!

What did you have for the rationale in *Lucy*? I would have put something to the effect that the court seems to justify its decision on the common-sense notion that, "Come on, the parties obviously intended that Wood would sing for his supper. If he didn't, Lucy would be too vulnerable because she had given him an exclusive. Even though he didn't come out and say so, we will imply a promise to use reasonable efforts."

Viewing cases as opportunities to practice doing law, don't overlook the intellectual dividends that can flow if you *challenge* the court's reasoning. Can you think of any reasons why Wood would *not* want to promise Lucy that he would use "reasonable efforts?" Can you think of any reasons Lucy might have agreed to give him an exclusive contract even though he didn't promise "reasonable efforts"?

A Way to Check Your Brief

A good way to check your brief is to put it in the following form:

We decided X (holding) because

> *1. Of these operative facts and*
>
> *2. For these good reasons (rationale).*

If you do put your briefs in this format, you may find some strange constructions:

*We decided to imply a promise of "reasonable efforts" on Wood's part **because** Lucy designed parasols.*

This raises the issue of whether you should always follow the traditional format: facts, issue and holding, rationale.

Alternative Format

How do we know what facts are operative unless we know the issue? What had been just an interesting tidbit becomes the smoking gun *if* the issue was "Is Lucy a woman of many talents?"

*We decide that Lucy is a woman of many talents **because** she designs parasols.*

Consider putting the issue first, and then the facts. It then becomes much easier to tell which facts are operative and which are tidbits.

Another problem with the traditional format is that it suggests that facts, issue, and rationale are all quite distinct. They aren't. They often meld together. For example, a statement of the issue must include at least some operative facts or it will soar off into "Will this contract be enforced?" That said, however, the categories can be helpful.

The last problem with the traditional format is that it doesn't handle the *holding/dicta* problem very well.

Holding/Dicta

Holdings are statements of law necessary for the decision in the case; *dicta* are statements of law which aren't necessary for that decision. Recall *Walker–Thomas*. The court discussed two matters: first whether the courts had the power to void unconscionable contracts and, second, the elements of unconscionability (lack of meaningful choice coupled with unreasonably favorable terms). Which the holding and which the dicta?

The holding was that the courts have the power; it was needed to decide the case. The dicta was the discussion of what constitutes unconscionability; it was not necessary to decide the case because the court did not decide whether the contract was unconscionable. Why do we split these hairs?

It goes to the heart of *stare decisis*. When something is really at issue, when the case turns on it, the court will think long and hard about it before reaching a decision. The reason we follow prior decisions is that we respect that effort. Compare that to a statement of law that has the quality of, "Oh, by the way, did you know that...."

Dictum is not ("are" not, for you real hair splitters) worthy of the same respect because it is not the product of long, serious thought; this is because nothing in the case turned on it.

To see how this works out, assume a case following *Walker–Thomas* where the issue is how to define unconscionability.

Lawyer One: Your Honor, in *Walker–Thomas* the court defined unconscionability, and you should follow that definition.

Lawyer Two: No, Your Honor, that discussion of unconscionability was dicta.

Judge: That's right. The court didn't have to define unconscionability to decide the issue before it. Therefore, that definition doesn't bind me.

The distinction between holding and dicta is a useful analytical ploy. It forces you to think deeply about the precise issue. But don't ignore dicta. Much of the law you will learn will come from judicial asides. That is why the traditional briefing format doesn't always work; had your brief of *Walker–Thomas* not covered the elements of unconscionability, you would have missed the main point.

Clutter

Should you include citations, dates, names of judges, and procedural history? Or are they just clutter?

Wood v. Lucy, Lady Duff–Gordon

New York Court of Appeals, 1917

222 N.Y. 88, 118 N.E. 214

Opinion by Justice Cardozo

Is this information necessary?

No, hardly ever. It won't help you review, nor does it further your understanding of the case. In Constitutional Law courses, it's interesting to see how a particular Justice's philosophy plays out in several areas. However, in most courses, who wrote the opinion is of little interest. That said, in the development of common law principles, some courts are more equal than others. The opinions of the New York Court of Appeals (the highest state court in New York) with Justice Cardozo and the California Supreme Court under Justice Traynor carry particular weight.

Dates are important *if* you are studying the historical development of a particular legal doctrine. Sometimes you are. *Usually* you aren't. Most cases are included in casebooks not to show you what the law *was* but to show you what the law *is*.

Legal education generally ignores history. Reading old cases as current law may give you the sense that the problems facing the law have always been the same, that the law itself is above history, that it is the product of neutral rational principles rather than the clash of competing philosophical, economic, and political positions. It isn't.

Oliver Wendell Holmes, in his great essay, "The Path of the Law," said it best:

> *I cannot but believe that if the training of lawyers led them habitually to consider more definitely and explicitly the social advantage on which the rule they lay down must be justified, they sometimes would hesitate where now they are confident, and see that really they were taking sides upon debatable and often burning questions.*

Law cannot and should not escape its historical context. Yet we tend to teach law as a set of timeless principles. I lament this with great fanfare. But, bottom line, I am part of the problem. Don't include dates. Include them only if you think them important. And be explicit as to why the date is important. Do you feel the case would not be followed today because it reflects different times?

Procedural History of the Case

Some profs *insist* on it and, well, it's their nickel. For my money, don't *routinely* include the procedural history of the case.

Jury found for plaintiff. Defendant appeals on basis of improper jury instruction.

Appellate court reversed and plaintiff appeals. Affirmed.

This tells you nothing about the law and simply takes up space. Your interest is in what the error was in the jury instruction.

This is not to say, however, that procedural history is irrelevant. I return to the notion that I developed in the last chapter. There are things that you should understand about a case (such as which party cited which case) that you need not "take away" from the opinion. The procedural history of a case is one such thing. Forcing yourself to sort it out will help you to understand how courts operate and will help you understand which party is arguing what.

The procedural history of a case can also tell you some very interesting things. In Lucy, Cardozo concluded:

The judgment of the Appellate Division should be reversed.

What does this mean?

Lucy won at the lower court. Reading the flowing prose of Justice Cardozo, we are swept along, "But of course a promise should be implied." Before

Cardozo, the courts were reluctant, in the name of party autonomy, to "imply terms" to contracts. Cardozo was working a major *shift* in the law, but he doesn't seem to be making a ripple. Recall our earlier discussion about the reluctance of courts to overrule prior decisions. Instead they distinguish them or, as here, add certain refinements which in fact change the basic rule. In the common tradition, *our revolutions are pretty much invisible.*

In addition to the procedural history of a case, be sure you are clear about *what happens next.* Often the decision will put an end to the matter, once and for all. But what about the case of *Wood v. Lucy*? Has Wood won his case? Think.

Final Pointers

1. Leave wide margins so that you can add points from class discussion and make further notes when you review.

2. Don't expect to write your brief the first time you read the case.

3. Some advise *not* to brief a case until you have read all of the cases in the same assignment. This helps you see how the particular tree fits in the forest.

4. Include a "puzzling points" section at the end. What don't you understand about the case? Do you agree with it?

Here is a format you might try out. If you find that it doesn't always work (and it won't), this discovery doesn't make me an idiot; it makes you a genius. It shows that you are not mechanically filling in the blanks; it shows you are struggling with the material.

1. Issue/holding (What legal issue did the court have to resolve and how did it resolve it? Note: in some cases you will find more than one issue.)

2. Operative facts (don't include the kitchen sink . . . unless the case is about a plumber).

3. Rationale (in your own words).

4. Procedural history and what happens next (when of interest).

5. Puzzling points.

And that's all, folks!

CHAPTER 11

BEING THERE: CLASS

You will teach yourself the law; I will teach you how to think.

Professor Kingsfield, *The Paper Chase*

Let the wild rumpus start!

Maurice Sendak, *Where the Wild Things Are*

As an undergraduate you sat in class, mildly entertained, taking good notes, as the prof lectured. You left, if not a better person, at least a more knowledgeable one. Law school classes aren't like that.

The dreaded "Socratic method" replaces the lecture. The prof calls on a student to recite an assigned case: facts, issue, holding. Then the questions.

Prof:	If the facts showed X instead of Y, would the court have come out the same way?
Student 1:	Yes, because blah, blah, blah.
Student 2:	I disagree. The case wouldn't come the same way because blah, blah, blah.

Prof:	Ok, is this case different from the one we studied yesterday?
Audience:	(murmuring): Wait a minute, what's the answer? Would the case come out the same way if X, not Y?
Student 3:	I think they are consistent because blah, blah, blah.
Student 4:	Not so. They are inconsistent because blah, blah, blah.
Prof:	OK. What policy does the case further?
Audience:	(murmuring): Wait a minute, what's the answer? Are they consistent or not?

No answers. But that's OK. The goal was not to come away knowing that X would make a difference or that yesterday's case was inconsistent with today's. The goal was to teach how lawyers and judges work. *Law is not something that we know; it is something that we do.*

Expect frustration and confusion ... but also movement, excitement, and flashes of insight. Come away exhausted, confused, but that much closer to being a lawyer.

Jump in, try out ideas, and let the wild rumpus start!

Warming up

Take five minutes *before* class to review your briefs of the cases you will discuss. That way you won't waste valuable time trying to remember who the plaintiff was or what the dispute was about.

Being called on

Law school classrooms are often portrayed as scary places: professors gnash their terrible teeth, roll their terrible eyes, and skewer helpless students in front of hundreds of classmates, all aggressive, competitive and judgmental. Stories abound. One of my favorites is where the student, now a law professor, successfully answered the professor's first five questions only to trip up on the sixth.

"That just shows you didn't understand *anything* from the very beginning!"

I once had a student so intimidated by what he had seen in *The Paper Chase* and read in *One L,* that, before applying to law school, he searched scores and scores of law school bulletins, looking for the magic words: "We do not employ the Socratic Method." No luck.

We've mellowed. In the '60s and '70s there was a strong backlash against the rigors of the Socratic Method suggesting that it—well, for the lack of a better word—destroyed students. While some Kingsfields remain, most of us employ Socratic Method Light. Some alert you that you will be up the next day and others call on folks in alphabetical order. Some call only on volunteers.

Finally, we limit ourselves to *five* questions.

Trial lawyers advise witnesses, "Don't guess," and this is probably good advice in the classroom. If you are asked a question, and don't have a clue,'fess up—trouble's certain if you wing it. (There are follow-up questions.) The class is *not* about you: if make a fool of yourself, no one will care; classmates are dealing with their own fears.

I'll have more to say about the Socratic Method and the terror of being called on in Chapter 13, *Fear and Loathing in the First Year.*

Of course, the best way *not* to be called on is to volunteer. Volunteers are seldom cold called.

Volunteering

> *Put me in Coach, I'm ready to play,*
>
> *Today.*
>
> *Look at me,*
>
> *I can be,*
>
> *Centerfield.*
>
>   John Fogerty

Go to a third grade class: the teacher asks a question and *every* hand shoots up. Go to a law school class: the professor asks a question and everyone looks at their shoes. Curious.

Class is your *opportunity to play!* Jump in, test your ideas, think on your feet. You owe it to yourself and your classmates. Even though it may not feel like it, you have things to contribute.

Don't wait until you *know the answer* (that day
may never come) and don't wait until you have
something really good to say. When *we* think of
something we likely tell ourselves, "That's obvious,
everyone has thought of that. That's not really good
at all and I'm not raising my hand." Most likely,
however, no one else has thought of it.

Don't worry about asking *dumb* questions. They
are a virtue. Profs know their stuff and will zip on
down the road thinking everyone understands what
it took them a long time to understand. Brave souls
are needed to slow them down with dumb questions
(most likely everyone's confused). Staying with our
baseball metaphor, take one for the team!

Studies show that minorities, women, and even
certain parts of the classroom tend to volunteer
less. But once one does, others follow.

Volunteer *early* (or otherwise you might convince
yourself that you never will), but don't volunteer
often. There is a cost. While your arm waves, in
order to hold on to your comment, you will of
necessity be blocking what others are saying. Further classmates, and often even the professor, re-
sent frequent flyers. After you have volunteered
some, until you have something unique to offer,
curb your enthusiasm.

This raises an important point: the need to listen
to others; not to find fault, but to learn. You can
learn, perhaps more, from those who you have
previously pegged as morally and politically bank-
rupt. I've taught many years; seldom does a class go
by that I don't learn something from a student's

comment, insight or, indeed, argument. The ability to listen carefully, to silence the critical commentary of one's own internal voice, to understand another's position, is simply an essential lawyer skill. Practice now.

Taking notes

Another essential skill is taking notes.

Lawyers take notes as bullets whiz. As an opposing witness testifies, you'll listen for improper questions (in order to object) and to the answers, deciding whether they are consistent with the witness' prior statements and whether they help or hurt your case (and, if they hurt, whether there is anything you can do about them on cross). Clearly you can't transcribe the testimony; at best you can "jot" key points, perhaps a word or two, simply enough to remind you of where you want to go on cross-examination. *Learn to jot.* To wit:

"X instead of Y?"

"Cases consistent?"

"What policy?"

This way you can keep up as the discussion jumps from one topic to another rather than being bogged down trying to transcribe what the prof said about *X.*

"Yeah, but won't I forget?"

Locker room

Unless your short-term memory is worse than mine, you will not miss anything important *if* you conduct a *mini-review* after each class. Right after class, or surely some time the same day, take ten minutes to read over your class notes, filling in the points you missed.

"X instead of Y?" X made a difference in the sense of blah, blah, blah, but it didn't make a difference in the sense of blah, blah, blah.

Laptops

There will be temptations (MySpace, Instant Messenger, Breaking News, and, of course, Solitaire), and you will kid yourself: "A quick look, nothing more; it is, after all, a *News Flash* (Car runs out of gas in Orange County)." "I can do two things at once; in fact it *helps* me to do two things at once. I did it as an undergraduate and I was gang-busters!"

You *can't* do two things at once (at least not very well), and the harder you work in law school, the better lawyer you will be. Would you want take a cruise on a ship designed by an engineer who had played Solitaire during Basic Buoyancy?

Once you turn off the Internet and the games, there are still dangers. Some sit staring at their screens like grim court reporters, fingers poised, committed to transcribing *every* word. You'll miss subtleties. Anna Quindlen, in *Blessings*, writes of an elderly woman:

"After so many years of living alone, she had to remind herself that part of saying the right thing was reading the face of the person to whom you were speaking. It was no wonder that her own

mother, who had tended to look down at her own rings whenever she talked, had so often gotten things wrong."

Without the gestures, the grimaces and the grins, you hear the words but get things wrong.

Some students, finding that they tend to transcribe on their computer, take notes by hand.

Then there's the matter of *class participation*. It is important for your classmates and, indeed, for your professor, for you to offer an insight, answer a question or two. If your focus is on the screen, you will be something of an outsider, missing the movement and excitement of the class; volunteering becomes more of a knock on the door than an excited utterance. Further, and perhaps surprisingly, you participate by "being there." You have no idea how much you contribute to the class *merely* by looking at the professor. Professors, like Quindlen's character, need to read the audience, its gestures, grimaces, and grins. "Am I making things clear?" "Is it time to move on?" "Is my favorite footnote really that boring?"

The final potential problem with computers is that they may prevent active review. Handwritten notes cry out for margin notes, arrows, and additions. The need is always to be *involved* with the material, not just *rereading* your notes but *reworking* your notes, restating the rules, considering new hypos, asking if what you learned yesterday is consistent with what you learned today. This requires *writing*, not just cutting and pasting.

Bottom line, if you are using a laptop, fine, but consider some pledges:

I will <u>not</u> keep my hands on the keys at all times.

When a question is asked, I will think, not scroll.

I will look up and participate.

I will only write down key points, and never, not once, complete sentences.

Don't get the notes but miss the class.

CHAPTER 12

STUDY AIDS, STUDY GROUPS, OUTLINING AND MESSY CASEBOOKS

Write!

Reading, you skim along and all is rosy. Put pen to paper (or fingers to keyboard). Things get messy. "Wait, that point really doesn't make sense. And how did the court get from point A to point C? I thought I understood that."

Underlining and decorating your book with color markers gives you a sense of accomplishment but leaves the real work of understanding to a later day. Do it now.

Reading, write, in the margins: key facts, issues, rules of law, and puzzling points. Don't observe; participate. Writing, like the prospect of being hanged, concentrates the mind.

A well-used casebook is a mess.

Canned Briefs, and Commercial Outlines

Most profs advise *not* to rely on canned briefs or commercial outlines knowing, full well, that you will believe the second-year student who assures you that someone in his class used nothing but canned briefs ("Didn't even buy the book!") and did great. Probably the most important advice in this entire book: *Never believe second-year students.*

Study aids cover more than you need to know. I recall a short story:

> *A man commits murder in the victim's living room. "I must wipe my fingerprints off the glass I was drinking from!" Fair enough, he does. "What about the table? Did I touch it? Why take a chance?" He wipes the table. "Maybe I went into the kitchen! I don't think I did, but I can't be too sure, it will take just a few minutes!" The next morning, the murderer is found in the attic ... slavishly wiping off old trunks.*

There are scores and scores of legal doctrines that you won't cover. Treatises do. You'll get further and further from what you need to know, eventually becoming an unfortunate character in one of Poe's short stories.

Study aids "leave the driving to us." To learn how to practice law, do your own work. It does no good to let someone else take batting practice for you.

Make study aids your *last*, not your first, choice. If you are having a particularly difficult time with an area, a treatise might help. Once you have finished a topic, a Nutshell or commercial treatise might help you see how others have organized the material, and how others have described the rules.

Outlines and old exams

"Outlining" is a grand law school tradition and, like briefing, a brilliant educational device. Outlines combine case briefs, class notes, and any outside reading you have done. There is nothing magical about outlining except *doing* it. Its value is not the product but the production. It is yet another way to be actively involved with the material. ("Where does this interesting tidbit fit? Should it go under Topic A or Topic B and, come to think of it, what's the difference between A and B?") As for the major categories, the pompous Roman Numerals, the Table of Contents of your casebook can be helpful.

Some find it helpful to review old finals or example tests given in some books. Writing the answers helps, although, as a student, I would look at an old exam and simply freeze—there was simply no way I could answer it. On the real test I thanked my Little Voice shouting "You're doomed!" and moved on.

One idea worth pursuing. With a group of friends, take a couple of hours to review old exams. Don't just discuss the questions, write your answers. Then each reads their answer. This way you will see different approaches to writing exams. Nothing concentrates the mind like specific examples.

If you are going to take a multiple choice test, old tests and books showing models might be very helpful. They will give you a good sense of the format and how you should approach it.

Study Groups

One of the best things about practicing law is talking cases with colleagues. After law school I practiced with a Legal Services Program. Every Friday afternoon, we sat around the table in our small law library and talked cases. I was representing a group of low-income families, mostly farm workers, and their complaint was that a large cattle feedlot had moved next to their small community along with flies, smells, and general health hazards. The Friday meeting went something like this:

"How is your feedlot case going?"

"Great! I found a wonderful case, right on point. It holds a feedlot's a public nuisance. I'm moving for an injunction next week."

"But won't you have a problem with the Knowles case?"

"No, I can get around Knowles by arguing X."

"Yeah, but if you argue X, won't they come back with Y?"

"I thought of that. If they do, I'll argue Z."

"I dunno. Do that and they'll come back with W."

Exciting, hard-headed legal analysis. A newspaper reporter, who sat in, had a slightly different take:

"Oh, no! They've overrun the Nitpicks! Retreat to the Quibbles!"

So be it; some people don't appreciate Mozart. Once you get into your studies, law will be about the only thing you want to talk about, to the great

consternation of friends, significant others, and reporters.

Many enjoy study groups. While law school is
often an "all men are islands" kind of place, in fact
much legal work is done in teams. Working with
others is a tricky business. Some may dominate;
others seek free rides. Study groups will require you
to negotiate, often implicitly, the critical dynamics
of working with others, including, perhaps, some
explicit breaks:

> *"Let's stop for a few moments. This group doesn't
> seem to be working out. We never get as far as we
> plan. There are too many distractions. What can
> we do to improve this?"*

Or, more to the point:

> *"Kenney, shut up!"*

A few tips:

1. Encourage "dumb questions." Learn. Don't
    maintain image.

2. Don't play it by ear. Structure helps. Will you
    go over more than one subject? Will you dis-
    cuss cases or work on problems? When is
    quitting time?

3. Consider discussion leaders. "Next week, you
    do Property, I'll do Contracts." Planning and
    leading a review session can be quite edu-
    cational.

4. It is *not* a good idea to divide the first-year
    curriculum among the group to prepare out-

lines. "Kingsfield, you take Contracts." true value of outlines is writing them.

5. One really fun thing to do, near the end of the semester, is to play "Worst Case," "Funniest Case," "Most Pathetic Plaintiff," "Most Dastardly Defendant." It is a marvelous way to review.

Don't feel bad if you're *not* in a study group. You can do brilliantly without one, and they are not for everyone. Some people work better alone. So be it! But, outside the formal structure of study groups, be sure to "talk law" with other students every chance you get.

How much time?

About halfway through the first semester one of my students came to me.

"I'm doing all the reading and briefing and have even started on my outlines. But I still have time for my family and going to an occasional movie. What am I doing wrong?"

Don't get all caught up in the law school hype. Sure, it is demanding, and, sure, it will probably take more time and intense preparation than you are used to. But you don't have to become a mole.

Several years ago a national study showed law students averaging about two-and-a-half hours of study for each hour in class. Assuming you are carrying 15 units, this works out to about 53 hours per week. This is surely a full-time load and is probably enough already. Don't think that your classmates are studying all the time. We all like to play games with each other. Some will claim that they hardly study at all, others will claim that they study all the time, have already finished their outlines, and have found secret study aids that make the Rule Against Perpetuities look simple and even help them lose weight.

Time management, in school and then in practice, is a *major* issue. As I spend all of my time on this book, I'm probably not the one to ask. However you might want to take a look at a book by my colleagues Kay Kavanagh and Paula Nailon, *Excellence in the Workplace: Legal and Life Skills in a Nutshell*. It has many great ideas on managing your time (and no promotional fee was paid).

While we are all urged to take time to smell the flowers, a quick word in defense of workaholics. Their families may suffer but workaholics are some are the happiest people I know.

A leading cancer researcher was asked, "What are your hobbies? Your outside interests?"

"None. I'll cure cancer."

If you, like me, planned your entire undergraduate life around a single guiding principle, "No classes before 11," you will be shocked to learn that studying in the *early* morning hours is the most productive. After you wake up, you are as alert as you will be; thereafter, it's all downhill. If I start working around 6 a.m., I get as much done in one hour as I can in two or three in the late afternoon or evening.

Trees and Forests

Usually your focus will be quite narrow, on a particular case or, indeed, a particular paragraph. Every now and then, step back and try to get an orientation as to where you are and how a particular case fits with the others you have read. Consult the table of contents of your casebooks. Treatises, study aids, nutshells and law review articles can also help place the tree in the forest.

As you wander the halls of your first year, you are something of a tree *yourself*. How can you find the forest?

Journals

Law study is turbulent and overwhelming. Expect moments of exhilaration and expect moments of deep self-doubt. Every now and then, quit the hurly-burly and step back to reflect on what is happening to you. Consider keeping a journal. Take 20 to 30 minutes a few times a week to be with yourself and your thoughts.

My students, after initial grumbles, tell me they got a great deal out of it. Graduates tell me that they reread with great interest.

Write your thoughts, because, until you write them, you really don't know what they are. In your head they are just vague impressions and fragments of ideas; on paper they take shape and content. Write *now* while you are experiencing what will be an intense and highly significant period in your life. Next year it will be too late:

"First year? I liked it, at least some of it, I think."

Many journal entries will be first-year gossip. But occasionally force yourself to attempt something in the nature of an essay.

- *Reflections on cases.* Did you find it just? Were there certain aspects of the case that you found of special interest that your classmates and professor did not?

- *Reflections on law school.* How is it affecting you? Is it what you thought it would be? How does law school compare with undergraduate education? What about competition? What of male/female reactions in the classroom? Do you participate in class? Why or why not?

- *Reflections on lawyering.* Based on what you see, do you think you will like being a lawyer? What do you think the lawyers who handled a particular case were feeling? Were thinking? Could they have done something to avoid litigation?

Sit right down and write yourself a letter, to you as a third-year student. What will you tell the person you shall become? "Why I came to law school" might be a good topic. In the years to come, before you run off and join the circus, reread your letter.

Finally, what if you think keeping a journal is a waste of time? Write an essay: "Why keeping a journal is a waste of time."

You can't win. It's my book.

CHAPTER 13

FEAR AND LOATHING IN
THE FIRST YEAR

Visualize yourself as a cute, lovable baby, lying in your crib, playing with a teddy. Next to you is another crib. You look over and are delighted. A friend! Someone to share the unfolding wonders.

"Hey, wait just a minute!" you suddenly realize, "That baby's standing! I can't do that. I can't even pull myself up. I'll never make it. I'll never walk! Hey, you, you're not so cute, you know. Pudgy in fact. Show-off. Stuck-up! . . . . Brat!"

If you don't get this story, you haven't started yet.

Why was I afraid?

Imagine, is all that I can answer.

You have a stake. You have given up a job, a career, to do this. Or you have wanted to be a lawyer all your life.

You've studied hours on a case that is a half-page long. You couldn't understand most of what you read at first, but you have turned the passage inside out, drawn diagrams, written briefs. You could not be more prepared.

147

And when you get to class that demigod who knows all the answers finds another student to say things you never could have. Clearer statements, more precise. And worse—far worse—notions, concepts, whole constellations of ideas that never turned inside your head.

On many occasions I discovered that I didn't even understand what I didn't know until I was halfway through a class. Nor could I ever see how anyone else seemed to arrive at the right answer. Maybe they were all geniuses. Maybe I was the dumbest guy around.

The student? Perhaps a late-admit. From a non-accredited college. No. A professor. From an accredited college, Stanford. Scott Turow. He survived and so will you. He went on to great things as a lawyer/novelist. Isn't it nice to know that someone whose books routinely appear on the *New York Times Bestsellers List* once sat where you sit, terrified?

Why is the place so scary?

Partly, it's the hype. Professor Kingsfield, dreaded Contracts Professor of *Paperchase*, bellows at his first-year class:

Your minds are filled with mush. You will teach yourself the law. I will teach you how to think!

That doesn't bode well.

Law school is a brand new game. Doing graduate work, say in education, philosophy, or social work, you would know what to expect and would be confident in your abilities. But how are you going to do in law school?

During those long months of your first semester, you will work in the dark, receiving very little feedback as to how you are doing. Legal education makes little or no use of TA's. The good news is that professors do their own teaching; the bad news is that they do their own grading. Because they spend much of their time involved in scholarship and various forms of service, they have little time to give feedback in terms of reading term papers and midterms. It is not unusual to sit in a large class, perhaps over 100, awaiting the *one and only* test. By way of contrast, medical education makes extensive use of experienced students to teach novices, the saying being "See one, do one, teach one."

Some schools offer at least one small section in the first semester; and, in the second and third years, there will be seminars and clinical courses that have a lower student/faculty ratio and hence more feedback. With these exceptions, the general model holds: large classes followed by a single final.

To help you get through those first long months, I will look at the psychological tensions of the first year. In your darker moments, you believe "I'm the dumbest guy around" and "Everyone here is viciously competitive, except me and my friends." And you will, most likely, assign a wildly inappropriate meaning to grades. Most fear of being called on in class. I will explain why we teach the way we do, the so-called Socratic Method, and I will urge you to help us out, by raising your hand and volunteering.

"The Dumbest Guy Around!"

Take heart! Most everyone will feel that way every now and then, even that smug guy from Princeton.

In the old days, deans would welcome students:

"Look at the person to your right, look at the person to your left. Only one of you will be here second semester."

But that's not much of an issue anymore. We now *pre-flunk,* thanks to the LSAT. Still the "ferocious, grasping sense of uncertainty" remains. Why?

Insecurity is universal. So wrote Carl Rogers, the founder of non-directive counseling. Despite all of our brilliant successes, we know, deep down, that we really aren't that "hot"—thus far, its been luck and bluff. But law school feels different; those "demigods" will expose us, once and for all.

Not to worry. You will sneak through yet again.

As to those "notions, concepts, and whole constellations of ideas that never turned inside your head," but seem at the finger tips of your classmates, realize that there are *many* constellations of ideas. The ones your classmates express may never have turned inside your head *but* the ones that you have probably never turned in *theirs*.

Looking around the room, seeing all of your accomplished classmates, all of whom are smart, you may feel a little like jelly. Take comfort: *you* are that smart, educated, and stable person everyone is afraid of. That sentence is worth rereading, maybe even underlining.

"Law Students Are Viciously Competitive"

Fear quickly becomes loathing. Don't reject people simply because they had the effrontery to come to law school. You may reject your classmates as aggressive, competitive, humorless and, worst of all, compulsive, studying all the time. Now, of course, *I* wasn't that way as a law student, nor were my close friends. I am sure *you* and your friends aren't that way, either. But we can agree that everyone else is.

Competitiveness and aggressiveness are not just psychological projections. Your classmates are competitive, and so are you. It will not do simply to deny these feelings, "Oh, I don't care what grades I get or how I do; I just want to get by!" Some students take denial to the extreme of not trying; they do a minimum amount of studying and miss class frequently. (If you refuse to try, then failure will be less painful. On the other hand, there is always the possibility of the ultimate seventh-grade fantasy—an "A" in Contracts and an "F" for Effort.)

You are competitive, or you wouldn't be in law school. You have achieved recognition and pleasure in competing successfully in the past. This is not shameful. Accept this part of yourself; however, do not let it consume you. Scott Turow almost did. He told a friend, *"I don't give a damn about anybody else. I want to do better than them."*

My tone was ugly.... What had been suppressed all year was in the open now. All along there had been a tension between looking out for ourselves and helping each other; in the end, I did not expect anybody—not myself, either—to renounce a wish to prosper, to succeed. But I could not believe how extreme I had let things become, the kind of grasping creature I had been reduced to. I had not been talking about gentlemanly competition. There had been murder in my voice.

That night I sat in my study and counseled myself. It's a tough place, I told myself. Bad things are happening. Work hard. Do your best. Learn the law. But don't suffer, I thought. Don't fear. And for God's sake, don't give up your decency. (Another sentence worth rereading.)

The Socratic Method

Where there is understanding,

    Let me sow confusion.

Where there is light,

    Darkness.

No, we are *not* committed to a terrible misreading of the Prayer of Saint Francis.

The "Socratic Method" involves a professor randomly calling upon students to "state the case," and then to answer a series of follow-up questions, either directed at the coherence of the case itself or its future application. Critics argue that this method terrorizes and humiliates, teaching future lawyers, by modeling, that ours is a profession of bullying and aggression. Other critics argue that the process of demanding justifications and meeting argument with counter-argument leads to extreme relativism.

> *Suppose the student is confronted by the question, "What does 'honorable' mean?" He gives the answer he has been taught, but he is argued out of his position. He is refuted again and again from many different points of view and at last is reduced to thinking that what he called honorable might just as well be called disgraceful. He comes to the same conclusion about justice, goodness, and all the things most revered. We shall see him renounce all morality and become a lawless rebel.*

So wrote Plato in *The Republic*. Sure, Plato was something of an alarmist but, still, it's true that things haven't gone well for Athens.

We are *not* trying to inculcate relativism; the goal is *not* to expose your ignorance; the goal is *not* to ridicule. The goal is *to force you to justify your positions, to consider other points of view, and to realize that even the best of arguments suffer from "inconvenient facts."*

To illustrate, take a familiar case: a tenant is suing the landlord for negligently maintaining a common stairway. The landlord sets up as a defense a clause in the lease in which the tenant agreed not to sue the landlord for negligence. Is the clause valid?

Student: I don't think the tenant should be held to her promise not to sue if that promise was buried in the small print in the lease.

Professor: Why not?

Student: It just isn't fair.

Professor: Why not?

Here the student may feel that she is being attacked. Still worse, the student may feel that she is being argued out of her sense of fairness. This is not the professor's goal; rather it is to force the student to bedrock, to force her to understand what she means by "fair."

Student: Well, it seems to me that one reason we enforce promises is to protect free choices. If the tenant didn't know what she was signing, then the whole justification for enforcing promises collapses.

Behind our sense of justice often lie good sound reasons. For the professor to insist upon their verbalization is not to attack them.

Professor: Good. But what if the evidence showed she read the contract? Would you still think the agreement unfair?

Student: Yes. The facts show that she was poor and probably not that well educated. She really didn't know that she was giving up valuable rights.

Professor: Good. But isn't that a little paternalistic? If the law doesn't enforce her promise because she is poor and not well educated, aren't we saying that she is legally incompetent? That she doesn't have that most basic of rights, the right to mean what she says?

The professor is not attacking the student, not trying to trip her up and humiliate her. Nor is the professor trying to argue her out of her position and turn her into a mouthpiece for landlords. The professor is attempting to force her to consider other points of view, to adopt the "yes.... but" form of reasoning. *"Yes,* my initial reaction is valid, *but* there are counter-considerations."

Max Weber, the great sociologist, wrote that the "primary task of a useful teacher is to teach his students to recognize *inconvenient facts.*" The teacher should force students to understand what their opinions and arguments entail. Weber continues:

If you take such-and-such a stand, then you have to use such and such means in order to carry out your conviction. Now, these means are perhaps such that you believe you must reject them. Does the end "justify" the means? Or does it not? The teacher can confront you with the necessity of this choice.

The teacher can force the individual, or at least we can help him, to give himself an account of the ultimate meaning of his own conduct. This appears to me as not so trifling a thing to do, even for one's own personal life. Again, I am tempted to say of a teacher who succeeds in this: he stands in the service of "moral" forces; he fulfills the duty of bringing about self-clarification and a sense of responsibility.

Having argued that the tenant should be excused from her promise, it is discomforting to have the professor point out that the argument entails paternalism. In Weber's analysis, the professor is not suggesting that the promise should be enforced; the professor is forcing the student to realize the important values which would be sacrificed if the promise were not enforced. *"The teacher can confront you with the necessity of choice."*

Of course we screw up. Teaching law is not easy. We don't lecture; we'll suddenly see nuances we hadn't seen before. All is movement, and you never know what comes next. In the hurly-burly we'll reject what the student believes is a valid point; undoubtedly, we are too abrupt with students who seem to be meandering; and, undoubtedly, the shock and dismay we occasionally experience shows. These are but inadvertent and unfortunate slights and insults caused by the intellectually challenging and unplanned nature of Socratic discourse.

When the Socratic Method Happens to You

Knowing that your professors are in the service of "moral" forces doesn't much reduce the terror. Two things might:

1. You won't look as nervous as you feel.

2. No one will notice if you make a fool of yourself.

In Moot Court or Trial Practice students are frequently videotaped. The universal reaction: "I sure didn't look as nervous as I was." Do your classmates appear nervous?

Confront, however, the dreaded fear: You make a total fool of yourself. You bumble, meander, and eventually give up. The professor moves on and asks the person behind you what has to be, and I'm not making things up here, the easiest question you have ever heard.

Shattered, you walk from class. You overhear smatterings of conversations and are greatly relieved.

*"They're **not** talking about me and what a fool I was. They're talking about the cases and lunch. But wait! It's worse than I feared. They just don't **care**!"*

Finally, *volunteer* some.

For class to succeed, students must share their insights, questions, and experiences. You can't sit on your hands and then complain that the class is boring. A good class is as much your doing as it is the professor's.

Don't wait for the "right moment," the moment when you are sure of the answer or the moment when you have something terribly insightful to say. *These moments will never come.* You will never be sure of an answer and, as for insight, most of us are convinced that if we thought of something, it must be painfully obvious.

Fear also keeps our hand in place and our graze on our notes. So what if you are wrong? Play the fool and the world continues to turn. This is a valuable lesson even if a disappointing one. The willingness to take risks is absolutely essential to effective lawyering. Who was foolish enough to first assert that separate means unequal? To argue that, despite tradition and practice, police must warn defendants of their right to remain silent? To suggest that manufacturers of goods could be held "strictly liable" for injuries their products cause? Law demands creativity; creativity demands we try new things; creativity demands we play the fool.

As Ms. Frizzle of *The Magic School Bus* advises:

"Take chances! Make mistakes!"

Grades

Finally, you are *not* your grades. "Of course not," you laugh nervously.

Just you wait.

You work really hard all semester. Suddenly it all comes crashing down into a letter or a number. "So that's it, huh. I'm a C."

No, you are not a C. You are whoever you were before you came to law school, the same person who, as a small child, took such good care of the puppy. Only you're different: you have a lot more knowledge and a lot more skills. You are well on your way to becoming a competent professional.

Remember why you came to law school. You didn't come to be a successful law student; you came to be a successful lawyer. Some students, disappointed in their grades, forget this and drop out in place. Keep working hard on your studies; you will know more law and will have better lawyer skills when you really need to, when another individual puts important matters into your hands. From now on, it's about your clients.

If you do well on your exams, more power to you. Feel good; celebrate. But you are at risk as well. As I will discuss in my chapter on Careers, if you are at the top of the class, you may take a job, not to fulfill a life's dream, but rather to continue to prove that you are the "right stuff." Then there is the matter of pomposity. Don't become a character of Shakespearian dimension, walking the law school halls

".... dressed in an opinion

Of wisdom, gravity, profound conceit—

As who should say, 'I am Sir Oracle,

And when I ope my lips, let no dog bark!' "

On your way to the Law Review office, just remember why you came to law school and that you're the same kid who was always picked last.

———————

"I'm enjoying every facet of law school, the classes, my classmate, everything. I'm not worried about flunking out and I'm sure I'll do just fine. I

still have my old friends, time for movies. What am I doing wrong?"

If none of the things I have discussed apply to you, wonderful. If you are not panicking, maybe it is because you *do* understand the situation. That said, this chapter has been a downer. It focused on the negatives. It started with Professor Kingsfield, who, I admit, is one of my heroes:

Your minds are filled with mush. I will teach you how to think.

He's right and you will come to know it. When you aren't complaining, you'll be talking law and loving it.

You are going to meet many wonderful people and make life-long friends. Expect bumps and moments of despair. You are mastering a new and difficult discipline. At first you will be doing it wrong; you will garble facts, misstate issues, and confuse holdings. After much hard work, you will do it right.

"Hey, look at me! I'm standing, too!"

PART 3

EXAMS

Then comes the dreaded day, the dreaded words, "You may begin."

Years ago a national humor magazine had, as its cover, the cover page of the New York Bar Exam. Quite authentic. Quite foreboding, even for those of us who passed our bar exam years ago. One's hands still trembled. Opening the magazine, however, we found something like:

> We were joking. You have passed the Bar. All you have to do is sit here for the next three days, acting busy. Others in the room are not getting this message; the exam is so hard none of them will pass.

Don't expect a last-minute reprieve. We're serious.

Law school exams are different, at least from other exams you have taken in the past. However, they are not much different from what you have been doing all semester: figuring out how the law resolves disputes in specific factual situations. An exam question is like an abridged case: the legal analysis is gone and only the statement of facts remain.

In this part, you will be given an exam to take and then two answers to analyze. But before that, it's well to ask what is your goal on the exam, as knowing where you are going will help keep you on track. We will also take a quick look at the famous, but often unworkable, IRAC approach to exams.

Multiple-choice exams are becoming more and more popular, with law school following the lead of many state bar examiners who devote the first day of their exam to the Multistate Bar Exam which asks multiple-choice questions over basically legal areas. Should you study differently for such exams? How should you approach them?

The final chapter of this part, *Zen and Exams*, basically tells you, when the day arrives, to forget everything you have learned about taking exams and simply take it. As for the title of the first, *Writing Law School Exams: The Only Skill Worth Having*, it's a *joke*!

CHAPTER 14

WRITING LAW SCHOOL EXAMS: THE ONLY SKILL WORTH HAVING!

Question 1

Acme Construction Inc. *allkdfj pqwiur nbvmznx kdk ieur pire jdjo ghjhgfiyr oiyu re otjhg lkpqyr pqlxh plvhgfd qwert yuiop asdf fgh zxcvb mjuik opk kiuy juyhgr dqwsxcgy plmbht fdghj qmpzwno hyde nhyu cdew mkoiy asdfqwer.* Discuss. Be concise but don't overlook anything. Pay particular attention to *kuzt op mdzopor yuiopt.*

Law school exams are written in Greek.

Looking around the room, everyone has started. Sweat runs into your eyes; drops smudge the only words you understand.

Take a deep breath. Remember this: All law school exam questions relate (somehow) to the material you covered in the course. You're *not* in the wrong room. Eventually the words will resolve into English.

Don't worry that you didn't get enough sleep. Most students have a hard time dropping off the night before. You won't be alone. But no one has ever, not ever, fallen to sleep during a law exam.

However, you will get hungry and thirsty—law exams are often four hours. Take munchies, extra paper for notes to help organize your thoughts, know your exam number (law exams are usually anonymous), and, once you get your copy of the exam, make sure all the pages are there—it is best to answer *all* the questions.

Goals and Format

Other than staying awake and well nourished, what will be your goals on exam day?

"That's easy. To show how much I have learned."

Nope.

To strut was our undergraduate strategy. It will be a hard habit to break but it is important to do so. Otherwise bad things happen.

Law school exams are timed; you don't want to waste the little you have on peacocking irrelevant legal doctrines no matter how difficult they were to learn.

More basically, if you believe that your goal on exams is to regurgitate knowledge, you will study to *memorize* rather than to *understand*. As we have seen in previous chapters, the key to becoming a successful law student, and to becoming a successful lawyer, is not *memorization, memorization, memorization*; it is *application, application, application*.

So what is your goal? *To help the reader thin. through the problem.*

All good legal writing is alike. Your goal is *always* to *help* the reader (here, the professor) understand how the law would impact a specific factual situation. You'll confront fact patterns which end with folks injured, disappointed, or mad. (There are *never* happy endings—eventually what will this do to your view of the world?) How can you help the reader understand how the law would impact—not necessarily resolve—such conflicts?

First, tell the reader the *legal issue* that must be resolved; second, tell the reader the *law* or the *legal principles* that would be used to resolve it; finally, help the reader understand how the law or the legal principles would *play out*.

Issue

First, identify the *legal issues* that must be resolved. Most questions have several, some buried. Discuss each *separately*. I will stress the need to think through how these issues relate to one another. This is where scratch paper comes in.

Law or Legal Principles

Second, tell the reader what *legal rule* or, if the legal rule is ambiguous, what *legal principles*, a court would use to resolve the issue. There is no need to memorize exact wording; it is enough to give the reader a fairly accurate statement of the law or policies. As to form, again, there are no magic words:

"The law is that . . . ." or
"The courts have held that . . . ." or
"The U.C.C. requires that . . . ."

Analysis (Your Best Thinking)

This is the heart of your answer, helping the reader think through how the law or principles would play out. This format seems easy enough but let's consider common mistakes.

Common Mistakes

Jumping into your analysis without passing "Go."

Assume that an individual, Mr. Dan, signed a contract to purchase a refrigerator from a door-to-door seller. He is being sued on the contract. An answer might *begin*:

Mr. Dan signed the contract in his house. It is hard to get rid of sellers once they are in your home. Mr. Dan didn't go to a store to buy a refrigerator and hence he probably hadn't thought the matter through.

The student has jumped right into the analysis without telling the reader the issue or the law. This is a *very* common error, often made by students who know better. *Why do students make this error and how can you avoid it?*

Let's reconstruct the student's thinking. Reading the problem, the fact that Dan signed the contract in his house *jumped* out. Mulling it over, it popped into the student's head that consumers are at a disadvantage dealing with such sellers; first, because it is often hard to get them to leave without buying; and, second, because they haven't been shopping for the item, they probably don't know a good price.

These elements smack of lack of meaningful choice; hence, the doctrine of unconscionability may apply. (We examined this doctrine in our discussion of *Walker-Thomas*, Chapter 9.) Why didn't the student tell us that she was discussing this doctrine? There are two possibilities, both correctable: either the student knew *too little* or she knew *too much*.

First, the student may have *not have known* that she was addressing the issue of unconscionablity. Facts jumped out; they *seemed* important; she wrote them down. She should have asked *"So what?"*

Dan signed at home. **So what?** *Well, this means he didn't have much of a choice.* **So what?** **Well, maybe there is an issue of unconsionablity.**

On the other hand, the student may have omitted stating the issue and law because she knew perfectly well that she was addressing the issue of lack of unconscionability and had simply assumed that the professor would know that she was without her telling him. Why should she treat her professor as a dope and explicitly tell him the issue she is addressing?

Because good things happen.

First, her analysis will be sharper as her analysis will be grounded in the law. As she is now self-consciously writing about lack of meaningful choice,

other *points* and *facts* that are relevant will come to
the fore. Second, by explicitly stating the law, other
elements of the the law might *jump* into her mind:
for a court to throw something out on the basis of
unconscionabilty, two elements must be present:
lack of meaningful choice *and* terms unreasonably
favorable to the stronger party.

Facts lead to law; law leads to facts.

Let's rewrite, stating the issue and the law.

*Does Dan have an unconscionability defense? For
a contract to be unconscionable, there must have
been lack of meaningful choice and* (Oh yes! Now
I remember) *terms unreasonable to the stronger
party. Did Mr. Dan have meaningful choice? He
signed the contract in his house. It is hard to get
rid of sellers once they are in your home. Mr. Dan
didn't go to a store to buy a refrigerator and hence
probably hadn't thought the matter through.* (Oh
yes! Now I see why it was important): *The facts
tell us that Dan had just returned from work; he
was probably tired and this is another factor
pointing to lack of meaningful choice.*

A third advantage of stating the issue at the top
is that it will act as a topic sentence to keep you on
point. Most questions will trigger several legal issues–say that Dan might have a lack of capacity
defense as well. Without a clear statement of the
issue you are addressing, you might *meander* between issues, making a mess of things, discussing
lack of meaningful choice in one sentence, lack of

capacity in the next, and returning to meaningful choice in the next. *Discuss each issue separately!*

Once you state the issue and the controlling law or principles, you turn to your analysis. What is the most common mistake here?

Failure to consider both sides

Students sometimes take sides or close too quickly on an issue; their analysis remains superficial. The solution? *Be a self-critic.* When you are making an argument, your Little Voice should whisper *What would the other side say? What would the salesperson say about Dan's lack of meaningful choice?*

"So what?" forces you to ground your analysis in law, **"Yes** ... **but"** leads you to competing arguments and hence deeper analysis:

Yes, *in many ways Dan didn't have a meaningful choice,* **but** *he did have a meaningful choice in the sense that the terms of the contract were clear and he understood them.* **Would these factors lead a court to reject his claim?**

Rubbing contention against counter-contention *forces* your analysis deeper *–what does "lack of meaningful choice" entail?*

IRAC and Its Discontents

Thus far what I have given you is close to the famous *IRAC* approach to exam-taking, without the *C*.

*I*ssue, *R*ule, *A*nalysis, *C*onclusion

I have not come to praise IRAC, but I have not come to bury it, either. First, its weaknesses.

I leave off the "C" because it tends to suggest that you must resolve the case (*"Plaintiff will win"*) and, worse than that, that you must come to the *correct* conclusion. A recent book on law school exams skewers this notion of correct conclusions with its killer title: *Getting to Maybe.*

Remember, you are not the "decider." Your job is to help the reader understand how a court might resolve the conflict. That reader wants your best thinking on the issues presented and is not particularly interested in your conclusions unless they further your analysis: "Having looked at the plaintiff's and defendant's arguments as to this point, it strikes me that the plaintiff has the better arguments in that . . . ."

Of course a question may *ask* for your conclusion as in "Which of the two arguments is best?" But your grade will not turn on your conclusion as much as on your analysis of the two arguments and on the support you give for your conclusion.

The mantra IRAC can mislead in other ways as well. "Issue" may lead you to think in terms of the "big issue": "Did the plaintiff acquire the land by adverse possession?" This does not focus your analysis at all as the doctrine of adverse possession has several elements and *each* will trigger a separate issue: "Was the plaintiff waving the flag of adverse possession?" "Was it waved for the requisite time?"

As to "rule," this can mislead you into thinking that there will be one rule to apply but often there will be two possible rules to apply (perhaps a "majority" or "minority" rule) and at least part of your analysis should go to which rule should be applied (and then, perhaps, to apply it). While one might state the issue "Which of these rules should apply?" there is no *rule* to follow in making that call ("Longer rule wins!"). Here you will be stating *legal principles* or *policies* that would impact the decision. Similarly, you may be given a statute and asked to apply it to a fact pattern and the case will turn on how the court interprets two or three of its keys words. While you can state the issues, you really can't state a *rule* as this too will turn on questions of policy.

Knowing its dangers, if you are using IRAC in a given problem, be wedded to *ideas*, not to *form*. There is no need to always start with the issue; you can start with the law:

> *For a contract to be unconscionable, there must have been lack of meaningful choice and terms unreasonably favorable to the stronger party. Does Dan have an unconscionability defense?*

And sometimes it works to have your analysis *precede* your statement of issue and law and, indeed, sometimes you won't *need* to even state the issue when your statement of law makes it clear.

The value of *IRAC* is not its form but its simple reminder that you must, somewhere, tell the reader what *issue* must be resolved, by what *legal rule* or *legal principle*, and then help the reader think thorough the matter with your analysis. Finally, *if* it furthers your analysis, state your conclusion.

Fischl and Paul, *Getting to Maybe*, would bury IRAC. They point out that there are several kinds of exam questions that simply don't lend themselves to it. For example, you might be given two arguments and be asked to comment on which is best. Or you might be given a legal principle and be asked to come up with a fact pattern that would show its limitations. There are many variations of law questions and a slavish commitment to IRAC will do real harm.

Spotting Issues and Information Overload

Read aggressively. You are not sitting back, reading a short, short story; you are on a hunt. As you read, legal tidbits will jump out; note them in the margins. Consider rereading the question, now that you know what's being asked. There is little filler in law school exams: if the defendant kicked the plaintiff's *ugly* dog, why was it *ugly*?

Most likely you will find that, rather than knowing too little, you know too much. You may find yourself drowning in a sea of issues and law. Best to have a separate sheet of paper for rough notes: make a list of the major points (issues) that you will address, leaving room for sub-points. Don't expect this to be complete before you begin writing; new matters will pop into your mind as you write—jot them on your separate sheet and return to what you were writing. Law exams are timed (don't spend too much time thinking before writing) and law answers are fluid (don't expect to know everything you are to write before you start).

Relationships between Issues or Topics

Most questions will trigger several issues or topics. What's the relationship between them? There are, for example, two elements in the unconscionability doctrine: (1) lack of meaningful choice and (2) unreasonable terms. What is the relationship between them? Must Dan show both apply to prevail or is it enough if he establishes one?

Let's say there are three issues, A, B, and C. To prevail, must the plaintiff win on all three issues (A *and* B *and* C) or is it enough if the plaintiff prevails on only one (A *or* B *or* C)? Or are we dealing with some form of new math: ([A *or* B] *and* C)?

After you have identified the issues a problem presents, be clear on the relationship between them before you start to write. Then, when you move from one issue to the next, tell the reader the relationship between the issue you just discussed and the one you are about to discuss. I'll show you a neat way of doing this later in the next chapter.

*All Legal Writing is **not** Alike*

While the *goal* legal writing is always the same, to help someone come to a conclusion, the *form* may vary. Legal exams are different in two ways. First, there is no need, as there would be in a brief or memo, to recite the facts. *Don't recite the facts at the top of an exam*. You're simply wasting time. Of course, as you go along, you will flag relevant facts to support your analysis. Second, on exams you state the law in your own words—there is no need to memorize statements of law. On briefs and memos, cite specific language; don't paraphrase in your own words, even if you can add flare to Restatement prose—admittedly a rather low bar.

So, should you go back and memorize my advice? No, apply it! Read on.

CHAPTER 15

PRACTICE TEST

What follows is a typical (at least for me) law school exam question. I follow it with two possible answers which I will analyze in the next chapter. If you wish, you can try your hand at writing an answer before you see my answers, or you might wish to wait until after you read them.

Isn't the latter cheating? No. It is one thing to read something and say, "That's good." It is something more to articulate why it is good. However, you must learn not only to recognize good writing and how to *describe* what constitutes it. You must *write* it.

In art museums, you will see aspiring artists copying the pictures of the masters; aspiring poets copy the work of masters as well, calling this "playing the sedulous ape." Play the ape: find a good piece of legal prose and *copy it* just to get a hands-on sense of how it is put together.

Rules of Law to Apply

These legal rules will come into play in answering the practice test. Reread them a couple of times before you begin writing your answer, and it is OK to refer back to them while you are writing.

1. If one is sued for breach of contract, it is a good defense to say, "I wasn't making a serious offer, and the person who is now suing me should have known it!" The law is that, after looking at the surrounding circumstances, if a reasonable third party would conclude that the person making the promise was not serious, then that promise is not enforceable.

2. The Statute of Frauds requires that some, not all, agreements be in writing. It generally goes something like this:

    The following contracts are invalid, unless the same, or note or memorandum thereof, is in writing and signed by the party to be charged:

    1. An agreement for the sale of real property.

    2. * * *

Cases interpreting the Statute of Frauds have indicated that it fulfills two purposes. The first purpose is to protect against false claims. A writing is good evidence that the parties actually agreed and that no one is making things up. The second purpose of the Statute is cautionary. People shouldn't enter into important legal transactions orally, such as the sale of realty. Written contracts ensure greater reflection on the part of the contracting parties.

3. Contracts for an illegal purpose are void and unenforceable. For example, a "contract," as in "there is a contract out on the Godfather,"

is unenforceable. Even if the assassin does his part, he can't sue to recover his promised fee. Such contracts are illegal on their "face" in that the illegality appears in the agreement itself: "I'll shoot him for $5,000." Some courts have extended the rule to prevent someone who has performed a contract in an illegal manner from suing on it.

The Question

Sleazy Sam and Billy Knowles ran into each other at the Lazy J Bar. After several drinks, Billy said, "You know, I think I'll blow this town and get into pictures."

"Oh, yeah? How are you going to support yourself in Hollywood until they discover your major talent?" asked Sam.

"Why, I'll sell my house. You can have it for $60,000. Last week it was appraised at $120,000."

"You must be joking; that deal is too good to be true," replied Sam, having another drink.

"Man, it's just that you don't have the money."

"Look, I can have $60,000 cash at the end of the week."

"Bring it by."

"Are you serious?"

"Sure," laughed Billy.

"Well, I need a new place for my bookmaking activities."

"That's illegal, but what you do with the place is your business," said Billy. "Let's shake." The men shook and left the bar.

Three days later Sam received the following letter from Billy:

Dear Sam,

Of course I was joking when I promised to sell you my house for $60,000 cash at the end of the week. In any event I don't want to do it. So there.

Yours truly,
(Signed) Billy Knowles

Discuss.

———————

Taking an exam, before you start writing, it is well to jot down some ideas on a separate piece of paper which will then serve as a rough outline. Do some jotting now. It's okay to go back and read the law and the problem.

Model Answers

As you work your way through these two examples, jot down what you *like* and *don't like* about them.

Answer Number One

This case is about Sam and Bill, who met in a bar and began to talk about the selling of Bill's house to

Sam for $60,000. The issue is whether the alleged contract is enforceable or not.

First, Bill was clearly drunk.

Second, Bill was joking. He said as much in his letter to Sam. Who on earth would sell a $120,000 house for $60,000 in order to get into pictures? Sam was going to use the house for bookmaking activities, and that's illegal. And remember that Sam didn't think Bill was serious because he asked him, "Are you serious?" Sam knew Bill was joking.

Because this deals with the sale of real property, the Statute of Frauds applies. The first English Statute of Frauds was enacted nearly 300 years ago to prevent fraud. In California the Statute is Civil Code § 1624. Many commentators in law reviews have argued that the statute, which has been adopted with modifications in many states, causes more fraud than it prevents. That is, it allows people who have made promises to get out of them simply because they are not in writing. Courts often try to get around the Statute of Frauds.

Bill will clearly win.

Answer Number Two

[Ed. Note: I put words of contrast in bold to illustrate their importance.]

There are several issues to be considered in this question:

1. *Did Bill make a serious offer to sell his house to Sam?*

2. *The Statute of Frauds applies; does the letter from Bill to Sam satisfy it?*

3. *Is the contract void because Sam intended to use the house for an illegal activity?*

The first issue is whether Bill was making a serious offer to sell his house. If he wasn't, then he has a good defense to any suit Sam files. The test will be, considering all of the circumstances, would a reasonable person conclude Bill was making a serious offer? Bill will claim he was joking and that Sam should have known it. He will point out that both men accidentally met in a bar. There is no indication that they met to discuss the sale of the house. He will also point out that both men were drinking. (If Bill had been drunk, that would be another defense.) He will argue that no reasonable person would believe he wanted to sell a $120,000 house for $60,000 in order to go into pictures. Note that there was nothing put in writing—it is reasonable to assume that if Bill were seriously thinking about selling a house, it would be in writing.

On the other hand, *Sam will argue that Bill appeared seriously to want to sell his home. First, Bill initiated the discussion. Second, he mentioned that the house had been recently appraised—one does that when one is planning to sell. Third, Bill told Sam he was serious, and both men shook hands, a traditional way to conclude a deal. If Bill had been joking, he would have told Sam just that rather than shake hands. Finally, Bill himself thought the deal serious because he wrote the letter* *to Sam—had the joke been clear, he wouldn't have thought to write claiming it was a joke.*

Even if *it is found that Bill was making a serious offer, the agreement might still be unenforceable under the Statute of Frauds. The Statute applies because the deal concerns the sale of real property. It requires that some writing be signed by the party to be charged (here Bill). The original agreement was oral. However, Bill wrote Sam saying he wanted out of the deal. He signed that letter.* **The question becomes***, then, can a letter denying the seriousness of a prior oral promise be used to satisfy the Statute of Frauds?* **On the one hand***, it appears as though it might. One of the purposes of the Statute is to prevent fraud—by signing the letter, Bill admits he made the promise to sell the house. Sam didn't make up the agreement.* **On the other hand***, another purpose of the Statute is cautionary—to ensure that people reflect before committing themselves to important deals. Obviously a letter trying to get out of a deal cannot be said to fulfill any cautionary function: it comes too late.*

Assuming *Bill was serious in making the offer and* **even if** *his letter satisfies the Statute of Frauds, there* **is another** *possible defense, that of illegality. The law states that contracts illegal on their face are unenforceable.* **However***, this contract isn't illegal on its face—it is not for bookmaking, it is for the sale of a house. Assuming a seller knows that the buyer is to use what is purchased for an illegal activity, can he, must he, refuse to go ahead with the deal? I assume that contracts for illegal acts are not* *enforced in order to deter illegal activity. That policy would apply here and make the contract unenforceable.*

Before continuing, I would advise you to go back and reread both answers, noting in the margins what you liked and disliked about each. The more you put into this exercise, the more you will get out of it. Again, I hope you will take the opportunity to write an answer yourself.

Given the length of this chapter, and your growing weariness, I'm going to stop right here and pick up my analysis of the two answers in the next chapter. Get some rest.

CHAPTER 16

A TALE OF TWO ANSWERS

"Come on, Charles, was it the best of times or the worst of times?"

We'll look at the two answers given to the practice exam in the last chapter. Most would agree that Answer Two is better. I wrote both and the first illustrates common first-year errors:

1. Taking sides.
2. Failing to state the controlling law and making implicit statements.
3. Failing to note the relationship between issues.
4. Mixing legal categories.
5. Discussing law "because it's there."

The second answer will give you a feel for a really good answer. Don't be depressed by it; it took me a long time to write it, and I *wrote* the question.

Before you look at my analysis, reread Answer One, looking for the errors I just mentioned. Then reread Answer Two to see how it avoided them. OK, then don't.

Answer One

It begins:

This case is about Sam and Bill, who met in a bar and began to talk about the selling of Bill's house to Sam for $60,000. The issue is whether the alleged contract is enforceable or not.

This is a rather weak opening. How so? Jot!

The writer is clearing his throat, telling the reader nothing new, not focusing on the issues. ''Is the contract enforceable'' is so broad as to be meaningless. *Don't kill time, waiting for inspiration, by reciting the facts. Start writing when you have something to say.*

This smacks of *writing* without *analyzing*. Spend some of your allotted time, but not too much, thinking about and organizing your answer.

Look at the opening paragraph in the second answer:

There are several issues to be considered in this question:

1. *Did Bill make a serious offer to sell his house to Sam?*

2. *Assuming that the Statute of Frauds applies, does the letter from Bill to Sam satisfy it?*

3. *Is the contract void because Sam intended to use the house for an illegal activity?*

Why is this such an improvement?

Here, the student *planned* before writing. The student has a good sense of the issues to be discussed and probably a sense of how they all fit together. But don't be misled. It is *not* necessary to list all of the issues up front. You can simply start:

The first issue is whether Bill made a serious offer.

Still, before you begin writing, you should have a fairly good idea of all of the issues. Don't take off on the first issue you see.

Answer One continues:

First, Bill was clearly drunk.

I see two problems. Can you?

First, the student has *manufactured* facts—the question did not say Bill was drunk, simply that he was drinking. Get the facts straight and be aware of the critical distinction between *observed data* and *inference*. Don't jump to conclusions. Why do you think the student jumped here? (It is never enough to identify bad practice; one must also get at its root cause.) Here the student has taken Bill's side and figured his being drunk would help him get out of the contract. Always maintain your neutrality: *you don't care who wins*.

Second, the statement is implicit: *So what* if Bill was drunk? Is the student making a legal point or just an interesting comment? We don't know. Observe how the second answer avoids *both* of these problems:

"If Bill had been drunk, that would be another defense."

This doesn't assume Bill was drunk and tells us the *legal significance* of being drunk.

The first answer continues:

Second, Bill was joking. He said as much in his letter to Sam. Who would sell a $120,000 house for $60,000 in order to get into pictures? Sam was going to use the house for bookmaking activities, and that's illegal. And remember that Sam didn't think Bill was serious because he asked him "Are you serious?" Sam knew Bill was joking.

There are multiple problems here: no law, taking sides, and mixing categories. Reread to see how.

Law. There is no attempt to state the controlling law. Without some knowledge of the legal principles to be applied, the reader will not be able to understand how they would apply in the specific case. Merely calling the reader's attention to the fact that Bill was joking forces the reader to tie that fact to a controlling legal principle. Here is how Answer Two handles this problem:

The first issue is whether Bill was making a serious offer to sell his house. If he wasn't, then he has a good defense to any suit Sam files. The test will be, considering all of the circumstances, would a reasonable person conclude Bill was making a serious offer?

Unless your prof says otherwise, in stating the controlling law, you *don't* have to cite case names, Restatements, or statutes. Just alert the reader as to the governing law, using your own words to describe it.

Taking sides. Student Number One is simply making arguments for Bill. Ask: "What would the other side say when Bill's lawyer argued Bill was joking?" All the counter-facts will jump out. The problem with "taking sides" is that you fail to see the other side's point of view and without rubbing contention against counter-contention, your analysis is doomed to remain superficial.

Keep in mind, *"Yes,* that's true, *but . . . . "*

Mixing categories. The business of illegality *(Sam was going to use the house for bookmaking activities, and that's illegal)* is thrown into a discussion of seriousness. Not good. Legal analysis is *analysis by category.* "Illegality" and "seriousness" are *separate* legal categories; each, on their own, could make the contract unenforceable. Always keep categories separate. Good statements of the issue can act as topic sentences and help keep you on point. (We will see that the same *fact* can be used in more than one category, for example the lack of writing going to the seriousness issue and triggering the Statute of Frauds issue.)

One cause of mixing categories is the failure to state the issue and controlling law at top. If you do, most likely you will stay on point. Answer One continues:

> *Because this deals with the sale of real property, the Statute of Frauds applies. The first English Statute of Frauds was enacted nearly 300 years ago to prevent fraud. In California the Statute is Civil Code § 1624. Many commentators in law*

reviews have argued that the statute, which has been adopted with modifications in many states, causes more fraud than it prevents. That is, it allows people who have made promises to get out of them simply because they are not in writing. Courts often try to get around the Statute of Frauds.

This paragraph reads like a good undergraduate essay. A fatal flaw.

Writing law always *involves the interplay of law and fact.* Recounting the history of the Statute of Frauds does not help the reader understand how the law would impact the controversy between Bill and Sam. Note that *"So what?"* applies to long discussions of law as well as long discussions of fact. You must *explicitly* tie the law you are discussing to the facts of the case, and you must *explicitly* tie the facts you are discussing to the law.

Fortunately, there is usually little need, in law exams, to cite specific code sections ("Civil Code § 1624") or, for that matter, specific case names. Case names may be important in some courses, such as Constitutional Law. In most first-year courses, however, case names are not significant. Ask your professor.

Finally:

Bill will clearly win.

If it were that clear, the question would not have been asked.

A final criticism of Answer One is that it fails to show the relationship between the issues and, when it introduces a new issue, fails to indicate its legal significance. Consider the first sentences of the first two paragraphs.

First, Bill was clearly drunk.

Second, Bill was joking.

What is the legal significance of Bill being drunk? He would have a defense to the contract action, and it would be helpful to the reader to know this. Let's rewrite:

First, if a person makes a promise when he is drunk, this would constitute a defense.

We can rewrite the second topic sentence as well:

Second, if Bill was joking, the law says that individuals are not to be held to their jokes.

But what is the relationship *between* the *intoxication* issue and the *prankster* issue? It could be either an *and* relation or an *or* relation. To successfully defend the action, must Bill show both that he was drunk *and* that he was joking, or is it enough if he shows one or the other?

To show an *or* relationship:

Second, assuming Bill could not show he was drunk, if he could show he was joking this would constitute a defense.

To show an *and* relationship:

Not only must Bill show he was drunk, in addition he must show he was joking.

Compare the two major transitions in Answer
Two:

1. *Even if* it is found that Bill was making a
    serious offer, the agreement might still be
    unenforceable under the Statute of Frauds.

2. Assuming Bill was serious in making the offer
    and even if his letter satisfies the Statute of
    Frauds, there is another possible defense,
    that of illegality.

I call these *IRS* transitions. Not only do they
introduce the next topic, but also relate it to the
last topic or topics discussed *and* tell the reader the
legal significance of the topic.

  *I*ntroduce—*R*elate—*S*ignificance

Forcing yourself to use IRS transitions not only will
help the reader understand your writing, but also
will help you to think through the relationships. I
return to this topic in my chapter on legal writing.

Answer Two

(After listing the issues to be discussed):

*The first issue is whether Bill was making a
serious offer to sell his house. If he wasn't, then he
has a good defense to any suit Sam files. The test
will be, considering all of the circumstances, would
a reasonable person conclude Bill was making a
serious offer? Bill will claim he was joking and that
Sam should have known it. He will point out that
both men accidentally met in a bar. There is no
indication that they met to discuss the sale of the*

house. He will also point out that both men were drinking. (If Bill had been drunk, that would be another defense.) He will argue that no reasonable person would believe he wanted to sell a $120,000 house for $60,000 in order to go into pictures. Note that there was nothing put in writing—it is reasonable to assume that if Bill were seriously thinking about selling a house, it would be in writing.

This is really good. How come?

It starts off discussing the law. Again, *precise statements of law* are not required, nor need you memorize the language of statutes or Restatements or the key language from opinions.

The seriousness issue requires the student to apply a relatively clear legal standard to an ambiguous fact pattern. The paragraph shows good factual analysis. For example, note the use of the fact that the deal was not in writing. There is a *separate* issue concerning the Statute of Frauds, but here the fact of no writing is skillfully used as evidence of lack of serious intent. Well done!

On the other hand, Sam will argue that Bill appeared seriously to want to sell his home. First, Bill initiated the discussion. Second, he mentioned that the house had been recently appraised—one does that when one is planning to sell. Third, Bill told Sam he was serious and both men shook hands, a traditional way to conclude a deal. If Bill had been joking, he would have told Sam just that, rather than shake hands. Finally, Bill himself thought the deal serious because he wrote the letter to Sam—had

*the joke been clear, he wouldn't have thought to
write claiming it was a joke.*

This paragraph answers the essential question,
"What will the other side say?" (or, to state the
matter differently, uses *"Yes, but"* analysis).

Is it necessary to reach a conclusion as to which
side has the better arguments? Not necessarily.

This is a tricky point. Physicians, trained to come
to correct answers ("Yuck! It's TB!"), often don't
make good law students. In law, when we are trying
to help someone decide a matter, *analysis,* not *conclusions,* rock. Take the issue of whether Bill's
letter satisfies the Statute of Frauds. The competing
contentions would be:

> *Bill: My letter could not satisfy the Statute of
> Frauds because the goal of the Statute is to
> force people to reflect before they enter into
> important deals. My letter was written after
> I made my hasty promise. To allow it to
> satisfy the Statute would defeat its purpose.*

> *Sam: Not so. The main purpose of the Statute of
> Frauds is to prevent false claims from being
> made. It requires that before one person can
> sue another for the breach of certain kinds
> of promises, that person must produce writ-
> ten evidence that the promise was made.
> And there is that evidence, Bill's letter.*

Developing the competing contentions is your main
work. It helps the reader see how a court would
approach the issue, and it shows that you know how

to analyze problems as a lawyer would. To further that analysis, it may be proper to reach a conclusion—not because it is necessary to reach the "right" conclusion, but rather to round off the analysis, to show the reader that you have a legal sense that some arguments are better than others. Two important lessons come from this discussion:

1. *Don't freeze up and not mention an issue in fear that you won't reach the proper conclusion.* ("Gee, maybe the letter Billy wrote will satisfy the Statute of Frauds. I don't have a clue. Better not mention it.") Mentioning an issue, even if you haven't a clue, helps the reader who may have a clue. In terms of an exam, the issue might be an important one—bringing it up will count for something.

2. *Don't simply assert your conclusion; always justify it.*

Take the following conclusion:

I think that Sam will win the Statute of Frauds issue.

Well and good. Perhaps, in a real court, he would. Yet, as written, the conclusion tells us nothing about the only thing we are really interested in: the student's ability to analyze problems. Perhaps the student simply made a lucky guess—after all, the odds aren't all that bad. Compare:

I think Sam will win the Statute of Frauds issue. Although Bill's letter was written after the promise, and hence could not fulfill any cautionary function, it seems that the main thrust of the Statute is to prevent false claims. Here we know Bill made the promise because we have his signed letter to prove it.

In sum, while analysis may stand without conclusions, conclusions seldom stand without analysis.

Continuing with Answer Two:

Even if *it is found that Bill was making a serious offer, the agreement might still be unenforceable under the Statute of Frauds. The Statute applies because the deal concerns the sale of real property. It requires that some writing be signed by the party to be charged (here, Bill). The original agreement was oral.* **However**, *Bill wrote Sam saying he wanted out of the deal. He signed that letter.* **The question becomes**, *then, can a letter denying the seriousness of a prior oral promise be used to satisfy the Statute of Frauds?* **On the one hand**, *it appears as though it might. One of the purposes of the Statute is to prevent fraud—by signing the letter, Bill admits he made the promise to sell the house. Sam didn't make up the agreement.* **On the other hand**, *another purpose of the Statute is cautionary—to ensure that people reflect before committing themselves to important deals. Obviously a letter trying to get out of a deal cannot be said to fulfill any cautionary function: it comes too late.*

Another job well done. Nice transition. It shows we are dealing with an **"or"** relationship between seriousness and the Statute.

It is worth pausing to note that this question illustrates two kinds of exam questions:

1. Where the law is clear and the facts muddled.
2. Where the facts are clear and the law muddled.

The "seriousness" issue is an example of the first. There we had a clear legal standard and had to apply it to an ambiguous fact pattern. Here the facts are clear and the law is ambiguous. The fact of the letter is clear but its legal significance is not: would it satisfy the Statute? The model answer uses the proper mode of analysis. Because the Statute does not tell us what kind of writing it requires, we must turn to the **purposes and goals** of the Statute to resolve the issue. Would they be furthered or defeated by allowing the letter to count?

Continuing with Answer Two:

Even if *Bill were serious in making the offer and* ***even if*** *his letter satisfies the Statute of Frauds,* ***there is another*** *possible defense, that of illegality. The law is that contracts illegal on their face are unenforceable.* ***However****, this contract isn't illegal on its face—it is not for bookmaking, it is for the sale of a house. Assuming a seller knows that the buyer is to use what is purchased for an illegal activity, can he, must he, refuse to go ahead with the deal? I assume that contracts for illegal acts are not enforced in order to deter illegal activity. That policy would apply here and make the contract unenforceable.*

This starts well. There is a good transition. We know that even if Sam wins on the serious issue and on the Statute of Frauds point, he still may be a loser if he blows the illegality point. The discussion of illegality would be much improved had the student asked, "What will the other side argue?" There are powerful arguments against Bill's position here; so powerful, in fact, that courts will likely reject the defense, although that is an issue I will leave to your Contracts course.

One thing to note about the discussions of the letter and of the illegality. *Neither* used IRAC. This is because there are no "rules" at play: there is no rule that tells us whether a letter of revocation can satisfy the statute, and there is no rule that tells us whether a court should extend the illegality defense to a case like ours. These matters must be decided as a matter of policy.

A student wedded to IRAC would have made a mess of things. Be flexible!

Finally, one last point. You are to discuss *all* issues that are *fairly raised* in the problem *even though* you may think one would be determinative. For example, even if you were convinced Bill would win his case on the Statute of Frauds point, you must still discuss seriousness and illegality because they are fairly raised in the problem.

Like Orwell's barnyard animals, all issues are *not* equal. Some call out for more analysis. For example, there is simply more to be said about whether Bill's letter should satisfy the Statute of Frauds than there is to be said about whether he was serious. The Statute of Frauds issue presents a tricky legal issue; the serious issue simply asks for the application of a rather clear rule to some messy facts. Writing exams, don't try to treat all issues equally; spend more time on the demanding ones.

That said, discuss *all* of the issues, even the minor ones. The prof may see more in an issue than you do and by at least mentioning it, you will get credit. The downside with this advice is that it may lead you into discussing *false issues*. If Bill lacked mental capacity, that would be another possible defense. However, there is nothing in the facts that suggests that he lacks capacity and hence it is a *false issue*—you won't get any credit for discussing it. However, as there is generally no penalty for false issues, the real cost is wasting time. And, again, what you might see as a false issue might be central to the prof. If you are uncertain about whether something is an issue or not, *err on the side of inclusion*.

So, what's a poor law student to do? Spend more time on the "demanding issues" and avoid "false issues." Buy low, sell high. How are you to know which is which? By working hard during the semester!

CHAPTER 17

MULTIPLE CHOICE EXAMS

The world is still deceived with ornament. In law, what plea so tainted and corrupt, But, being seasoned with a gracious voice, Obscures the show of Evil?

Shakespeare, Merchant of Venice

Many bar exams devote a day to the Multi–State Bar Exam, a multiple-choice test covering basic first-year courses. Multiple-choice exams are also becoming popular in law schools. They're tough.

Fine, but what do they have to do with Shakespeare? We'll see.

Preparing for Multiple Choice Tests

Review old or model multiple choice exams. The ones you take in law school won't be your mother's, the ones you aced in high school. Don't meet that strange beast on exam day.

Reviewing multiple choice exams, no doubt you will try to answer the questions. Well and good. But, more importantly, *reverse engineer: how did the question try to lull you into the wrong answer?*

I hate to break it to you, but those professors who you love dearly (who wouldn't?) are *not* your friends. They *want* you to check the *wrong* box.

Otherwise, no curve. Drafting a multiple-choice exam, they must make all of the answers plausible; there need to be siren songs. I will mention some later. For now, when reviewing multiple-choice exams, focus on how they tried to trick you, on the snares, delusions, and ornaments.

Studying. Should you study differently for multiple-choice? That's a hard question. First let's see how these exams differ from essay exams.

They favor the turtle, not the hare. It's possible to bluff on essay tests, with brilliant points concealing matters you didn't fully understand. No such luck on multiple-choice exams. *Sure and steady wins these races, not spurts of insight.*

I'm not sure how one studies to be the hare, but another facet of multiple-choice has a clearer impact on study. It is difficult to write essay questions that cover *all* issues covered in a course; *objective tests can be comprehensive*. To assure course coverage, some professors scurry back to their offices to write a multiple-choice question after *each* class.

Essay exams allow you to show what you *do know*; objective tests expose what you *don't*.

In terms of your studying, this might mean two things. Preparing for an essay exam, relatively confident that only the major doctrines will be covered, you might give short-shift to some of the backwaters, those curious doctrines or cases that seem to address only very specific or very infrequent factual situations. On multiple-choice, there are no backwaters.

Second, you should probably focus a tad more on memorization. It is much easier for objective tests to trigger specific elements of various legal doctrines. Hence, it might to advisable to memorize elements.

Beyond that, be leery of claims that you should study differently. Both essay and objective exams require an understanding of the law, the ability to read carefully, to spot issues, and to analyze problems. This comes from immersing yourself in your studies.

Taking Multiple–Choice Exams

Two initial matters: First, be clear about whether there is a *penalty* for guessing and, second, be sure to keep track of your *time*. Is a little extra time built into the exam, which would allow you to revisit questions that stumped you?

As you are about to begin, remind yourself that you will likely be "deceived by ornament" and, to quote the Bard once again:

A goodly apple, rotten at the heart, O, what a goodly outside falsehood hath!

Questions are in three basic parts: facts, question, and choices. These babies are drafted with care: all have goodly outsides, but some, of necessity, are rotten at heart.

The facts

Each fact matters. Of course, I will advise you to read the question closely, perhaps even twice. More helpful would be to ask why folks blow past key facts and what, if anything, can be done about it.

Why do you blow by key facts? If, in reviewing old multiple-choice, you missed a question because you overlooked a key fact, ask, "How come?" What you have to say to yourself is so much more valuable than anything I will say.

Perhaps you read too quickly. Perhaps you jumped to conclusions (the fact that someone drank a bottle of vodka does not mean he was "drunk"). Perhaps you took sides; once you do, you overlook or devalue facts or arguments that favor the other side. To assure an accurate reading, read *slowly*, don't *jump* from fact to conclusion, and, as much as humanly possible, try to *remain neutral*: it should make absolutely no difference to you if the widow and her small children are to be thrown into the street to make room for a huge, multi-national corporation hell-bent on polluting the neighborhood.

Reading the question

Don't assume that the professor will ask the question you would have asked. Reading the question, you might think, "This will be an assumption of risk question" only to find: "Who will be this season's NBA coach of the year?" Okay, bad example, but it will stick. Be sure you understand the question; it may not be the one you anticipated (and might not even be the best one someone could ask).

There is a bewildering range of possible questions. Some ask you to identify one correct answer out of four or five choices. Others ask you to identify, out of four or five good arguments, the "best" argument; or, out of several significant facts, the "most significant." Note, in making your selection, that the "best" argument need not be a winning argument or even as good as ones you can think of; it is the best of those given.

Is this your final answer?

All of the answers will be tempting. One ploy would be to try to answer the question yourself *before* you look at the possible choices. Next, read all of the choices; if yours is there, you are probably right. However, if you don't see it, *don't jump at the first one* that seems right. On a well-drafted exam, all will seem right.

If you were drafting such an exam, how would you trick students?

You might list as one of the choices a perfectly accurate statement of law which, however, does not specially apply to the facts at hand.

You might draft a statement of law that is partially accurate, which does fit the factual situation, but which does not have <u>all</u> of the required elements.

You might draft choices designed to catch the student who has jumped to conclusions–an answer which would be correct <u>if</u> our vodka drinker was drunk.

Frequently, it will come down to eliminating answers. Despite Dearly Beloved's best efforts, often you will be able to eliminate all the choices but two; and those two, alas, are utterly indistinguishable. (This I know; I have taken such tests). What to do?

My colleague, Dan Dobbs, has some good advice. First, *reread* the facts and the question; you may pick up something, a fact or an omission, that you didn't previously notice. If that doesn't work, try to construct a *hypothetical* set of facts on which one of the contending answers would operate but not the other. This will show you that they are not the same and may point the way to the correct answer.

As a last resort, consider skipping the question and come back to it. Later questions may throw some light on it. However, given that time's winged chariots are always an issue, your may not have time to come back. It might be best to answer the question, mark it, and return to it if you have time.

As to *guessing*, if there is no penalty for wrong answers, go ahead. However, if there is a penalty, consider the odds. Typically you gain one point for a correct answer, lose one for an incorrect one. A wild guess is out: if there are five answers, your chance of getting it right are one in five, *meaning that if you guess on five questions,* you'll lose four points while picking up only one. Not good.

However, if you are able to eliminate all choices but *two*, apply the "preponderance of the evidence test" and if one seems a tad better, go for it. If you can eliminate all but *three*, up your criteria to "clear and convincing" and skip the question unless one of the three stands out. You will have to be right two out of three times to win.

Finally, there probably is something to the notion that your first instinct was correct. Either that or guess "B".

CHAPTER 18

ZEN AND THE ART OF EXAMS

> *In a comedy the lead asks, "Pass the butter."*
> *Opening night, he got a huge laugh; second*
> *night, nothing. He asked the Director, "What*
> *went wrong?" "Opening night you asked for*
> *the butter. Tonight, you asked for the laugh."*

We've covered a lot.

— Expect *panic* but you're in the right room.

— Your *goal* is not to strut nor to come to a correct answer; it is to help the reader understand how the law would play out in a given situation.

— *IRAC* seldom works but stating issues and the law (or legal policies) somewhere near the top helps focus your analysis.

— *"So what?"* grounds your *factual* discussions in *law*, and your *legal* discussions in fact. *"Yes ... but"* helps you to develop both sides and deepen your analysis.

— *IRS* transitions help, both you and the prof.

— Take scratch paper, drinks, and snacks ... but not your pillow.

— The best advice concerning multiple-choice exams comes from Shakespeare.

"Fine, but where's the Zen?" Zen requires patience.

After the panic, you will *enjoy* the exam. It will be a fascinating intellectual puzzle. It will push you, confound you, and ultimately delight you. *Exams are not awful*. The *prospect* of exams is awful. *Grades* may be awful. Exams themselves are adrenaline, discovery, and adventure. The hard part about exams is generally not having too little to say, but having too much to say.

Some use "checklists," ones which reduce the bloomin' confusion of law into one mnemonic device, perhaps "Tippecanoe and Tyler too." Checklists are thought to be a good way of picking up the issues. There are dangers. While there may be a "Tippecanoe"on the exam, dollars to donuts, there won't be a "Tyler too." But, because you are looking for it, you might think you see it. And there will be issues on the exam that you didn't put in your mnemonic, perhaps an "I like Ike." However, to be fair, preparing a checklist is yet another way to focus on the law and that has to be good. Further, a checklist can help you remember the various facets of a legal doctrine.

Don't believe second-year students. "Professor Scalia is a hopeless liberal, so always take the bleeding-heart position," or "Professor Cro–Magnon isn't that sophisticated; you really have to draw pictures for him." Second-year students don't know what worked for them. Perhaps Scalia, deep down, loves hard-headed, heartless analysis, and the very thing that prevented the student from doing much better on the exam was his wishy-washy, bleeding-heart position. And, as for Professor Cro–Magnon, how many stick drawings of bison can one person take?

No one is smart enough to psych out the professor. Don't try a special writing or analytical style based on what you think the professor wants. You're going to be busy enough just sorting out the problem.

What to do just *before* the exam is to start? Last-minute review is not a good idea, because the last doctrines you review are ones you are likely to see on the exam even if they are not there (and last-minute review is, alas, too late). Before their big moment, opera singers bellow a few notes and ball players practice their mean stares (for opponents) and their innocent "Who, me?" expressions (for refs). During your warm-up, repeat, and repeat, "So what?" and "Yes.... but.... "

What to do just *after* the exam? Learn from experience. Think about how you did rather than immediately going to a movie or beginning your next project. After your first exam ask (and better still, write about):

What did the exam teach me about the way I studied? Did I spend enough time analyzing the questions? Did I carefully consider the facts and address the important facts in the discussion? Did

I develop both sides of the arguments? What did I do well? What should I do differently on my Torts exam Tuesday? Is it Tuesday? Oh, no, it was yesterday!

Of course, there are no controlled studies as to what is effective exam writing. However, some hunches are better than others. (However, to reassure yourself as to this matter of "no controlled studies," look at the lower right-hand corner of the title page of this book: make sure it doesn't say, in teeny-tiny print, Placebo Edition.)

Now, the Zen. *Be with the exam. Ooommm.* Looking for what you know will be on the exam, knowing that you are writing for Professor Cro–Magnon, reminding yourself to write IRS transitions, all of that, and all I and others have had to say about exams, *noise.*

Having worked through these chapters, you have learned a lot about writing exams. When you first learned how to hit a ball, you had to instruct yourself: place my feet this way, hold the bat a little higher, turn my head a little further to the right. On game day, all of that is gone; it is simply you and the incoming ball.

Better still, don't go for the laugh, go for the butter!

PART FOUR

LEGAL WRITING AND
ORAL ADVOCACY

All legal writing is persuasive writing. You have
to persuade the reader to keep going.

Kay Kavanagh

This Part deals with legal writing and oral argu-
ment. Both rest on your ability to do legal analysis.
Seldom there is bad legal writing or bad legal argu-
ment; often there is bad legal analysis. Instead of
"Legal Writing," think "Written Legal Analysis,"
and instead of "Oral Argument," think "Oral Legal
Analysis." Expect old friends, "Yes, but..." and
"So what?" and a plethora of "on the other hands."

Often your goal will be to convince someone,
usually a judge, to make a particular decision. We
begin there. "How do judges decide? What factors
are at play?" Policy and precedent play a big role
but, in the highly theoretical world of law school,
we often overlook the critical importance of facts.

Good lawyers must become good storytellers and novelists help.

The next four chapters deal with the mechanics of legal writing. The first discusses goals, how to get better and, perhaps most important of all, how to get started. Chapter 21 gives you some general writing tips, such as IRS transitions and avoiding common errors in legal prose. Chapter 22, lovingly entitled "Murder Your Darlings," deals with editing. The next chapter gives you some exercises to practice what I preached.

The last two chapters deal with the scariest thing of all: oral argument. There will come a time when it's your turn to shallow once and say, with a confidence you may not feel, "May it please the court?" What are your goals, other than not passing out? Here actors help: what do they teach, not about insincerity, but about sincerity?

CHAPTER 19

SPILT MILK: HOW MOTHERS, AND JUDGES, DECIDE

"No, Mommy, please don't send me to my room. I didn't mean to spill the milk. It slipped out of my hand. When Ben knocked over his soup, he didn't have to go to his room. Send me to my room only if I'm really bad. If you send me for this, I'll spend my whole life in my room—no one wants that."

There you have it: the big three, instinctively. Arguing spilt milk in the kitchen or free speech in the Supreme Court, all you have are *facts* (it was an accident), *precedent* (Ben walked), and *policy* (save the Big One).

Mom will have a different take on things. She'll *distinguish* Ben's case ("He's younger") and, as to policy, she might argue that, unless small infractions are penalized, worse things will happen (a child-care version of the "broken windows" theory). And, as to what happened, Mom might have seen things differently.

Of the three—facts, precedent, and policy—which is the dog and which the tail?

If you answered *facts* are the dog, you win.

John W. Davis, the most famous appellate lawyer of his day, the man who argued more cases before the United States Supreme Court than any other lawyer, stated the matter clearly:

"The statement of facts is not merely part of the argument, it is more often than not the argument itself."

How come?

Facts (aka "Stories")

If you're the mom, you want to do the right thing. Sure, you want to be consistent with what you have done before, and you worry about how what you do now will play out in the future, but your major concern is simply being fair. Judges want to correctly apply the law and create good precedent. But they also want to do justice, to do the *right* thing for the litigants. In stating the facts of your case, your goal is to get the judges to feel that justice is on your side and to leave them feeling, perhaps without realizing it,

"You know, it just seems fair that the plaintiff win. Let's see if the law allows it and, if it does, whether our decision would create a good precedent."

Appellate briefs open with a *Statement of Facts* and oral arguments begins with "The facts are these." Beginners, *unlike* John W. Davis, want to hurry ("I assume the Court is familiar with the facts"). They want to get to the good stuff, the law school stuff, precedent and policy. *Don't make this mistake.* (Legal education distorts by suggesting that precedent and policy are more significant than fact. Why? Profs can't ask probing questions about facts, and they don't make good exam questions. Similarly, legal education distorts by suggesting that the real action is in appellate courts, rather than in Trial Court, Tuesday morning–but I digress.)

"Statement of Facts" sounds boring and mechanical. Think *story!*

When you are done with your story of the facts, tell it, or read it, to a ten-year-old and then ask, "Who is in the right?" If it isn't your client, rewrite.

Let's practice.

- Defendant Paul is a local Chief of Police.

- Plaintiff Davis is a photographer for a local newspaper.

- To help local merchants protect against shoplifting during the Christmas season, the defendant distributed a flyer showing the pictures of "Active Shoplifters."

- Plaintiff had been arrested for shoplifting but was never convicted.

- Plaintiff's picture was on page two of a five-page flyer.

- Plaintiff has sued defendant for violating his civil rights.

Tell the defendant's story. What facts will you stress? In what order? Will you leave any out?

Don't keep reading. Give the matter some thought.

Now tell the plaintiff's story.

Here's the story told by the United States Supreme Court:

Defendant Paul is the Chief of Police of Louisville, Kentucky. For the purpose of alerting local area merchants to possible shoplifters who might be operating during the Christmas season, he distributed to approximately 800 merchants in the Louisville metropolitan area a "flyer" of active shoplifters. The flyer consisted of five pages of "mug shot" photos, arranged alphabetically. In approximately the center of page two there appeared photos and the name of the plaintiff, Edward Charles Davis III.

Who do you think won the case? Now consider the same story, this one told by a law review writer:

Plaintiff Edward Charles Davis, a photographer for the Louisville Courier–Journal and Times, was arrested in Louisville, Kentucky on a charge of shoplifting. He pled not guilty. The charge was "filed away with leave [to reinstate]," but he was never called upon to face that charge in court. With the onset of the Christmas season defendant Paul, the Chief of Police for Louisville, prepared a five-page flyer containing the names and mug shots of "Active Shoplifters." Copies of this bulletin were distributed to merchants warning them of possible shoplifters. In fact, the flyer was composed not only of persons actually convicted of shoplifting, but included persons who had been merely arrested. Plaintiff's name and mug shot were included in the flyer.

Who wins this case?

Lawyers tell more stories than J. K. Rowlings and Stephen King (but not as well). They tell stories to opposing counsel during negotiations, to juries during trials, and to judges during appellate arguments. Study stories. How does the Supreme Court's story create sympathy for the defendant while the law review's leads one to root for the plaintiff? *Reread* them. Some hints:

1. List the adjectives that were used by both and highlight the pleas for justice.

2. From whose perspective are the two stories told?

3. Look for the facts that both discussed? Where and how?

4. Were there any key facts left out?

Okay, my first hint was a trick. There were *no* adjectives and *no* pleas for justice. What do you make of them apples? *Facts* convince, not adjectives or rhetoric. Adjectives and rhetoric often make things worse; first by concealing the cold hard facts and, second, by suggesting desperation.

We tend to be sympathetic with the first person we meet. The Supreme Court first introduces us to the defendant and immediately tells us some nice things about him: he is the Chief of Police and was trying to protect local merchants from shoplifting. Bravo. The law review story starts with the plaintiff and immediately tells us some nice things about him: he has a responsible job and, while he was arrested, he was never convicted. Nice guy.

If we see this as a case of a good cop, trying to do his best in fighting crime, certain facts jump out, others recede. Neither the Justice who wrote *Davis* nor the law review writer were *consciously* slanting their statement of facts. The slanting occurred unconsciously once they, for whatever reason, became sympathetic to one of the parties. When we take sides, even unconsciously, the facts (and eventually the law) *tend* to line up.

In the Court's version, for example, we learn that the flyer was fairly long, five pages, and that the plaintiff was *not* singled out. Indeed his *"photo"* appeared on page two. In the law review version, we are reminded that it was his *"mug shot"* and we are never told exactly where it appeared; for all we know, it could have been featured on page one. Merchants were *"alerted"* in the Court's version, while they were *"warned"* in that of the law review. Finally, while the law review leads with the fact that the defendant had never been convicted of any crime, the Court's version has yet to mention it.

This tendency for facts (and then the law) to line up to support one's side is the root of the whole matter. Again, John W. Davis: "A case well stated is far more than half argued."

The Supreme Court presents us with an image of a well-meaning cop at risk, while the law review presents the image of a wronged, innocent man. Which is the correct image?

If you answered the hard-working Chief, wrong. If you answered wrongly-accused Davis, wrong again. *Both* images are correct! There is a famous gestalt drawing that includes the images of both a young woman and an elderly woman. Some see one, some see the other. *Both are there.* Stating your case, the trick is to bring your woman to the fore, *without* adjectives, over-writing, and pleas for justice.

Of course, even in the best of cases, a little rain must fall. After discussing how to stay dry (relatively), we will suggest that you can give more punch to your facts if you use *specific details* and work hard on your *opening*. (In oral argument, *exit lines* are just as critical; otherwise, like old soldiers, you just fade away.)

Dealing with Inconvenient Facts

You are a trial attorney and are about to call your client to the stand who will testify as to the horrible bodily harm inflicted on her by the defendant's negligence. "By the way," she whispers to you, "I had a great game of tennis yesterday." What do you do?

"Shut up about that!" Not the best move and surely not an ethical one. Rather than trying to suppress evidence, you might try whistling in the dark: when your client is on the stand, ignore the issue by not asking how she is currently doing, hoping that your opponent doesn't stumble upon this gem. Perhaps he won't delve into her current condition, fearful that she will merely detail great suffering. But this course is very risky. If your opponent strikes gold, the jury will conclude (rightly), that you were trying to put one over, and your *entire* case crashes.

The other alternative is for *you* to raise the issue. Among trial lawyers, this is known as "drawing the sting," the theory being that the jury will conclude, if you brought it up, it can't be that bad. Plus you can put spin on it.

Question: What did you do yesterday?

Answer: Played some tennis.

Question: Tennis? With your injuries?

Answer: Yes, I am trying so hard to get well, to recover my health.

Some lawyers, however, draw so much sting *nothing's* left but a pile of inconvenient facts and apologies. It is dangerous to ignore bad facts, hoping they will go away, *and* it is dangerous to spend too much time on them? So what's a poor, underpaid lawyer to do?

My test: *Will the court feel betrayed if it learns what I omitted?* Had I read the Court's version and concluded that the cop was my guy, I would have assumed that Davis was a shoplifter. I would feel betrayed if I later learned that Davis had never been convicted. "Hey, they were trying to put one over on me." You never, never once, want a judge (or jury) to conclude that you are up to no good: your *entire* case will suffer, not to mention your career.

On the other hand, I would not feel betrayed because the law review writer didn't tell me that the picture was on page two.

In bringing up inconvenient facts, don't always try to spin them. Sometimes it gets ridiculous. Once I was in a lower court, waiting my turn. The guy before me was representing himself on the charge of running a stop sign.

"Your Honor, that wasn't my fault. My car doesn't have any brakes."

Never expect that *all* the facts will support your side. If they did, there probably wouldn't be a case. A frank admission does wonders to convince the Court that you are playing above board: "Frankly, your Honors, Davis was never convicted of shoplifting and this hurts our case."

When we get to the matter of dealing with *prior cases*, I will repeat this point: admitting that some cases go against you is far preferable than turning blue trying to make them fit your theory. Admitting that they hurt your case has the further advantage of giving you the opportunity to present them in a way suggesting that they really don't hurt that much, thus stealing some of your opponent's thunder suggesting that they are the root of the whole matter and that they totally destroy your position. Think *preventative maintenance.*

Placement matters. Don't lead and don't conclude with harmful facts; put them somewhere in the middle. (What we hear or read first and last tends to stick–and surely this obvious point should not go last, but there you have it.)

Tell your story from the viewpoint of your client and, as to inconvenient facts, be candid, but not too candid. How to make your story more spiffy?

The Importance of Opening Lines

"It was the best of times, it was the worst of times."

"All happy families resemble one another; every unhappy family is unhappy in its own way."

"It is a truth universally acknowledged, that a single man in possession of a good fortune must be in want of a wife."

Novelists work hard on their opening lines. They only come once. Novelists want to grab interest, state a theme, and get things moving. They would never, ever, open: "This is a story about the French Revolution." As lawyers, they would never begin their story: "This is an appeal from the Third District Appellate Court in Ohio which reversed an entry of a partial Summary Judgment, by Superior Court in Toledo, in favor of the two defendants who were brought in by way of cross-complaint."

Begin with pizzazz. State your basic theme.

"This case is about a police officer who was doing his best to protect small business owners from shoplifting. He mistakenly put a man's photo in the middle of a flyer showing shoplifters. Now he's being sued. For money damages.

"Mr. Davis, a photographer for a local newspaper, awoke one morning to find himself turned into a giant cockroach (whoops, wrong book) . . . awoke one morning to find himself falsely accused of being a shoplifter. He found his 'mug shot' posted all over town."

Probably best to write your "story" and opening lines *last*, when you have a better feel for your case. And remember this: simplicity and brevity. Most cases come down to very simple propositions: "One man, one vote," "Our Constitution is color blind," "No one should profit from his own fraud." What is the essence of your case?

"I didn't mean to spill the milk."

"You weren't paying any attention to what you were doing."

The Power of Language

In Contracts you will learn, or have learned, that plaintiffs must mitigate their damages. Called off a job, they must stop. They cannot go on working and hence *pile up damages*. The phrase triggers an image: a sweaty guy in overalls, shoveling up a pile of damages. We won't let him get away with that! But what if we called what he was doing *"complet-*

ing the contract"—doing the job he promised to do, the job the breacher promised to pay him for. Now we see an innocent man working and sweating, while the guilty breacher sneaks off, trilling his moustache and laughing the laugh of all villians!

"Mug shot." "Photo."

Judge Jerome Frank noted the hypnotic power of words. Why were early common law courts hostile to arbitration clauses? Because an early judge labeled them an attempt to *"oust"* the jurisdiction of the courts. Well, no one is going to put up with that. Of course, arbitration clauses could have been characterized as *"parties freely choosing an alternative forum."*

Can you spiffy up your story with powerful phrases?

Specifics, not Abstractions

In *The Merchant of Venice*, Shylock comes to claim his "pound of flesh." Asked why he would have Antonio's flesh rather than his money, Shylock responds:

> *He hath disgraced me, and hindered me half a million; laughed at my losses, mocked my gains, scorned my nation, thwarted my bargains, cooled my friends, heated mine enemies, and what's his reason? I am a Jew. Hath not a Jew eyes? Hath not a Jew hands, organs, dimensions, senses, affections, passions? fed with the same food, hurt*

with the same weapons, subject to the same dis-
eases, healed by the same means, warmed and
cooled by the same winter and summer, as a
Christian is? If you prick us, do we not bleed? If
you tickle us, do we not laugh? If you poison us,
do we not die?

Textbooks on writing often give examples of bad writing and ask you to rewrite. I think the opposite approach would work, too. Rewriting something good to make it bad might help you understand what was good about it in the first place. Try rewriting Shylock's lines, making them horrible. ("It was a dark and stormy night and this guy Antonio pretty much dissed me.") Here's my rewrite of Shylock:

Antonio's a bigot. He has treated me very unfairly,
simply because I'm Jewish. But being Jewish is
no different than being anyone else. Like, I have
feelings too.

Forget the rhythm of the language; I ain't Shakespeare (nor was meant to be). But note Shylock's *specifics*: losses, gains, friends, enemies, eyes, hands, organs, dimensions, senses, affections, passions, food, weapons, diseases, healing, warmed, cooled, bleed, laugh and die. We don't need anyone to tell us that Antonio was a bigot; we know he was because we know what he *did*.

Telling your story, stress specifics, not abstractions; talk nouns and verbs, not adjectives and adverbs. If justice is really on your side, your proclaiming it in a grand sweeping manner won't convince the court. *Facts tell.* Recall the stories told of the police and the photographer: convincing without adjectives and without pleas for justice.

Writers, and you are one, are advised: *Show, don't tell.*

A compelling factual statement motivates the court to rule in your favor; now you must establish a rationale that permits it to do so. You must discuss both the past (precedent) and the future (policy).

Precedent

"The Statute of Frauds requires this kind of contract to be in writing. This one wasn't. It may be a stupid law, and it may be quite unfair in this case, but there you have it. I win!"

The common law is littered with remains. Thinking the law squarely behind him, policy and fairness be damned, the lawyer smugly sits down only to have the court come up with an exception; perhaps an estoppel, perhaps an implied promise, perhaps a new duty. *All* cases can be distinguished or, if not, overturned; and *all* statutes are ambiguous or, if not, many can be found unconstitutional.

You are never safe.

Oliver Wendell Holmes, in his classic article, *The Path of the Law* (1896), argued that courts should not follow precedent blindly and that "it is revolting to have no better reason for a rule of law than it was laid down in the time of Henry IV." He argued a deliberate reconsideration of the worth of the rules.

When you get the dragon out of his cave on to the plain and in the daylight, you can count his teeth and claws. But to get him out is only the first step. The next is either to kill him, or to tame him and make him a useful animal.

Never trust dragons; they may turn out to be paper. To jump eons and metaphors, beef them up. Convince the court that they are still useful animals: tell the court why the cases and statutes are still good policy.

"The Statute of Frauds requires this kind of contract to be in writing. This one wasn't. The writing requirement isn't just some kind of technical requirement. It protects important societal interests, such as . . . ."

Dealing with Adverse Authority

You are sitting in front of your computer, researching the law as it applies to a client's case. Things are going swimmingly, you have found several decisions that are in your favor. All of a sudden, out of nowhere, and totally unprovoked–*beep*!– a case that totally destroys your position. What to do? Look around the room furtively, and hit "delete"?

What is the case for "delete"? Something better than, "They put the key there so they must have wanted folks to use it." What about your loyalty to your client? Isn't it disloyal to disclose a case that hurts? And what about, if your client's opponents can't find the case, why should your client pay you to do their work? And, if we say, "You can't delete" won't that mean lawyers will become research-shy, not adequately researching the law in fear of finding a bomb?

None of these arguments won the day. As an Officer of the Court (whatever that might mean—you can't order folks about or even give them parking tickets), you have an obligation to call to the Court's attention adverse *controlling* authority. Of course, you can still hit "delete"—no one will search your hard drive and you can always sleep soundly, "The case wasn't controlling—distinguishable .. the defendant spelled his name *Browne*."

I'll come back to this when we discuss oral argument. It goes to the root of the whole matter. As a lawyer, what is your role? If you were Master of the Universe, would you keep, or delete, "delete"?

As I indicated in our discussion of facts, don't lose credibility by trying to make everything fit into your theory. All litigated cases are close and all have conflicting authorities. If you can't distinguish an adverse case convincingly, don't try. Nothing goes better than "The case of *Smith v. Browne* is inconsistent with our position. Nonetheless, we should still prevail because. . . ."

Eats Pittsburgh

One common error is interpreting an element in a case, and more frequently, a phrase in a statute, in such a fashion that the interpretation turns around

and destroys itself. I call this "Eats Pittsburgh"—
for reasons long forgotten.

Let's say a burglary statute requires a "forced
entry" and the defendant crawled through an open
window. Was this a "forced entry"? If the court
interprets "forced entry" as *any* entry that requires
physical force (and crawling through a window requires physical force), it has effectively defined the
element out of existence: all entries require physical
force, including walking through an open door. We
know that this interpretation must be wrong because we know that the legislature wanted to somehow distinguish between breaking down a door and
simply walking through an open one. If it had not,
it would not have included the requirement of a
force entry.

Policy

Under the doctrine of *stare decisis*, whatever your
court decides will become precedent. If it adopts
your reading of the cases and statutes or your new
theory of liability or defense, will that produce
justice for not only the current litigants but also
future ones? By now you have had your fill of policy
arguments, so I will flag only a couple of concerns.

"Policy arguments" are more than "I think it
would be a swell idea." By that I mean, if possible,
ground your policy arguments in legislative or judicial pronouncements. If you are arguing that ruling
in your favor will "save whales," cite statutes or
decisions that suggest that saving whales is a good
idea. These authorities need not be directly on point

as long as they reflect the same policy; for example, a state statute funding a "whale rescue" program or one protecting seashore environments.

Second, be aware of *slippery slope* arguments. Many legal arguments focus not so much on the merits of the particular dispute but on where it might lead.

"If we invalidate this lease clause that exculpates the landlord from liability for negligence, the next thing you know we'll have all kinds of tenants in here demanding that we rewrite their leases, even the amount of rent."

There are *three* responses to all slippery slope arguments. Write them out. They will be on the final. (Yeah, but if *they* are on the final, then *everything* will be on the final.)

1. All slippery slope arguments are reversible.

"If you refuse to invalidate this clause, then you will never invalidate a clause, even one involving forfeitures of first-borns in the event of late rent."

2. Slopes have dumps and holdings can be limited.

"Your Honor, this exculpatory clause is unique in that it relieves the landlord from liability for personal injury. There is a strong policy to encourage landowners to take reasonable steps to avoid such injury. No such policy is involved in other lease terms, surely not the amount of rent."

3.   Some slopes may be worth the ride.

"Your Honor, now that you mention it, that would not be such a bad idea."

I recently saw a wonderful response to a slippery slope argument. The judge asked something like, "Counselor, if we do what you would like us to do in this case, in our next case, won't you come in here on the behalf of Acme Corporation arguing that we have already committed ourselves to the destruction of Western Civilization?"

"No, your Honor, I won't do that. I don't represent Acme."

CHAPTER 20

WRITTEN LEGAL ANALYSIS: GOALS, GETTING BETTER, AND GETTING STARTED

A lawyer's teenage daughter threw the gauntlet: "Dad, you can't write and I'm taking one of your briefs to my creative writing teacher to prove it!"

A week later, the verdict. Smugly. "I was right, Dad. My teacher says you can't write! He says your sentences are too short, your paragraphs are too short, and besides, anyone can understand it."

That is a true story, not to cast aspersions on any of my others. It raises a key question: *What is one's goal in writing?*

Writing a paper as an undergraduate, what was your goal, other than getting it in on time or, if not, within the prof's zone of tolerance?

— Showing that I understand the material.

— Showing that I am a good writer.

— Showing that I am real smart and/or creative.

— Showing that I have a killer vocabulary and am a master of metaphor.

If you were in graduate school, perhaps your goal was "to advance human knowledge" or, more candidly, to get a Fellowship.

Time to put away childish things. Tolstoy tells us that all happy families are the same; so too, all good legal writing: it helps someone make a difficult decision.

The world of law is a world of *action*. Clients do not come to grade you; judges do not want to be dazzled. They have decisions to make: should I take this plea? Should I issue this injunction? Your job is to *help*.

How?

First, tell the reader what *decision* he or she must make. In our world, what is the *issue* that must be decided?

Once you state the issue, put yourself in your reader's shoes: if I had to make the decision, what would help me? What would get in the way? Before my answer, what's yours?

It would help me to understand the prose (plain English—usually short sentences and short paragraphs); to follow the analysis (law is tough and no one has ever complained about being "written down to"); and to learn just what a pickle I'm in (one that alerts me to all of the competing policies, cases and arguments). And, of course, the shorter, the better—I have other decisions to make before I sleep.

What gets in the way? First, confusion as to goals (writing to impress, writing "like a lawyer"); second, taking sides (and hence overlooking counter-arguments); and third, and probably most importantly, flawed legal analysis.

I've read zillions of legal memos. Weak legal writing is seldom the overuse of adverbs, unclear referents, or split infinitives; it is mostly flawed *legal* analysis. "Legal writing" is not a separate subject; it is part and parcel of our larger endeavor, learning good legal analysis. Put another way, the hardest part of legal writing is doing the legal analysis. Once you understand how the law plays out, dollars to donuts, you will be able to do a pretty good job in expressing it. And, if you don't understand the law, dollars to donuts, your writing will be confused.

My topic is not "legal writing;" it is "Written Legal Analysis." In previous chapters I have discussed good legal analysis. A quick review. Legal analysis focuses on the *interplay* of law and fact. One tests one's discussions of law and fact by asking *"So what?"* ("As to my spiffy, indeed publishable, discussion of history of promissory estoppel, *so what*? Does it help my reader decide?")

Good analysis always considers *both* sides of an issue. Keep *"Yes ... but"* in mind. *Yes*, that is a very strong point on behalf of the defendant, *but* what are the counter-arguments the plaintiff could make? *Yes,* that's a good counter-argument, *but* how would the defendant respond? Not only does this ping-pong process force you to consider both sides, but it also deepens your analysis: the real analysis begins when we get to the nitpicks of the quibbles.

At top I told you that all legal writing is the same. Not to cast aspersions on the rest of this book, that's not 100% accurate. Legal writing involves three topics: *facts*, *issues*, and *analysis*. In your first year of law school, you will be asked to write *exams*, *memos* and *judicial briefs*. The three factors play out differently in these activities.

As to *facts*, on *exams* there is no need to recite them at top as your reader knows them (alas, all too well). Writing *office memos* and trial or appellate *briefs*, your reader is not familiar with the facts so you must, at top, recite them. How you state the facts, however, differs. In an office memo, be neutral; in a brief, tell the story so that the judge wants to rule in your favor. Recall, as I pointed out in the chapter on *Spilt Milk,* that the "statement of facts is not merely part of the argument; it is more often than not the argument itself."

As to analysis, in office memos you again are neutral while, in judicial briefs, *analysis* becomes *argument*. However, as we will see in the chapter on oral argument, this does not mean you only argue the strengths of your case. Often you need to bring up and discuss the weaknesses.

Before getting to the writing tips in the next chapter, let's first back up and ask a very broad question: "How can I get better?" And then a fairly specific one: "I have a memo due next week. Help!"

Getting Better

In an art museum, the tourist will say, "I like that;" the art professor, "Note how the artist uses color;" the artist, "I want to learn how to do that—get me a pad."

As we are now in graduate school, we are far above actually copying things out. But you, too, are an artist. It is one thing to read a piece of legal prose and "like it." It is something else to figure out why it is so good and to be able to comment on the style with flair. It is something quite different to actually do it yourself. When you read something that seems to work, *copy it.* In my chapter on exam writing, I offer a good piece of legal writing. When you get a chance, go back and copy it, word for word.

How else to get better? There are many terrific books on legal writing and many law schools have writing classes taught by dedicated and talented pros. Bravo. These are no doubt quite helpful. But *practice* is key. Stephen King, in his book *On Writing,* points out that he learned to write while washing motel sheets in Bangor, Maine, and that Faulkner learned while working in a post office in Oxford, Mississippi.

You learn best by reading a lot and writing a lot, and the most valuable lessons of all are those you teach yourself.

Of course, he doesn't tell you this until *after* you bought his book; but no matter, neither did I. As to reading a lot, you will: appellate cases, statutes, uniform codes, law reviews, and legal texts. Your focus will be on *substance* (the law); but pause, every now and then, to consider *style*. Become a *student of legal expression.* If it's clear, how is the author pulling it off? If it's confused, or terminally boring, how come?

Are topics clearly introduced? Do we know, not only that we are discussing Section 254 (D) iii, but why we are discussing it and how it fits into the larger picture? Does the judge stay on point? Do constructions force you to stop reading ("OK, the plaintiff said that, now which one was he?")? Do they force you to go back ("As we discussed previously")?

As a student of legal expression, take a close look at your own. Have friends read what you have written. If they say, "Like Wow! You must be real smart to be in law school," you lose. The winning ticket: *"You're not much of a writer. Your sentences are too short, your paragraphs are too short, and besides, anyone can understand it."*

Read your draft aloud. If it doesn't sound like you, you have fallen victim to the myth that legal writing must be highfalutin'. If you gasp for breath, your sentences are too long and your paragraphs too dense.

Finally, wait a week to read your draft. You will now read it as reader, not as author. "What does this mean?" Asked the meaning of a early poem, Robert Browning responded:

"God and I both knew what it meant once. Now God alone knows."

Getting Started

Time's winged chariots draw near and you're sitting at your computer, cursor flashing and blank screen mocking. "I'm not worried about getting better: I'm worried about flunking out."

First thing. Turn off the computer and go for a walk. Tell yourself that you will start first thing tomorrow. As Norman Mailer advises:

"If you tell yourself you are going to be at your desk tomorrow, you are by that declaration asking your unconscious to prepare the material."

Don't just sit down one morning, look at the problem, and begin writing. Blink, blink. Read the problem a day or so before and let it simmer. Talk with friends. Try out ideas. Dream on it. Think about it at dinner, even if it irritates those who want the salt.

Starting too early is one problem but so, too, is starting too late. Writing is a fluid process. We see new relationships and learn new things as we compose. And, after the draft is done, ideas continue to percolate. Leave time for an edit and a second draft. (Stephen King usually polishes off a short novel between the first and second drafts of a larger one—nice work if you can get it.)

Once you sit down, don't freeze up. *Start!* Don't worry about good legal *writing*; struggle with the legal *analysis*. Don't freeze up: "I don't know how to deal with that nasty statute that threatens to destroy my entire position." You don't need to know *everything* you will write before you write *anything*. Like many authors, Stephen King doesn't have an overall plan before he begins:

The situation comes first. The characters—always flat and unfeatured, to begin with—come next. Once these things are fixed in my mind, I begin to narrate. I often have an idea of what the outcome may be, but I have never demanded of a set of characters that they do things my way. On the contrary, I want to do things their way. In some instances, the outcome is what I visualized. In most, however, it's something I never expected.

Yeah, but King writes fiction!

A state Supreme Court Justice told me that he was writing an opinion dealing with the issue of whether a girl could join the Boy Scouts.

"After the oral argument, I thought 'No way.' But by the time I finished writing my opinion, she was in."

CHAPTER 21

WRITING TIPS

- *Quote, don't paraphrase; put law in context*
- *Don't force the reader to puzzle or go back*
- *Avoid "The butler did it!"*
- *Use IRS Transitions*
- *No meandering*
- *Be Explicit*

Quote the law and put it in context

Let's say a homeowner refuses to pay the last installment on his home-remodeling contract. The contractor bribed the Building Inspector to expedite paperwork. The homeowner raises the defense of illegal performance of contract. As a statement of law, consider:

Cases have held that people cannot profit from their own wrong.

This would be an adequate statement of law on an exam because there is generally no need to cite specific cases or recount specific language. But if things really matter, as they do in office memos and appellate briefs, how is the reader to know that you got the law right? *Cite* sources.

In the case of <u>Riggs v. Palmer</u>, it was held that no one shall be permitted to profit from his own wrong.

This is better. However, the reader still has to take your word as to what the case held. If you can find *specific* language, quote it:

In the case of <u>Riggs v. Palmer</u>, it was held that "no one shall be permitted to profit from his own wrong."

Great language and we know the court used it. Before applying that language, what don't we know about *Riggs v. Palmer?*

Just about everything! What were the facts? What was the wrong? How was the person trying to profit from it? When you are citing a key case for a proposition of law, alert your reader to the context, not in great detail but in broad strokes. An introductory sentence or with parenthetic clause, will do:

In the case of <u>Riggs v. Palmer</u>, it was held that 'No one shall be permitted to profit from his own wrong'(<u>murderer denied inheriting his victim's estate</u>).

Return to our hypo. The homeowner is resisting paying the contractor for *completed* work because the contractor had bribed a building inspector to expedite paperwork. The homeowner's lawyer quoted "no one should profit from his own wrong." If you were the judge, wouldn't you be a tad miffed to learn that that language came from a case where a murderer was trying to inherit from his victim's estate?

Good legal writing is replete with quotes, not paraphrases. Quotes assure readers that they are reading the law, not just your interpretation of law. Legal research is really a scavenger hunt, a hunt for tasty morsels. But beware "cut and paste."

Word and Word Perfect, Westlaw and Lexis, are all terrific but....

Once you find your morsel (statutory or case language on point), don't cut and paste. *Copy the language yourself.* That's hard work and that's its virtue. You will read more carefully, copying only what you need. "Do I need that quote?" "Can I omit subpart B?" Copying discloses ambiguities and implications. "Wait a minute. I can interpret that word differently." Analyze *now*, not at a date to be named later.

Three matters of style. Quotes of more than 50 words (Okay, long ones) should be indented and single-spaced. If you omit language from the quote that is not relevant (*as opposed to language that hurts you*), indicate with "....." If you add emphasis to any words to make them jump out, indicate by adding at the end "(emphasis added)" or, if the emphasis was in the original quote, "(emphasis in original)."

Don't force your reader to puzzle or go back

Who's on first?
No, who's on second.

How many times have you been happily reading a case only to be abruptly stopped by: "The appellee argues...."

"Who is the appellee?" After rooting around for several minutes, "Oh, the appellee is the perpetrator," and all seems right with the world. "Wait a minute! Who is the perpetrator? The guy who axed his uncle?"

Avoid abstractions that force your reader to stop (and I find particularly difficult "former" and "latter").

Along the same lines, never force your reader back. How many times have you read, "The same argument that I made 20 pages ago applies here"? How many times have you gone back? Simply remind the reader of the previous argument in a phrase or sentence: *"The same argument I made 20 pages ago, to the effect that the world is flat, applies here."*

Avoid "The butler did it!"

You are not Agatha Christie nor were meant to be. Mystery writers carefully scatter clues (*x, y and z*) only to reveal, usually on the last page, that the butler did it. This, of course, forces the reader—at least the argumentative reader—to go back, reviewing the clues to see if they really add up ("I don't even *remember* a butler!")

There should be no surprise endings in legal writing. They may work in jury argument but not in legal writing. Here your goal in writing is simply to help someone make a difficult decision ("Who did it?"). Lead with your conclusion.

I conclude that the butler did it because of x, y, and z.

Now readers can test your conclusion as they go along: "Does *x* point to the butler?"

Briefs begin with the conclusion you want the judge to reach and often office memos do so as well–they can be a good overview. On law exams, however, conclusions are less necessary, unless they are "maybe."

Use IRS Transitions

> *The fish are jumpin'*
> *And the cotton is high,*
> *Oh, your daddy's rich,*
> *And your ma is good lookin',*
> *So hush little baby,*
> *Don't you cry.*

What a muddle! Sloppy work, George! Should baby hush *only if* the fish are jumpin', the cotton high, the daddy rich, *and* the ma good lookin'? Or will one, say jumpin' fish, do the trick? Or perhaps it takes a combination: ma good lookin' *and* high cotton?

From lawyers, even those who got music, we can ask for something more: IRS transitions. They are simply marvelous because they force you to think through the relationships between various items and, once you have, to tell them to your reader.

As was pointed out much earlier in this book (and don't go back), many rules of law are comprised of several elements and the relationship between those elements will be either *"and"* or *"or."*

Let's say you have spent some time discussing whether the fish are jumpin' and you want to move on to the question of the cotton.

Next, let's talk cotton.

This works to introduce your next topic but does nothing to show the *relationship* of cotton to the fish *nor* does it tell us the *significance* of the cotton. Compare:

For baby to hush, it is not only necessary for the fish to be jumpin', but also the cotton must be high.

This flags that the relationship between these elements is *"and"*. If it were *"or"*:

Even if the fish are <u>not</u> jumpin', if the cotton is high, baby should hush.

IRS transitions do three things: introduce the topic (cotton), show its *relationship* to the last topic (fish), and shows the *significance* of the topic (the impact on the crying).

I: They *i*ntroduce the topic;

R: They *r*elate that topic to the prior topic; and

S: They *s*hown the *s*ignificance of the topic.

You don't need a IRS transition between each topic. Sometimes the relationship and significance will be obvious. But, unless you have a good reason not to use such a transition, use it. *Err on the side of clarity, always.*

Like hitting a fast ball or playing the piano, IRS transitions are easy to understand but hard to do. Practice. See the chapter, "Writing Exercises."

Recently a student pointed out another benefit of IRS transitions: they help show how the specific and detailed discussion fits into your overall analysis and thus help solve the forest/tree problem endemic to legal writing. Why didn't I realize this before? Partly because Gershwin songs kept running through my head and partly because I focused too much on the tree, on how IRS transitions worked between paragraphs. My bad.

No Meandering

You're not James Joyce nor were meant to write stream of consciousness. Once you have a good IRS sentence, stay on point. Never start off on one topic and then, before you are done with it, mosey into another.

> *Even if the fish are <u>not</u> jumpin', if the cotton is high, baby should hush. Was the cotton high? The facts indicate that it was ready for harvest and hence was probably high. Ma had been Ms. South Carolina. Of course we would have to know a great deal more about the soil condition, the kind of cotton, and the season's rainfall records, to reach any definite conclusion as to its height.*

One reason you might do this is that the mind is like Windows: when you are writing on one topic,

the other is still running and occasionally something from it will "pop" into your mind. Unless you
have some other place to write it down, it barges
into your prose. While writing, always have a note
pad handy.

Be Explicit

With Shakespearean flair, you write,

*"Mark you well this: ma had been Ms. South
Carolina."*

This is an *implicit* statement. Your reader is
forced to tie the *specific fact* (her stunning victory)
to a *factual conclusion* (she's good lookin) and, once
that is done, then tie the *factual conclusion* to its
significance (that baby should hush). But your reader may not do this, may simply yawn, "Oh, how
'bout that. She was Ms. South Carolina," and just
keep on going.

Ironically, implicitness is caused, on the one
hand, by knowing *too much* (starting in the middle
of the story) and, on the other hand, knowing *too
little* (the problem of free radicals.)

Starting in the middle of the story. Toddlers begin
"Then Pat said...." assuming that you know everything that they do, who Pat is, what was said
before, and what they had for lunch. Although your
readers are lawyers, even as a first-year student you
will know much more about the particular area of
law you are analyzing than they do. You will know
more! Having thought long and hard on the matter,
it may be very clear to you how the fact (or legal

point) fits in the legal analysis—realize your readers are first-time players.

Free radicals. On the other hand, too much knowlejdge might not be your problem but too little. Your prose becomes implicit when you *don't* know how the fact (or legal point) fits in your legal analysis. It just seems important so you put it in. I have previously described this as the *free radical* problem. Demand of yourself, *"So what* she was Ms. South Carolina?" Tie your intuitions to your analysis. Don't hope that the reader will do that for you.

Of course, there will be times when you can get away with implicit statements of law or fact, where the nexus between the two is so clear even a caveman can see it. Being too explicit *seems* to be writing down to our readers. However, law is tough and legal analysis difficult; be as explicit unless it is very clear you need not be. *Err on the side of clarity, always.*

A spiffy slogan will help:

> *Every fact you write,*
> *Every law you cite,*
> *Before the final dot,*
> *Ask, "So what?"*

Put a spiffy tune behind it and we may have something! But not *Porgy and Bess*.

CHAPTER 22

MURDER YOUR DARLINGS

On dark and stormy nights, novelists sweat blood and tears to compose compelling scenes, thrilling encounters, desperately trying to avoid the hackneyed opening. Then comes the cold, cruel light of morning ... and editing. "Yes, my love, my creation, you are quite brilliant, you dazzle, my best so far, but, alas, you don't fit."

In the trade it is known as "murdering your darlings."

Expect to do some of that yourself. Rereading your draft, hopefully after a week of "cooling off," you will spot phrases, sentences, and even paragraphs ready for rewriting ... or the block.

"Me? You're gonna delete me? You're kidding. You spent so much time getting me just right. You did! I'm the key to the whole thing; without me the center will not hold and things will fly apart. Look at that fat paragraph over there! Why, it's nothing but fluff. Cut it. Leave me. In fact, *expand me!*"

As a lawyer you will edit a lot and, frankly, plagiarize a lot. Asked to do a will or create a partnership, you will look in a form book and tailor it to your own situation. Working with forms, or editing your own work, it is fairly easy to see what

247

doesn't fit and what can be improved. But with your nose pressed close to the text, how do you see what's not there?

Seeing What's Not There

Before you begin editing (or plagiarizing), it might be a good idea to jot a list of issues and points that the draft *should* include. Omissions will now jump out. Better yet, make an outline: doing so will trigger more thoughts. If you were writing a chapter on editing, what would you include?

Seeing What's There

Words, words, words, paragraphs, paragraphs, paragraphs. Back up—does the structure make sense? Don't try to edit on-line. Print a hard copy.

Highlight your issues, legal authorities, and the first sentence of each paragraph. Reread the highlights. Does your draft hold together? Make sense? Check the *order* in which your points are made. You have considerable choice; just don't begin at the beginning and push through to the bitter end. The first and last points you make are the most likely to be remembered. Put important points either first or last; points in the middle tend to be overlooked and forgotten.

As to your *issues*, can you state them more clearly? Assume you can and read critically. As to *legal authorities*, do you put the reader in direct contact with the law by quoting and not paraphrasing? Do you begin in the middle of the story, failing to realize that your reader is much less familiar with the legal area than you? As to your *topic sentences,* are they IRS transitions, ones which not only *introduce* the new topic but also *relate* it to prior discussions and also show its legal *significance*? It's OK not to have IRS transitions, but only if you have a reason not to.

Once you have considered the overall structure of your draft, *reread* for substance. Assume either a slow judge ("Say what?") or a vicious opponent ("Gotcha!").

Meandering. Make sure that your discussions stay on point. Does the analysis address the topic flagged by the topic sentence? Don't come and go, talking of Michelangelo.

Explicitness. There is no room for interesting facts, standing alone; there is no room for brilliant legal analysis, standing alone. Reading your draft, is it clear how each fact you discuss relates to the controlling law and how each legal principle you discuss relates to the facts of the case? Ask, *"So what?"*

Both sides. Even when you are writing an argumentative brief, you must consider, and respond to, your opponent's arguments. Here the saying is, *"Yes,* that's true, *but...."* Stop after each point you make and ask, "How could I respond to that?"

Your final edit is for style. Your targets: dead metaphors, pretentious diction, vague abstractions, and excess verbiage.

As to each sentence, ask, "Do I have big words where shorter ones can do?" "Can I say this in fewer words?" "Can I make it more concrete?" "Can I make it more punchy?"

At first, this will be difficult to do because, reading what you have written, it will seem just fine. Be aggressive; doubt each and every sentence. What follows are examples of bad writing and how to cure them. *Don't* try to memorize them: they are here simply to prove that what initially looks just fine, ain't.

Zap pretentious phrases:

At the present time	*zap now*
In the event	*zap if*
In the majority of instances	*zap usually*
With the exception that	*zap except*
For the reason that	*zap because*
In my considered opinion	*zap I think*

Zap intensifiers, adjectives and adverbs:

"It is very important to note"	*zap "Note"*
"The lecture was boring."	*zap "It put me to sleep."*
"The defendant lacked ethics."	*zap "She stole $1,257,876.24."*

Not only are you making your prose more spiffy and hard-hitting, but you are also reducing clutter and making it shorter. *Short is good.* We aren't paid by the word. Picking up a long brief, judges (who were once law students) skim. "Omit needless words," preached Strunk and White, the authors of the classic *Elements of Style*. Omitting needless words does not mean omitting detail or treating subjects in outline form. It means that *each word must tell*.

Your goal? Cutting 10%. Stephen King's first rejection slip read: *"Not bad, but puffy. You need to revise for length. Formula: 2nd draft = 1st draft— 10%."* If 10% works for him, it should work for us.

Passive verbs can trigger excess verbiage. The *active* voice is generally quicker than the passive:

The case <u>was reversed</u> by the Supreme Court. Passive voice: eight words.

The Supreme Court <u>reversed</u> the case. Active voice: six words.

Verb derivatives create problems:

He <u>made a decision</u>.
He <u>decided</u>.
They <u>took action</u>.
They <u>acted</u>.

Any sentence with *more than one verb* is a target. Clauses (a group of words with a subject and a verb) can often become phrases (a group of words without a verb).

"When the lawyer was conducting her cross-examination, the witness got up and left." 14 words.

"During cross-examination, the witness got up and left." 9 words.

Zapping is one activity in the third stage. Another is asking yourself, "Is it clear what, or whom, I am talking about?" Look for abstractions such as appellee, promisee, assignor, former, latter, and "The argument I made four pages ago."

Finally, last step: Step back and ask, "Is there any way to make this more *visually* inviting?" There is nothing worse than turning a page and seeing nothing but type, type, type. White space tells the reader, "Hey, this isn't going to be that bad." Break up long paragraphs. There is nothing better than an occasional paragraph of one or two sentences.

'Tis.

CHAPTER 23

WRITING EXERCISES

Time now to practice. In the first exercise, I ask you to critique an office memo. Then we will compare notes. The second exercise allows you to practice your IRS transitions. Finally, I'll give you some very wordy phrases which, in my considered opinion, in a great majority of instances, should be zapped.

Exercise One: Critiquing a Memo

A family built a new home and had moved most of their belongings inside. However, they were not yet living in it, in the sense that they were sleeping elsewhere, awaiting new bedroom sets. On the day in question, the family had left the house around 4 p.m. Sometime thereafter, Larry Durbin stole several items from the home, having gained entry by crawling through an open window.

The question: Has Durbin committed Residential Burglary?

To: Senior Prosecutor
From: Humble and Most Obedient Junior
Re: State v. Durbin

Statement of Facts
(Omitted)

Statement of Law

The state Criminal Code provides:

Section 1: Residential Burglary in the first degree is:

A.   Any armed robbery of a residence in which a person is threatened. An armed robbery is committed with the use of a gun, knife, bat, or any other object capable of inflicting injury.

B.   Any robbery of a <u>residence</u> that (i) occurs at night and (ii) in which entry was accomplished by force.

Section 2: Upon conviction of residential burglary in the first degree, the defendant shall be sentenced to not less than 5 years nor more than 15 years in the State Prison. An individual who has been convicted of a prior felony or who was convicted under Section 1(A) shall not be eligible for probation.

Conclusion

The defendant is guilty of first degree residential burglary.

Analysis

The house is a residence even though the family had yet to spend the night. They had moved most of their belongings in, and they clearly intended to make it their home.

Crawling through an open window requires force. The Supreme Court of a sister state interpreted a similar statute and held that a great deal of force is not needed, only a slight amount. State v. Stiggall (citation omitted). Here we have a slight amount for sure.

The only problem I see with this case involves Section 1(B)(i). This is because the family left the house around 4, and it is usually light until 6 or so.

What do you think? Play the role of senior prosecutor and critique. Only then read my take on it.

My Critique

Let's begin with one's *goal*. The goal of legal writing is to *help the reader decide a difficult issue.* If you were the senior prosecutor, what would you want in the memo? A clear statement of the controlling law, indications where the law might be ambiguous, a good development of both sides of the issues and *no clutter*.

The good news is that by copying, not paraphrasing, the controlling law, the author put the reader in direct contact. However, don't copy everything. Because the question doesn't involve punishment, Section 2 can be dropped; as there is no suggestion of armed robbery, Section 1(A) can be omitted. Consider:

Section 1: Residential Burglary in the first degree is:

A.   (Dealing with armed robbery—omitted)

B.   Any robbery of a <u>residence</u> *that (i) occurs at night and (ii) in which entry was accomplished by force.*

This cuts down on the clutter. The author correctly flags what was omitted but failed to indicate that the word "resident" was not highlighted in the actual text:

Any robbery of a <u>residence</u> *. . . . (Emphasis added).*

The "Conclusion" isn't helpful. (Note: by not reminding you what the conclusion was, you had to go back and reread. My bad–but, of course, you didn't. Your bad.) The goal of this memo is to help "Senior Prosecutor" evaluate the case; Junior's bare conclusion doesn't help.

Had Junior, before the analysis, stated the conclusion and *briefly* noted its basis, that would help. The reader could sing along.

Turning to the "Analysis:"

The house is a residence even though the family had yet to spend the night. They had moved most of their belongings in, and they clearly intended to make it their home.

The word "residence" should be highlighted, thus reminding the reader that this is a key part of the law. The question "So what?" isn't answered: *so what* if it was a residence? Finally, "yes ... but" analysis was not used: *Yes,* they moved in their stuff, *but* before people spend the night, the house seems more like a storage shed.

When you consider opposing arguments, your analysis goes deeper: what is meant by "residence?" Why did the Legislature make robbing a residence a more serious crime than robbing a storage shed? We can get a better sense of what was meant by "residence" if we know that purpose.

After discussing the issue of "residence," the memo moves on:

> *Crawling through an open window requires force. The Supreme Court of a sister state interpreted a similar statute and held that a great deal of force is not needed, only a slight amount. State v. Stiggall (citation omitted). Here we have a slight amount for sure.*

First, a yucky transition: how does "force" relate to the first topic, "residence" and what difference does it make whether or not force was used? Try your hand at an *IRS* here.

Second, there is a failure to develop opposing arguments: *yes,* crawling requires force, but so does walking, which would mean that the force requirement would always be met and Pittsburgh would be gone. Often a failure to develop opposing arguments stems from becoming an advocate as opposed to impartial evaluator: once one declares, "The defendant is guilty," one has an interest in defending that conclusion.

As to the *Stiggall* case, it would be far more effective to quote *specific* language from that case (thus assuring the reader you are not misreading it) and far better to give a brief indication of the context in which those words were uttered.

> *State v. Stiggall (defendant drove a truck through the doggie door)* . . . . .

Finally, because *Stiggall* comes from a sister state, it is not controlling authority. One should discuss whether a local court should follow it. Even if the case was "controlling," one should face the issue of whether it is a sound decision (cases can be distinguished or overruled).

Finally, what of:

> *The only problem I see with this case involves Section 1(B)(i). This is because the family left the house around 4, and it is usually light until 6 or so.*

Where can one begin? "Section 1(B)(i)" forces the reader either to stop and go back to the statute to see what it says or, as is more likely, skip the whole thing. Be helpful:

> *The only problem I see with this case involves Section 1(B)(i) <u>which requires the crime to be committed at night</u>. This is because the family left the house around 4, and it is usually light until 6 or so.*

Note that the argument is implicit. The reader must do the work, jumping from the fact (that it might have been light) to the factual conclusion (the crime might not have occurred at night) to the legal conclusion (then it ain't Residential Burglary).

This is because the family left the house around 4, and it is usually light until 6 or so. Thus the entry might not have occurred at night and thus there was no Residential Burglary.

In making a jury argument, one might decide to be implicit, hoping that a juror will connect the dots and hence become a strong defender of the position. However, in legal writing, *always err on the side of clarity.*

Exercise Two: IRS Transitions

IRS transitions are easy to understand but hard to do. They Introduce the new issue, they Relate it to the previous issue or discussion, and they show its legal Significance. Take the statute we used in the first exercise that defines "Residential Burglary" as:

A. Any armed robbery of a residence in which a person is threatened.

B. Any robbery of a residence that (i) occurs at night and (ii) in which entry was accomplished by force.

We can rewrite:

*A. Armed robbery **and** residence **and** person threatened **equals** guilt– **or** –*

*B. Robbery **and** residence **and** night **and** forced entry **equals** guilt.*

Assume, after you have discussed the "residence" issue, you want to discuss the "forced entry." You can simply introduce the issue (*The next issue is whether there was a "forced entry."*), but you can do much more:

> *Even if it is shown that a "robbery" occurred in a "residence," the defendant is not guilty unless it is also shown that there was a forced entry.*

Not all IRS transitions are alike. Some start with "Significance":

> *"The defendant will be guilty only if, in addition to finding a 'robbery' occurred in a 'residence,' it is found that a forced entry occurred."*

Some start with Introducing the topic:

> *"The next issue is whether a forced entry occurred, because, if it didn't, the defendant would not be guilty, despite the fact that a robbery may have occurred in a residence."*

Take ten minutes and play around with rewriting the sentence, sometimes assuming that the relationships between the elements are "ors": guilty if "residence" or "nighttime" or "forced entry." Play with different words. Here are some possibilities:

Words of Contrast

despite	even though	nevertheless	but
conversely	instead	though	although
notwithstanding	on the other hand	even so	however

Words of Addition

in addition	also	further	moreover
besides	too	and	more importantly

Words of conclusion

therefore	consequently	hence	as a result
thus	accordingly		

Exercise Three: Atari

Here are list of examples used in our last chapter. Practice your zaps.

At the present time
In the event
In the majority of instances
With the exception that
For the reason that
In my considered opinion
It is very important to note
The lecture was very boring.
The defendant lacked ethics.
The case was reversed by the Supreme Court.
He made a decision.
They took action.

'Tis.

CHAPTER 24

ORAL ARGUMENT

Just when you get comfortable, they spring Moot Court.

This will be your chance to stand, all by yourself, (sure there will be others in the room, *watching*), to stand before scowling law school professors, decked out in somber robes, to stand before them and explain the most complicated of legal issues, all the while fighting off a barrage of incomprehensible questions.

The idea is to introduce you to the joys of appellate argument. What's a poor law student to do?

Read your brief, quickly; remain conscious and not drool; win. All of these, alas, *fatally* flawed.

Don't rehash your written brief. Judicial decisions, like probably all of life's decisions, turn on two or three key points, not on all those points on the "pro and con" list and not on your wonderful treatment of that Idaho case in Footnote 23. Rehashing prevents you from focusing on the key issues, forces you to whip through, talking fast, to get to Footnote 23, and pretty much assures that you will keep your head down reading your script, ignoring the judges.

While losing consciousness and/or drooling tend to undermine your presentation, both are rare. Watching themselves on video, most law students remark, "Gee, I don't look nearly as nervous as I felt." Of course you will be nervous—even experienced lawyers get nervous and even, most probably, those smug professors. If your focus in on "how will I do?" then your attention will be on your shaky hands and sweaty brow. Shift your attention—take notes when your opponent is arguing and carefully listen to a judge's question (rather than, "Oh no, here it comes; I won't be able to answer that one!")

What about winning? *Shouldn't* this be your goal? *Believing* in your case, believing that you should win, is quite important. It is hard to rule against someone who obviously believes in their position. However, thinking of oral argument as a contest, a contest you must win, pushes you in bad directions. Like players of all games, you will be tempted to fudge, here manifesting itself in misstating law and fact. Like players of all games, you will get angry with your opponent and begin thinking in terms of skewing rather than convincing. Finally, if winning is your goal, you will tend toward defensiveness, taking each question asked by a judge as a hostile one and responding, almost knee-jerk, with "No." (In real life, in real courtrooms, "winning" manifests in arguing points long after they are lost and in trying to bully judges; thankfully, with their professors on the bench, law students seldom resort to such tactics.)

Okay. Is there a magic bullet, a goal to pursue that will help you avoid the pitfalls? *Yes*!

"To be helpful to the court."

When he argued before the Courts, that was the goal of John W. Davis, a man who argued more cases before the United States Supreme Court than any other lawyer of his generation.

To help? Was he nuts? Was his entire generation?

Back up. We are not playing games. We are doing serious stuff. Judges have heavy responsibilities: what they decide *matters*, not only to the parties before them but to folks yet unborn. Any case worth its salt will be a close one. You and your opponent are *experts* on the facts, on the law, and on the policy implications of the case. Judges need your *help* in understanding the complexities, and they need you to allow them to think through their reactions.

"I just want to be helpful" gets you off the hot seat. There is suddenly no need to get through your brief; you will focus on the points that seem pivotal. There is suddenly no need to fear that questions will destroy your case; you will welcome them as opportunities for you to help the judges think through the problems. Finally, your opponent transforms from Darth Vader into a colleague who is trying to do what you are trying to do–help the judges come to a proper decision.

Think of your presentation, not as *argument* but as *conversation*.

First, we will look at how to be helpful, then some matters of the substance of legal argument, and finally some pointers for when the Dreaded Day arrives.

Being Helpful

To be helpful, be candid and encourage questions.

Be Candid

Having done scads of research and hours of brief writing, all from your client's perspective, the odds are that you think your case is a slam dunk. "Why, all the cases and statutes line up on my side and, as to the very few that don't, they can be easily distinguished or interpreted around."

Almost all appellate cases are close, particularly those they select for Moot Court. *There is simply no way that you will win every point.* If you try, two bad things happen.

1. You will lose focus, wasting time defending Footnote 23.

2. You will lose credibility with the judges: like one bad apple, one implausible argument can infect the rest.

Concede what you can't win:

"Yes, my opponent is correct, the case did hold that. However, we believe that it is distinguishable."

"It is true, Your Honor, if you were to hold for my client certain expectations may be upset, but we

believe that they may not be as extensive as feared because of the following limiting features."

"I wish the cases were more clear in this area, but they are not. A fair reading of them, I submit, supports my position."

"That is a really good question, Your Honor, one I haven't even considered. Rather than try to come up with an answer on the spot, I would be happy to file a supplemental brief on it."

Concessions generate judicial goodwill and may rob your opponents of their best argument: "Why are you arguing that point, counselor? Your opponent has graciously conceded it."

Walk the extra mile. Instead of just disclosing "controlling authority" that goes against your position, as the Rules of Professional Conduct require, disclose "kinda adverse" authority: "This lawyer really wants to help me by telling me about all of the authorities that might apply. Thanks."

Of course, there are limits on candor. ("No, I don't like your hat.") Should you make arguments you don't believe in?

Tough issue. If you make arguments you don't find convincing, your lack of belief may show and undermine your credibility. ("This lawyer doesn't want to help me; this lawyer wants to fool me.") Further, as time is limited, it's best to stick with your winners. On the other hand, I have seen courts buy arguments that I thought were weak. If an argument is in the ballpark, and if there is time to argue it, I wouldn't drop it because I was not 100% convinced. Perhaps the judge will see more in it than you do. (That is why, by the way, you always include such arguments in briefs and in office memos.)

Never, however, beat a dead horse. (George Orwell tells us that a metaphor becomes stale when it no longer evokes the visual image it originally did— "beat a dead horse" is one of them, thankfully.) Making a bad argument has two bad consequences. First, your opponent might hoist you on your own petard (yet another stale metaphor). Second, the judges may conclude you're dumb or a bully.

Of course, identifying bad practice is one thing; it is quite another to correct it. Get to the root cause. Why do lawyers make bad arguments? Because they believe they must win every point. You don't.

A caveat on criminal defense. In order to protect the rights of the accused, criminal defense lawyers are allowed, often required, to advance arguments that stink. "Your Honor, my client is charged with violating a statute that prohibits 'obtaining money by false pretenses.' I move for a directed verdict as the state has only proved *one* pretense." Enough said.

To be helpful to the court, be candid. In addition, get the judges to voice their concerns.

Encourage questions and seek judicial involvement

Most cases turn on two, maybe three, main points. John W. Davis captures this notion with

"Go for the jugular!" Preparing for argument, what two or three points really matter? Focus on them.

But is your jugular theirs? Arguing a particular point, there are three possibilities, two of them bad:

1. The judges are *not* convinced of your position and *never* will be; you are wasting your time.

2. The judges are *already* convinced; you are wasting your time.

3. The judges are *undecided* and *need* further guidance.

How can you make sure it is 3, not 1 or 2?

Looking at the judges, and not your notes, or the flag, will help. Be aware, however, that we can misread signals: a smile may not indicate acceptance but rather, "This is ridiculous;" and a frown may not indicate rejection but rather, "Interesting point; let me think about it."

In an ideal world you could simply stop and ask, "Well, Your Honors, have I convinced you on that one yet? If not, do I have a prayer?" But oral argument is highly stylized, and you can't make that move. Rather, you will have to get the judges asking you questions so that you can address their concerns.

Watch some arguments. Lawyers are almost always better responding to questions than giving speeches. There is movement, creation, engagement. Answering questions improves your performance *and* makes you more effective. Again, your job is to the help the judges decide. If a point is troubling them and they don't ask, you won't be able to tell.

Some judges are reticent, too shy to interrupt, too unsure to voice their concerns. How do you smoke them out?

Want questions and invite judicial intervention. To get questions, first *want* questions. Judges are people, too, and human interaction is a subtle thing. If you fear questions, likely you won't get many. If you rejoice in them, they will come. During your argument, you can invite the judges to become involved.

"Your Honors, I plan to address the three issues in the following order. Would you like me to change that order?"

"That finishes my argument concerning issue one. Do you have any questions before I move on to issue two?"

Don't assume questions are hostile. Don't immediately answer, "No." Some questions will be friendly, trying to help you out. Others will be concealed arguments directed at other judges. Even those that flag weaknesses in your position are not necessarily hostile. The judge may be troubled by the point and wants your help in thinking it through. "Yes" is often better than "No."

Finally, if judges have the decency to ask you a question, don't blow them off with:

"Your Honor, I will answer your question in a few minutes. Right now I would like to keep talking about what I find of interest."

"Didn't you read Footnote 23?"

Don't fret never getting back to what you planned. You will and, if you don't, it probably doesn't matter.

Substance

Take away the Latin and legal argument isn't much different than arguing spilt milk in the kitchen: facts, precedent, policy. Never overlook the importance of facts: *"The statement of facts is not merely part of the argument, it is more often than not the argument itself."* And, as for slippery slope arguments of your opponent, remember the three responses. If none of this makes sense, reread the chapter on Spilt Milk.

Go for the Jugular and Murder Your Darlings

Preparing for argument, back up from your brief and ask two questions:

1. What are the two or three issues that will determine the outcome of the case?

2. What points should I concede?

When you ask these questions you will come to the painful realization that some of the best points in your brief won't play Saturday Night. But cut them or concede them you must. Novelists, editing their material, have a saying, "Murder your darlings." In our line of work, it's "Murder Footnote 23."

Know What You Want the Court to Do

"Assuming we agree with your position on the law, what do you want us to do? Let's assume

you've won. What should the last paragraph of our opinion say?"

Many a brilliant argument has crashed on this rock. Know what relief you want. Do you want the court to overrule a case? Declare a statute unconstitutional? Remand the case to the trial court and order a new trial? Do you want an order for some particular relief?

It is often best to *begin* your legal argument with a clear statement of exactly what you want the court to do. Often the real fight will not be about the merits, but about the proper remedy.

Themes and Exit Lines

Trial lawyers are great fans of "themes," reducing their case to a basic theme, one that can be stated in a few sentences: "This case is about the rush to judgment." They state their theme in their opening statement and, with great flare, return to it in their closing jury argument. While this can be overdone, consider a theme. It can focus on facts or on higher goals.

> *"Mr. Davis, a photographer for a local newspaper, awoke to find himself falsely accused of being a shoplifter. He found his 'mug shot' posted all over town. We ask this court to reverse the lower court and hold that he has a cause of action under the Civil Rights Act."*

> *"This case involves a very simple proposition: Our Constitution is color blind."*

You can open and close your presentation with your theme (but forget waving your arms and crying).

While spontaneity is the hallmark of great arguments, don't count on a brilliant closing riff to *pop* into your head when the judge says, "Two minutes." Unless you have written out and *memorized* your closing riff, you will be condemned to fade away, repeating and repeating snippets of prior arguments, or perhaps simply quitting the field with a rather pathetic:

"And That's All Folks!"

The Dreaded Day

Rehearsals

Hopefully you have rehearsed some. To think "I will then argue X" is much different than actually arguing it. Like writing, speaking slows the mind and, practicing before the bathroom mirror, you will get a much better sense of your argument and how to express it. When the time comes, you will know the major points you want to make and know how to answer the questions you anticipate. ("If I were the judge, what would I ask?") In real life, on big cases, lawyers will "moot" their argument with other lawyers in their firms playing the role of judge.

You can never prepare too much. That said, preparation is death. Perhaps I should explain.

A cast had just completed its second rehearsal before a live audience. The play was a comedy.

After the rehearsal, one of the actors asked the director:

"When I asked for the butter in the first rehearsal, I got a great laugh. Tonight I didn't. What happened?"

"The first time you asked for the butter. The second time, you asked for the laugh."

Great arguments are spontaneous, with both lawyers and judges coming to new insights. There is movement and excitement. The danger is that, if you have rehearsed your answer to a particular question, if you get it in your argument, rather than answering it afresh, you try to recall what you said before the bathroom mirror.

Prepare, prepare, prepare, but also know that often you must murder your darlings.

Warming up

In live theater, before they begin seating the audience, the cast is on stage, warming up, doing voice exercises, getting flexible, repeating snippets of dialogue. Courthouses (and law schools) aren't set up for this, but you might try finding an empty room. Do some riffs; get your voice limber.

Being there

When your opponent is arguing, the judges can still see you. Pay attention and be respectful. You can feign this by taking phantom notes. Never be bush: shaking your head, raising your eyebrows, or, indeed, picking your nose. (Sorry, it happens and I don't want an angry reader coming back and yelling, "You never said anything about not picking my nose!")

Creating Spontaneity

Don't read or commit your presentation to memory (except your closing riff). Although you might have written out your argument—probably a good idea—take only the briefest of outlines to the podium—in the unlikely event of a sudden loss of cabin pressure. Two or three words under Point A will trigger the major points you want to make *and,* free of the confines of a script, you may see new arguments as you go along, perhaps playing off a judge's question or an opponent's rant.

Encouraging questions, and being willing to change the order of your presentation, will also make things more exciting and more effective. Another device: if you are going second, listen closely to your opponent and then, when it is your turn, first thing, before you go into your prepared remarks, respond to one of their points–like a boxer coming off the canvas.

The major block to spontaneity is fear. "If I get away from my prepared remarks, I won't know what to say and, even if I do, I will never get back to where I was." *Don't worry.* If you have prepared, you will know what to say and will be able to get back to where you want to be. Have you ever even seen those oxygen masks, or used your seat as a flotation device?

Expect chaos. Embrace chaos.

Silence, pauses, beats and talk radio

If you ever get the chance, play the part of judge. You will learn just how iffy verbal communication is. Unlike reading, you can't stop, reread, or ponder. As speaker, how can you improve your chances of being understood?

Repetition, again, is no sin. Talk slow. Nervousness causes us to speak too quickly. When you first get up, don't immediately launch into your remarks; pause a few seconds, look at the judges, and take a deep breath. Then launch.

During your argument, take pains that it doesn't become a blur. Actors are taught the concept of "beat," a physical action that underscores a natural break in their dialogue. After a strong line, an actor may take a drink or walk across the stage to give the audience time to think. While you can't leave the podium, consider some physical act to mark transitions, perhaps looking down at your notes, adjusting your glasses, or a slight gesture. Variations in volume help, too. We generally raise our voices to make important points; try lowering your voice and watch everyone lean forward.

Pauses can be very helpful. There is a difference, however, between suddenly stopping and an effective pause. Pauses should be motivated: why are you stopping? To trigger a question? To allow a point to sink in? To gather your own thoughts? On stage, this is known as "using silence."

Getting comfortable with *silence* is critical. When people are expecting you to speak, seconds feel like hours (but they seem like seconds to the people). If you are uncomfortable with silence, during a client interview, you will ask another question instead of letting your client think about how to answer your first. During negotiation, you will make another offer rather than keep pressure on your opponent. During oral argument, you will blurt out an answer to a judge's question without thinking about it. When asked a question, *don't* immediately reply. Think about your answer. Occasionally, "That's a very good question that I hadn't considered. Let me think a few moments."

Finally listen to talk radio, for style, not necessarily content. The hosts are usually very good. Ask yourself, "What is the host doing to make things so clear? So convincing?"

Quotes

Don't read long quotes to the court. If you quote specific language, refer to the page in your brief where you quote the language so that the judges can sing along. If specific language is key, for example, in a case interpreting a statute, put it on a large chart that can be displayed on an easel during argument.

Fine, but what do I do with my hands?

Before you begin your argument, you will have a good idea of what you are going to say. So do actors. One of my favorite lines is that of Sir Toby, in *Twelfth Night*:

"Dost thou think, because thou art virtuous, there shall be no more cake and ale?"

But how should the line be delivered? Is Sir Toby angry, hurt, ironic, humorous? Stanislavsky, the founder of Method Acting, taught that once actors understand their characters' "intention," then gestures, facial expressions, and tone of voice tend to line up to support that intention; there would be no need to ask where their hands should be.

The acting metaphor works at another level as well. When a good actor is playing Sir Toby, it is not about the actor; it is about Sir Toby. When you are standing before the court, remind yourself that it is not about you, it is about your client. Being nervous is rather silly when your client has serious things at stake.

Let's end where we began (always a nice touch). What is your goal? What is your intention? Oral argument is not about getting it over with, not about being brilliant, and not even about winning. So, on that dreaded day, repeat:

I intend to help these judges understand the plight of my client and how the law supports my position. I intend to engage judges in conversation and to have them ask me questions. I intend to have fun, embrace chaos, and not be that poor, pathetic, colorless person that, deep down, I really am.

CHAPTER 25

ORAL ARGUMENT: AN EXAMPLE

If you are going first, you have a little more work to do. This overview will be from that perspective.

1. ***Introduce yourself and the client you represent.***

   "May it please the court, my name is C. Darrow and I represent Allprovidence Insurance, the defendant in the action below and petitioner here."

2. ***State the nature of the case*** (contract, tort, criminal) ***and briefly describe its procedural history***.

   "This is a suit on a life insurance policy on the life of Mr. Humpty Dumpty, brought by his widow. Our defense is that suit was barred by a suicide clause. At trial, it was our contention that Humpty did not have a 'great fall,' but rather that he took a 'great leap.' After a jury trial, judgment was for the plaintiff. We appeal on the basis that the judge improperly applied the 'plain meaning rule' and improperly excluded the testimony of one of the King's men concerning Humpty's dying declaration."

3. ***State the facts of the case***.

"In order to protect the widows and orphans, the true owners of Allprovidence, and in order to discourage suicide, the Allprovidence Insurance Company routinely includes a suicide clause in its policy, which bars recovery if the decedent took his own life. In this case . . . ."

In stating the facts, remember that the judges have read your brief and thus don't need all the facts recounted. Keep it short and succinct, focusing on the important and determinative facts. Even then, the court will cut you off with, "We are familiar with the facts, proceed with argument." But, given the importance of the statement of facts, don't go up there expecting the court to cut you off or inviting it to: "Does the court want to hear the facts?" Walk to the podium expecting to tell your story.

4. ***State the legal issues and preview the points you intend to argue***. A clear introduction to your legal argument is critical. Otherwise the judges may not follow it.

"It is our contention that the court below erred in applying the Plain Meaning Rule to Nursery Rhymes, thus preventing our argument that 'had a great fall' can be read as meaning 'took a great leap.' Unfortunately, the Yokel below is unfamiliar with Critical Legal Studies and trendy French Literary Criticism which suggests that texts can be read any way one wants."

*"Further, and as an **independent justification for reversal**, we assert the court below improper-*

ly excluded, as hearsay, Humpty's remark to one of the King's men, 'Being an egg I never got any respect. I'll make an omelet.' Although hearsay, we submit that it should have been admitted either as a dying declaration or as state of mind. Which issue do you wish me to address first?"

It is always a good idea to invite the judges to participate and always good to address their concerns, not yours.

5. ***Argue the case***. As with your written work, your oral argument will be improved by the effective use of transitions.

Not: *"The next issue concerns the admissibility of Humpty's dying declaration."*

But: *"That concludes my discussion of the Plain Meaning Rule. Unless there are any questions, I would like to now address the matter of Humpty's dying declaration. **Even if** this court decides that the court properly applied the Plain Meaning Rule, **it must reverse** this case if it finds that the testimony was improperly excluded."*

IRS transitions are best: they introduce the new topic, they relate it to the previous one, and they show its legal significance. The more *explicit* your argument, the more you *tie law and fact* together, and the more *concrete examples* you use, the clearer your argument will be.

6. ***Rejoice*** if the court asks you questions.

7. *Conclude and sit down*.

You will be allotted a certain amount of time. There is no requirement that you use it all. If you are done, sit down. Many first-year students do brilliantly until the end. Then, not having thought of a spiffy ending line, they thrash about aimlessly, repeating bits of prior arguments. Write and rehearse your last line. What do you want to leave the court with?

> *"Yes, Humpty was a good egg. But courts should not reward despair. Tell despondent eggs that their widows will not profit from their suicide; tell despondent eggs to stop exposing the incompetence of all the King's men!"*

Responding

If you are the person going second, after introducing yourself, unless there are factual matters you want to clear up, you can jump right into your argument. Before giving the overview of your argument, consider going after a specific point your opponent made during her presentation. This will assure spontaneity and zip.

Appellate arguments require clear introductions, clear transitions and clear summaries. This means repetition. Repetition is a virtue. As listeners, we can't go back to see how the arguments fit together. Often our minds wander. "What's for lunch?" Repetition is needed. Realize, too, that the judges, no matter how prepared, will not have the same familiarity with the law as you do. Give them a break and don't jump to the heart of your argument, which may turn on a rather fine point of law. Put that argument in context. As with legal writing, *begin with the basics*: "The Plain Meaning Rule basically provides that. . . ." rather than "The Plain Meaning Rule shouldn't apply here because. . . ." The latter construction forces the judges to go back and think, "What is the Plain Meaning Rule?" There is simply no need for them to have to do this. By the way, what is the "latter" construction and what's the problem with the word "latter"?

PART 5

LITIGATION

Perhaps nine-tenths of legal uncertainty is caused by uncertainty as to what court will find, on conflicting evidence, to be the facts of the case.

———

Jerome Frank

Doctrinal uncertainty is your daily bread.

"In *Globe*, involving a business contract and financial loss, the court held that a clause agreeing not to sue for negligence is valid. Would that holding apply in the next case, one involving a landlord/tenant relationship and personal injuries?"

Well, maybe. But once we figure out what legal rule to apply, the outcome is still not certain. Assuming the injured tenant gets around *Globe*, she still must prove that the landlord was negligent. On the basis of conflicting evidence, will the jury find that he was? *Well, maybe.*

In this part, we take a look at the factual side of things, the litigation process. Now you won't be trying lawsuits for years, so why spend time now? It will deepen your understanding of the legal doctrines you will study.

*"How will this doctrine play out in the court-
room? If it were my case, how would I prove it?
What witnesses would I call? How would the jury
be instructed? What would I argue to the jury?"*

These chapters will help with unfamiliar terms:
"motion to dismiss," "affirmative defense," "party
admissions," and "jury nullification" and will put
your Civil Procedure class in context. Along the way
I'll raise some ethical issues, some matters of jurisprudence, and highlight lawyer cunning. Hopefully
this will keep you awake.

There are no exams; don't try to memorize anything. You will revisit many of our topics in Civil
Procedure, Evidence, Legal Ethics, and Trial Practice.

We begin, naturally enough, with late-night advertising and the matter of fees. Next I'll show how
lawyers reduce the factual chaos into *Complaints*
and *Answers* and then describe how the law tests
for the legal adequacy of those factual stories, in
Motions to Dismiss and *Motions for Summary Judgment*. I'll introduce you to *Discovery*, and, in the
last chapters, I'll walk you through a trial.

Sit back, get a good light, and take a glimpse of
your future.

CHAPTER 26

CASE PLANNING:
THE INTERPLAY OF LAW
AND FACT—BACKWARDS

The Return of Ms. K

You remember Ms. K. She tripped. Recuperating, she watched a lot of TV. Late one night, during the reruns, after the ad giving the 1–900 number for an authentic psychic, the lawyer, C. Darrow appeared on the screen. Solemnly, indeed reluctantly, she broke the bad news:

"Insurance companies are sleaze! I hate to tell you, authentic psychics are frauds. I am your *only* friend." A warm, inviting smile:

"If you've been injured, been worrying you might get injured, or if the person who saved your life bruised your arm, hurry on down and we will see just how much money you get."

The next day, Ms. K hurried on down.

Lawyer Fees and Retainers

Rather than an *hourly fee* (used most often in business representation) or a *flat fee* (used often in criminal defense), *personal injury lawyers* work on a *contingency fee* basis. If settled prior to trial,

Darrow will receive 25% of the recovery, if litigated, 35%. If there is no recovery, Darrow gets nothing.

The idea behind the contingent fee is to assure access to the courts for folks who have been injured. If they don't win their case, they don't have to pay their attorney. Without a contingent fee arrangement, many people could not afford a lawyer. Some argue that contingent fees are a bad idea, because they encourage lawyers to bring unmerited lawsuits; and, even with meritorious cases, they put too much of a successful plaintiff's recovery in the lawyer's pocket.

Contingent fees are permissible only for personal injury cases and not, for example, in criminal, divorce, or child-custody cases.

However, even personal injury plaintiffs do have to pay *costs*: filing fees, reporter's fees for depositions, juror fees, and expert witness fees. Depending on the complexity of the case and the extent of discovery, these costs can run into quite a bit. If Ms. K wins her case, however, most likely the defendant will be ordered to pay these costs. If not, she's stuck.

Usually a large amount of money can be saved by both parties if they settle prior to trial; avoiding pretrial costs is a major incentive for settlement.

The tradition in this country is that *each side pays its own lawyer*, even if it wins. In many European countries, *loser pays both lawyers*. These rules have a big impact. "Each side pays its own" prevents people with small claims from getting legal representation ("Sure, I can win back the $400 you paid on the refrigerator, but my fee would be $2000.") "Loser pays" solves this problem but it discourages novel lawsuits: "If I sue Big Tobacco and lose, I will be out the money I paid my lawyer plus the zillions they paid theirs."

After they settle the matter of fees, Darrow and Ms. K sign a *retainer agreement*. It spells out the fee arrangement and states what Darrow is to do. Does the fee include appeals? A major source of lawyer/client fights is misunderstanding the lawyer's commitment. (Another is the failure of the lawyer to keep the client informed as to what is happening with the case: return your client calls *even if* there is nothing new to report.)

Hands are shaken. Ms. K leaves. Darrow, alone with her books, will start preparing for trial. She knows the chances are high the case will be settled but without some trial preparation, she won't know how strong the case is and won't know what a fair settlement would be. Where does she start? At the very *end* of the trial. What will the jury be told?

Jury Instructions and Their Politics

At the end of the trial, the judge instructs the jury. Lawyers prepare cases backwards. They begin with finding out *what* must be proved, by *whom* and by what *standard*. This is the stuff of jury instructions.

Visualize a warm courtroom, with jurors nodding off (and possibly you). The judge clears his throat and instructs:

*Ladies and Gentlemen of the Jury. I will now tell you the rules of law which you must follow to decide this case. (1) If you find that the defendant was **not** negligent **or** that the defendant's negligence did **not** cause plaintiff's injuries, your verdict must be for the defendant. (2) If you find that the defendant **was** negligent, **and** that his negligence caused the plaintiff's injuries, then your verdict must be for the plaintiff.*

Plaintiff claims that defendant was negligent.

Negligence is the failure to use reasonable care. Negligence may consist of action or inaction. A person is negligent if he fails to act as an ordinarily careful person would act under the circumstances.

Before you can find the defendant liable, you must find that the defendant's negligence caused the plaintiff's injury. Negligence causes an injury if it helps produce the injury, and if the injury would not have happened without the negligence.

If you decide for the plaintiff on the question of liability, you must then fix the amount of money which will reasonably and fairly compensate for any of the following damages proved by the evidence to have resulted from the defendant's negligence:

(1) The nature, extent and duration of the injury;

(2) The pain, discomfort, suffering, and anxiety experienced and to be experienced in the future as a result of the injury;

(3) Reasonable expenses of necessary medical care, treatment, and services rendered and reasonably probable to be incurred in the future; and

(4) Earnings which were lost by the plaintiff to date, and any decrease in earning power or capacity by the plaintiff in the future.

The plaintiff has the burden of proving by a preponderance of the evidence:

(1) That the defendant was negligent;

(2) That the plaintiff was injured;

(3) That the defendant's negligence was a cause of the injury to the plaintiff; and

(4) The amount of money that will compensate the plaintiff for her injury.

I will now tell you the standard of proof in this case. Preponderance of the evidence means such evidence as, when weighed with that opposed to it, has more convincing force and the greater probability of truth. In the event that the evidence is evenly balanced, so that you are unable to say that the evidence on either side of an issue preponderates, then your finding upon that issue must be against the party who had the burden of proving it.

Now that's a mouthful, and there is even more. The judge will also instruct as to witness credibility and the role of jurors.

"Where do jury instructions come from?" asks the precocious child. Appellate cases and relevant statutes. In most jurisdictions, you can find them in *form jury instruction books*. While these instructions seem quite dull, they mask vibrant political and legal battles.

Here the jury is instructed that Ms. K must prove both neglect and injury (*"burden of proof"*) and she must prove it by a "preponderance of the evidence" (*"standard of proof"*). These are not neutral or self-evident decisions; they turn on political assessments. Do we want to encourage or discourage personal injury suits? Do we want to shift losses, or do we wish to let them stay where they have fallen?

If we wanted to help people in Ms. K's position (to shift losses to folks who might be better able to absorb or prevent them), we could put the burden of proof on the defendant to prove he *wasn't* negligent.

On the other hand, if we wanted to further discourage people like Ms. K from bringing suit, we could increase the standard of proof required of her, from "preponderance of the evidence" to "clear and convincing evidence"; or even, as in criminal cases, to "beyond a reasonable doubt."

"Pain and suffering" awards are a hotly debated element of recovery. The huge jury awards one reads about are mostly for "pain and suffering." Insurance companies argue that they threaten Western Civilization. Others argue that huge jury awards do not harm American business but rather assures that it will be conducted in a safe manner. Both sides can keep you awake with compelling war stories and can put you to sleep with statistics.

Consider the following instruction:

*Ladies and Gentlemen of the Jury, you are to decide the facts of this case. I will tell you the law. It is your **duty** to follow the law as I give it to you even if you disagree with it.*

Again, this seems to be an unremarkable statement but, like so much of law, it masks great debates. Why not tell juries, "If you think the law is unjust, don't follow it"? This is known as *jury nullification* and, in the early days of our country, was a proud tradition: local juries protecting neighbors from the unjust edicts of the King.

We don't *tell* juries that they have the power to disregard the law. They can, of course, in the sense that they will not be held in contempt of court if they come in with a weird verdict. Woe to the lawyer who tries to argue jury nullification: "The law in this case would be unjust. Don't follow it." He will find himself in contempt of court. The issue of jury nullification turns on assessments of how much we trust legislatures will do the right thing. How much we fear juries will do the wrong thing? And how much we believe that general rules can capture the nuisances of justice? Fascinating stuff, but litigators just don't have time.

Investigating and Proving a Negligence Suit

From the jury instructions, Darrow knows she must prove:

    (1) That the defendant was negligent;

    (2) That the plaintiff was injured;

(3) That the defendant's negligence was a cause of the injury to the plaintiff; and

(4) That the amount of money suggested is needed to compensate the plaintiff for her injury.

The first two look fairly easy and may be established by Ms. K's testimony, "Before my fall, my leg and back were fine, but not afterwards." But how can Darrow convert physical injury into dollars?

Ms. K broke her leg, hurt her back, and incurred hospital and doctor's bills. She also missed 10 days of work. Darrow knows that it will be relatively easy to prove the amount of the "reasonable expenses of necessary medical care" by simply introducing the bills at trial. She can easily prove "lost earnings" by having Ms. K testify as to their amount. It will be more difficult to prove that the injuries will cause her lost income in the future, and it may be hard to convince the jury to put a high monetary value on the "pain, discomfort, suffering and anxiety experienced" by Ms. K.

The real problem for Darrow, however, is proving that "the defendant was negligent." Ms. K says she fell because the step at the top of the stairs was loose. Darrow and her photographer visit the scene and inspect the staircase. They will find that the top step, made of wood, is cracked so that, when one steps on its outside edge, it gives. But neither Darrow nor her photographer can tell how long the step has been cracked.

Does the mere existence of a cracked step prove, by a "preponderance of the evidence," that Landlord was neglectful? Without more, it seems pretty weak. If this is all she has, maybe Darrow won't even be able to get to the jury. If the judge thinks the evidence is so weak that no reasonable juror could find for the plaintiff, he can take it away from the jury after the plaintiff has presented her case, by granting a motion for a *directed verdict*; or even after the jury comes back with a judgment in favor of the plaintiff, by entering a *judgment notwithstanding the verdict—"a judgment n.o.v."*

Darrow needs more evidence of Larry's negligence. She would like to argue that Larry knew of the defective stair for months prior to Ms. K's accident, that he knew many people used the stairs, and that he was seen, beer in hand, laughing the villain's laugh, "After they eat cake, let them tumble!"

The odds are that Larry will deny knowing anything about the step's defective condition and will claim that he inspects them often (on his way to Temperance meetings), and that he has nothing but love for all his tenants, and that his heart goes out to Ms. K, but that, hey, it wasn't his fault.

In hopes of proving that Larry knew of the defect before the accident, Darrow will send an investigator to talk to other tenants. Did they ever report the condition to Larry? Were there other accidents on the stairs? Does Larry himself use the stairway, thus possibly having firsthand knowledge?

If Darrow can't prove Larry actually knew of the condition, what about arguing that, as a reasonable

landlord, he should have inspected the stairs period-
ically? Darrow will do legal research in hopes of
finding a statute or case imposing a duty of reasonable inspection on landlords. If she finds one, she
can ask the judge to instruct the jury:

Ladies and Gentlemen, a landlord has a duty to
make periodic inspections of common areas.

If Darrow can get this instruction, she has saved
herself a lot of work. Now she must prove only that
Larry didn't make the inspections, not that he
should have.

Assuming Darrow can't get the instruction as a
matter of *law* (because she can't find any statutes
or cases), she can argue to the jury that, as a matter
of *fact*, failure to inspect is negligence. It would
strengthen that argument if she could call other
landlords to testify that they always make inspections and think it would be unreasonable not to do
so.

Now she has something else to research: would
testimony of other landlords as to what they do be
admissible evidence? As many trial lawyers have
learned, everything you want to get before jury
might not be allowed into evidence. She will likely
write a *trial memorandum* to use at trial if the issue
comes up. (Note that this research can help in
negotiation: "Look, I will call three landlords who
will testify your client should have made inspections, and that testimony is admissible.")

Darrow realizes, however, that even if she can
establish a duty to inspect (either legally or factual-

ly), she still must show that the inspection would have disclosed the defect. She needs testimony that the stair was defective for a long time. She needs an *expert*. An expert need not have academic degrees nor even "book learnin'". An expert is simply someone who has special knowledge that will help the jury understand the facts of the case. Darrow will ask a carpenter to inspect the stairs and tell her, if he can, how long the step was broken.

Enter, stage left, *Quibble Weaver*.

While these investigations are going on, Larry has retained his own lawyer, Mr. Quibble Weaver. Of course, "Quibble Weaver" is a fictional name, but it isn't mine. It was the name given the lawyer in the first modern Italian novel, *The Betrothed*, written by Alessandro Manzoni in 1827. Even then and even there, lawyers took their shots. Quibble Weaver, indeed!

In any event, Darrow contacted Quibble looking for a possible settlement. Her initial overtures met sullen rejection:

"Larry Landlord wasn't negligent. Ms. K wasn't injured. Besides, there is a clause in the lease releasing the landlord from all liability."

"If that's the way it is going to be, see you in court."

Time to start drafting.

CHAPTER 27

COMPLAINTS, ANSWERS, PRETRIAL MOTIONS, AND DISCOVERY

Sometimes a case will settle before a lawsuit is filed. If one doesn't, it becomes time to ratchet up.

IN THE SUPERIOR COURT

IN AND FOR THE COUNTY OF KERN

STATE OF CONTENTION

Ms. K	.	**COMPLAINT FOR NEGLIGENCE**
Plaintiff	.	**AND STRICT LIABILITY**
vs.	.	
Larry Landlord	.	**Civil Action Number 1066**
Defendant	.	

. . . .

Comes now plaintiff and complains of the defendant as follows:

Count I

1. *The court has jurisdiction of this matter as all events complained of occurred in this county,*

    and both Ms. K and Larry Landlord are residents thereof.

2. *At the times herein mentioned, defendant owned the Owl Apartment Building.*

3. *At the times herein mentioned, defendant retained control in the Owl Apartment Building of the halls, lobbies, and stairways used in common by all tenants of the building and others lawfully coming onto the premises.*

4. *Plaintiff was a tenant of defendant on or about November 17 last year.*

5. *On that date, while plaintiff was proceeding down the common stairway provided by defendant for the use of all tenants, plaintiff was tripped by a defective stair on the stairway, thrown violently down the stairway, and in falling broke her leg and sustained injuries to her back.*

6. *As a result of such injuries, plaintiff sustained damages in the amount of $300,000.*

7. *Defendant knew, or with the exercise of reasonable care should have known, of the defective condition of the stairway, but negligently failed to correct, remove, or repair such defective condition, and such negligence by defendant was a proximate cause of plaintiff's injuries and the damages incidental thereto.*

Count II

1. *Plaintiff realleges 1–6 of her first cause of action.*

2. *Defendant is strictly liable for defective condi-*
   tions in the stairway, and said defective condi-
   tions were a direct cause of plaintiff's injuries.

   THEREFORE, plaintiff prays judgment against
the defendant for $300,000, for costs of suit, and for
such other and further relief as the court deems
proper.

                              C.   *Darrow*
                              Attorney for Plaintiff

———————

Reread Count II. What is Darrow up to? Why a
Count II at all? Isn't it the same as Count I?
Compare #7 in Count I with #2 in Count II. Read
carefully.

———————

The first thing a plaintiff must allege in his
complaint is that the court has jurisdiction to decide
the matter. As you will learn in your Civil Procedure class, whether a court has jurisdiction over a
defendant can be hopelessly complicated. In the
workaday world of lawyers, however, most defendants do not live out of state, and most do not
commit obscure torts offshore that, as luck would
have it, do harm in our town. Most defendants live
next door and do their nasty deeds in place; usually
jurisdiction is not at issue (except, of course, in law
school exams).

After the jurisdiction issue come the factual allegations that are needed to constitute a legal wrong. Note that *notice pleading* is all that is required. All you have to do is alert the defendant to your general factual contentions. It is, for example, enough to allege that the stair was "defective" and it is not necessary to say just how.

Returning now to the allegations in Count II, Darrow is asserting an *alternative theory* of liability. Unsure she can prove neglect, she is trying to avoid the problem by alleging that the landlord should be liable under the doctrine of strict liability. You will learn in Torts that, in cases involving very dangerous substances or activities, people can be liable for injuries they cause even if they were not negligent. This is true, for example, of people who store explosives. If the explosive goes off and injures someone, that person can recover without showing that the defendant was negligent. If you store explosives, and they go off, you are *strictly liable* for any injury caused. There is no need to show that you stored them in a negligent manner.

The law is always in a state of flux; Darrow hopes to convince a judge that the doctrine should apply to landlords and dangerous stairs. She does this by alleging that basis of liability. If Larry's lawyer is on his toes, he will file a motion saying that landlords are not strictly liable and then, as we are apt to say, the issue will be joined.

We'll see.

Proud of her work, Darrow takes it down to the County Courthouse, pays the County Clerk the filing fee, and files the complaint. The clerk gives it a case number, and we're off to the races. Darrow gives a copy of the complaint and a summons to a process server, who thereupon serves it on Larry Landlord.

Dismayed and no doubt quite fearful, Larry will take the compliant to his lawyer, Quibble Weaver, who now scurries to the law library. He has but twenty days to "answer."

IN THE SUPERIOR COURT

IN AND FOR THE COUNTY OF KERN

STATE OF CONTENTION

Ms. K	.	
Plaintiff	.	**ANSWER**
vs.	.	
Larry Landlord	.	**Civil Action Number 1066**
Defendant	.	

. . . .

Comes now defendant to answer plaintiff's complaint as follows:

1. *Admits allegations 1–4 inclusive.*

2. *Denies allegations 5, 6 and 7.*

3. *As to count two, denies all matters not admitted to in number 1 hereof.*

AFFIRMATIVE DEFENSE

As an affirmative defense to both counts, defendant alleges:

1. *That the lease between Ms. K and Larry Landlord, which Ms. K signed, provides: "The Landlord shall in no event be liable for any loss or damage which may occur to the Tenant."*

2. *Said clause bars plaintiff's suit.*

THEREFORE, defendant prays

1. *That plaintiff take nothing on her complaint.*

2. *That the court order plaintiff to pay defendant's costs of suit and order such other further relief as the court deems proper.*

> *Q. Weaver*
> *Lawyer for Defendant*

Weaver admits that the court has jurisdiction, that the defendant owned the apartment house and controlled common areas, and that the incident occurred on November 17. He denies the things he will contest at trial: the fall, the injuries, and the landlord's neglect. Ms. K, as plaintiff, will have the burden of proving them.

He also raises an *affirmative defense* concerning the lease provision protecting Larry from suits like this one.

Usually a plaintiff must prove all the elements of her case; sometimes, however, the law requires the defendant to bring up certain matters and then prove them. For example, the plaintiff must prove that the defendant was negligent. If the defendant claims that the plaintiff was *also* negligent (she was drunk) and this contributed to her injuries, the defendant must allege and prove it. Note, again, that these are political/legal decisions. One could, for example, require plaintiffs to prove not only that the defendant was negligent, but that they, the plaintiffs, were not.

You will spend time in your Civil Procedure class on how and why courts allocate issues between things the plaintiffs must prove and things the defense must prove (affirmative defenses).

Discovery

Trials used to be a whole lot more dramatic. Quibble could call surprise witnesses. "The defense calls Mrs. Ortelere."

At counsel table, Darrow would turn to Ms. K and anxiously whisper, "Mrs. Ortelere? Who is Mrs. Ortelere, and what does she know?"

"I dunno. She was my third grade teacher. My God, they're not going to bring *that* up?"

In 1938, the Federal Rules of Civil Procedure were adopted with the goal of taking the surprise out of litigation. The basic idea was that, if both sides of a lawsuit knew all of the evidence that would be introduced at trial, more cases would be settled; and, as to those that weren't, they would be decided on their merits rather than on lawyer gamesmanship.

To illustrate something of discovery, by way of *written interrogatories*, parties can ask each other questions:

> 1. *List all of the witnesses you intend to call at the trial and summarize what testimony you will elicit from each.*

If Weaver didn't list Mrs. Ortelere, she would not be allowed to testify, except in very rare circumstances.

In your Civil Procedure class you will learn all about the various *discovery* methods available to lawyers. They are quite extensive. One, for example, allows for opposing lawyers to inspect premises and another can compel a personal injury plaintiff to undergo physical examinations by doctors hired by the defense.

The most popular discovery device is the *deposition*. In a deposition, a lawyer is allowed to question opposing witnesses, under oath, in order to see what they will testify in court and to get a sense of whether they will make good witnesses. To assess how much his client might lose, Quibble wants to question Ms. K to see how sympathetic she will be.

Quibble will *depose* Ms. K in his office. Darrow will be there, and, before things start, she and Quibble will engage in that easy banter that lawyers love and clients hate ("What's my lawyer doing being nice to that sleaze?"). Once things start, Darrow probably won't do much except sit and listen. There is generally not much to object to in a deposition. Quibble can ask pretty much any question that can *lead* to admissible evidence, and that gives him a lot of room to question Ms. K about a whole manner of things. For example, he can ask her, "Tell me everything you were told by the neighbors about the stairs." As this calls for hearsay, such a question would not be permissible at trial; however, as it might *lead* to admissible evidence (calling one of the neighbors to testify), it is a fine question during discovery.

A court reporter will transcribe the questions and answers. Ms. K will be sworn in, and Quibble will try to pin her down, both as to the cause of her accident and as to the extent of her injuries. If Ms. K changes her story at *trial*, she can be *impeached* by these prior statements. Suppose, for example, she testifies *at trial* that she hurt her left arm during the fall. Quibble has the transcript of her deposition and is ready to *cross-examine*.

Cross Examination by Quibble Weaver

Q: *Ms. K, you testified on direct that you injured your arm during the fall, is that correct?*

A: *Yes.*

Q: *Do you remember coming to my office for your deposition?*

A: *Yes.*

Q: *Wasn't your attorney with you?*

A: *Yes.*

Q: *And you were sworn to tell the truth on that occasion?*

A: Yes.

Q: And I told you before we began not to answer any question you didn't understand, isn't that a fact?

A: Yes, I remember. You seemed like such a nice man at the time.

Q: During the deposition I asked you to describe your injuries. You told me of your back pains and your broken leg, isn't that right?

A: Yes, my back was quite painful. And my leg was really smashed up. It was terrible.

Q: I appreciate your injuries. Please just answer my questions. Now, after you indicated your problems with your back and leg, didn't I ask you whether you were injured in any other way?

A: Yes, you asked me that.

Q: And didn't you tell me, "No, I had no other injuries." Weren't those your precise words?

A: Yes, but . . . . .

Q: (Cutting her off) Thank you, nothing further.

If Ms. K has a good explanation for her inconsistency, her lawyer can bring it out during redirect. In the jargon of the trial bar, this is known as *rehabilitation*.

Redirect by C. Darrow

Q: Before you were cut off, I believe you were about to explain your inconsistency.

A: Yes. During the deposition, I was in pain. My back and leg hurt so much that I simply forgot about the injuries to my arm.

Trial lawyers will tell you that some rehabilitation is better than others.

Despite the spirit of the discovery rules, lawyers, like kids, still love surprises. Unlike kids, however, they don't like to be surprised; they like to surprise. Lawyers resist full disclosure. For example, before a deposition, a party will be told by her lawyer:

"Just answer the questions. Don't volunteer anything. You will want to tell your side of the story. But remember that the lawyer asking you questions will never be convinced by you, and it is his job to turn anything you say against you. But don't be nervous!"

Before trial, Darrow will undoubtedly depose Larry Landlord, hoping to find that he either knew of the condition or failed to make ordinary inspections of the stairs. Discovery is going per usual when suddenly Quibble makes a move designed *to end it all.*

Pretrial Motions Designed to Avoid Trial

IN THE SUPERIOR COURT

IN AND FOR THE COUNTY OF KERN

STATE OF CONTENTION

Ms. K   .

    Plaintiff   .

    vs.   .   **Civil Action Number 1066**

Larry Landlord   .

    Defendant   .

. . . .

DEFENDANT'S MOTION TO DISMISS COUNT 2 OF PLAINTIFF'S COMPLAINT

DEFENDANT'S MOTION FOR SUMMARY JUDGMENT

TAKE NOTICE THAT at 8:30 a.m. or as soon thereafter as the matter can be heard, on April 6 in Courtroom 4 of the Superior Court of the County of Kern, defendant will move the court to dismiss Count 2 in plaintiff's complaint as it fails to state a claim upon which relief can be granted. DEFENDANT WILL FURTHER MOVE that summary judgment be granted it as to Count One, dealing with allegations of negligence, on the basis that there is no triable issue of fact in this case. As attested to in the attached affidavit of Larry Landlord, Ms. K signed a lease that provided she could not sue for negligence.

                        Respectfully submitted,
                        Quibble Weaver

If Weaver wins this motion, there will be no trial.

Why have a lengthy and expensive trial if it is clear that Ms. K will lose? Procedural law allows for various moves to abort cases without trial if there really isn't a true factual dispute.

A quick aside. *"Procedural law"* refers to the rules which govern the *method* by which disputes are resolved; such as rules governing which court should decide the controversy (jurisdiction); what issues may be joined in the same lawsuit; and how long one has to answer a complaint. *"Substantive law"* refers to rules which determine the *outcome* of the dispute, the rules of contract, property, and dog bite. Substantive law governs our daily lives and those of our dogs.

The two most common procedural devices to test the legal effect and sufficiency of fact are *motions to dismiss* and *motions for summary judgment.*

Motions to dismiss a pleading as insufficient as a matter of law

The plaintiff files a complaint making certain allegations. A motion to dismiss basically says "no soap"—what is alleged doesn't make it as a matter of substantive law.

In this case, defendant is moving to dismiss plaintiff's second count. Plaintiff alleged that the defendant landlord should be liable on a theory of strict liability; that he should be liable even though the plaintiff cannot prove that he was negligent in relation to the stairs. Darrow wanted a fallback position in the event she could not prove negligence.

Clever idea. Defendant's motion to dismiss is saying, "Without showing negligence, there is no cause of action as a matter of law and hence the count should be dismissed. No need to have a trial on it."

In olden days, days of grace and style, motions to dismiss were called "demurrers." You will find that term in some opinions you read. It is still used in our more romantic states, such as California.

Motions for Summary Judgment

A motion to dismiss is solely defensive in that it can only attack the sufficiency of the facts alleged by the opposition. But what if there is an important fact not alleged by the opposition that would abort the case? How can you get it before the court? By a Motion for Summary Judgment. Along with the Motion you file an affidavit by someone who swears that the fact is true. If the opposing party files an affidavit saying the fact is not true, then the matter will be set for trial. However, if the opposing party doesn't file an affidavit denying the fact, the court deems the fact admitted. Then the question becomes, with that fact admitted, should judgment be granted to one of the parties? The test, as you will learn, is whether there remains "a triable issue of fact." If there is, judgment will not be entered; if there is not, then it will be.

Now, in our case, Ms. K did not mention the exculpatory clause in her complaint. To get it before the court, Quibble files an affidavit attesting to it. K can't deny it. The issue is joined: does the clause, as a matter of law, bar her suit? Yes, if the clause is legally enforceable; no, if it is not. Thus we are thrown back to the first chapter of this book. Seamless web and all of that!

Come 8:30, April 6, Darrow and Quibble arrive in Courtroom 4. Most likely they have each previously submitted a *Memorandum of Points and Authorities,* which are legal briefs arguing their respective positions. Does the case law suggest it would be appropriate to impose strict liability on landlords? Do any cases or statutes address the issue of exculpatory clauses in apartment leases? At the hearing, both lawyers will have the opportunity to quote precedent, argue policy, distinguish cases, wave their arms and predict doom. No doubt the judge will "take the matter under advisement." After a short interval the judge will enter judgment, in all likelihood striking the plaintiff's second count (nice try, Darrow) and denying Weaver's motion for summary judgment, holding exculpatory clauses unenforceable.

The matter is set for trial of plaintiff's remaining count, the one alleging negligence. Can Darrow make it out *factually?*

Trial's set for tomorrow. Get some rest.

CHAPTER 28

TRIALS

A tree falls in the forest. No one is there to hear. Does it make a noise? Despite the mush you learned in Philosophy 101, us lawyers can easily answer the question: "It depends on the jurisdiction in which it fell."

Jury trials go something like this:

1. Jury selection.

2. Opening statements.

3. Plaintiff's (or State's/People's) case-in-chief. Plaintiff rests.

4. Motions, such as a *directed verdict* motion, designed to test whether, at this point in the trial, a reasonable jury *could* (but not necessarily *would)* find for the plaintiff. If such a motion is granted, that's that.

5. Defendant's case-in-chief. Defendant rests.

6. Plaintiff's rebuttal (witnesses called to contradict new testimony given in the defendant's case).

7. Defendant's rebuttal (witnesses called to rebut plaintiff's rebuttal witnesses).

8. Closing arguments.

9.   Jury instructions. In some jurisdictions, jury instructions are given before closing arguments and in others some instructions are given before the trial starts.

10.   Jury deliberation.

11.   The thrill of victory, the agony of defeat.

Let's take a closer look at some of these phrases.

Jury Selection (Voir Dire)

The goal is an impartial jury. In the old days, whenever *they* were, jurors were neighbors. Who better to know the liar? The malingerer? In today's enlightened society, we seek an *ignorant* jury. We get it by questioning prospective jurors. This is known as "voir dire."

"Do you know any of the parties to this action?"

"This case involves an automobile accident. Have you been in an accident?"

"The plaintiff is asking for money damages for the pain and suffering she suffered as a result of the accident. The law allows for such damages. If you believed the evidence warranted damages for pain and suffering, would you award them?"
(Some people simply don't believe that these damages should be available.)

"This is a criminal case involving burglary. Have you been the victim of a crime? Do you have any relatives in law enforcement?"

In some jurisdictions, the lawyers conduct the voir dire; in others, judges do. Judges are replacing lawyers because lawyers use the opportunity to "try their cases" by converting what will become their closing argument into a series of questions:

"Now, if the evidence showed Ms. K suffered permanent leg damage, you wouldn't hesitate to compensate her fully for that injury, say in the neighborhood of $300,000, would you?"

After juror questioning comes juror selection. It is really juror *rejection*—those still standing after the rejections become the jury.

First come challenges *for cause,* and each side has an unlimited number. Say a potential juror is married to one of the police officers who investigated the crime. Defense counsel, no doubt insensitive to the dynamics of married life, would challenge this juror for cause. Of course, the prosecutor, equally blind to life's subtleties, would attempt to *rehabilitate* this juror:

"Even though you're married to the investigating officer, you could still be fair, right?"

"Are you married?"

It will be the judge's call.

What about pretrial publicity? Even if a juror has read about the case in the newspaper, she will be kept if the judge feels that she can put all that aside and render a verdict upon the evidence presented at trial. In cases involving major media coverage, however, the trial may have to be moved to another city.

In addition to challenges for cause, each side will have a limited number of *peremptory* challenges. Exercised when the lawyer feels, for whatever reason, that it would be best not to have the *person* on the jury, peremptory challenges are the stuff of war stories and crude stereotypes. In criminal cases, the prosecution wants Germans, preferably Lutheran, and retired high school vice principals, while the defense wants drunken fraternity boys of all faiths and denominations. Peremptory challenges have created the cottage industry of "juror consultants" who, in high-profile cases, do background checks on prospective jurors and, during *voir dire*, sit in the back and watch ever so closely for telltale twitches.

As you will learn in your Constitutional Law class, peremptory challenges cannot be used to systematically exclude individuals based on race or sex.

Opening Statements

Opening statements, known as "road maps," help the jury fit the various pieces of evidence into an overall story. "We will call Dr. Dread to prove that Ms. K sustained serious injuries. Dr. Dread is not a real doctor but he does play one on TV."

During their opening statements, lawyers are not supposed to "argue" their cases. Argument is the drawing of *factual inferences* and *legal conclusions* from the raw facts to be presented at trial. The line between "road map" (stating the facts, e.g., the stairs were in disrepair) and "argument" (drawing inferences, e.g., "This means the landlord was negligent") is often a fine one, and lawyers often cross over. However, grand pleas for justice, or for the need to send landlords "messages," are clearly argument and must be saved for closing, where the only limit, frequently ignored, is good taste.

Case-in-Chief: Hearsay and Examining Witnesses

In the plaintiff's case-in-chief, evidence must be presented to establish all of the elements of the plaintiff's case. In a typical personal injury case, they are:

a. That the defendant was negligent

b. That the negligence caused plaintiff's injuries

c. The extent of those injuries

The evidence can consist of *exhibits* (X-rays showing plaintiff's broken bones, photographs of the victim's injuries), *documents* (doctor bills) and, of course, *witnesses*, including *expert witnesses*.

Live witnesses are the most fun. A major limitation on what they can testify to is the *hearsay rule*. It basically prohibits a witness from testifying as to what others told him. Of course, in the real world, we love hearsay. Our ears go on high alert when we hear the rich and promising phrase, "Guess what I just heard?"

The hearsay rule prohibits the introduction of "an out-of-court statement introduced to prove the truth of the matter asserted."

"Sam told me that he had tripped on the stair two weeks before Ms. K did."

As this would be introduced to prove the matter asserted, that Sam did indeed trip on the stair, it would be inadmissible hearsay. To admit it would be unfair to the other side. Sam isn't testifying, and hence there is no way for Landlord's attorney to cross-examine him as to his ability to recall and as to his possible motivation for lying.

Hearsay comes in many variations. Irving Younger, a professor of trial advocacy, would tell the following story:

> *From a distance, bystanders saw a man crawl out of a bedroom window. They were too far away to identify the man but watched as a dog began to chase him. Bystanders followed but were unable to keep the dog and man in vision at all times. A few minutes later they came upon the dog at the foot of a tree; in the tree was a man. Can the bystanders testify to this?*

The hearsay problem doesn't jump out at you but, in essence, it is really as if the dog is testifying, "The guy in the tree is the same guy I chased from the house."

Younger would conclude, "It would seem that the testimony would be admissible because there really is no need to cross-examine the dog. We all know dogs never lie."

Younger would pause. "*But*, they have a great sense of humor!"

Like most legal rules, there are scores of exceptions to the hearsay rule; exceptions which will become the bane of your Evidence course. The two most common exceptions are *party admissions* and *prior inconsistent statements*.

Anything a party to a lawsuit said is admissible *against* that party. (A party is either the plaintiff or the defendant.)

"Now, you are a friend of Ms. K. Did she tell you what she was doing before she tripped on the stairs?"

"Yes. She said she was drinking beer and listening to Willie Nelson songs."

"How much beer?"

"She couldn't remember. But the song was Whiskey River."

This testimony is being introduced to prove the matter asserted, that Ms. K was drinking (a lot) before she fell. But because she's in the courtroom, she can take the stand and deny, or explain, her out-of-court statement.

A related rationale justifies the introduction of *prior inconsistent statements*. If a witness (any witness, not just a party) testifies one way at trial, the opposing lawyer can always bring up that witness's prior inconsistent out-of-court statement. This is why lawyers are fond of deposing opposing witnesses: if they change their story at trial, they can be *impeached* with their prior sworn deposition. This was illustrated in the last chapter.

In addition to the hearsay rule, the prohibition against *leading* witnesses on direct also helps ensure that the jury hears only what the witness has to say. When the lawyer calls his witnesses, he takes the witness on *direct* examination. Generally a lawyer cannot *lead* his own witness; that is, he cannot suggest the answer to him, as does the following:

"Mr. Plaintiff, isn't it a fact that you received severe back injuries in the accident?"

Only a dumb (or honest) witness would answer, "No."

On direct, you must ask *non-leading* questions (those that do not suggest an answer):

"Mr. Plaintiff, please describe the injuries you received as a result of the accident."

Leading questions are prohibited on direct because we want the witness to testify, not the lawyer. Leading on direct is permissible as to non-contested matters (where the witness lives) or in the case where the witness is having a hard time remembering.

After each witness, the opposing lawyer has the opportunity to *cross-examine*.

"Mr. Plaintiff, you testified on direct that you injured your back in the accident. Now, isn't it a fact that you had injured your back several weeks prior to the accident?"

On cross-examination the lawyer can, and usually does, ask leading questions. They are a great way to control the witness and force answers on unpleasant matters.

My beloved colleague, Paul Bergman, points to the irony. Inexperienced lawyers tend to ask leading questions on direct (because they know the answers) and non-leading questions on cross (because they don't).

Let's examine one piece of lawyer lore: *"Never ask a question on cross you don't know the answer to."* Rather than reasoned discourse, we get war stories:

The defendant was charged with biting off the victim's nose. An eyewitness, called by the prosecution, had testified on direct that indeed the defendant had done this heinous deed. On cross, the defendant's lawyer established that this witness was not looking in the direction of the defendant and his victim until after he heard a scream, thus throwing grave doubt on the testimony that he saw the crime. Then came the dreaded question: "If you weren't looking at the time, how can you know the defendant bit off the victim's nose?"

"Because I saw him spit it out."

Great story. Troubling story. It suggests that lawyers should use their craft to hide the truth and supports that debatable proposition, not with argument, but with audience laughter. Further, the story assumes that the prosecuting lawyer is *incompetent*. There is always *redirect*.

"Now, on cross-examination, it was shown that you didn't see the fight. So how can you testify that the defendant bit off the victim's nose?"

Cross-examination is needed, not to hide the truth, but to expose the truth. We humans take sides and, once we do, fudge our testimony: to recall a better look than we had. Wellman, in his classic book *The Art of Cross-Examination*, gives a striking example. Writing at a time when folks traveled by ship, he tells us that when two ships collide, "almost invariably all the crew on one ship will testify in unison against the opposing crew; and, what is more significant, such passengers as happen to be on either ship will almost invariably be found corroborating the stories of their respective crews."

Go Bears!

Cross-examination has been touted as the best known device for ferreting out truth (from weaseling witnesses). It usually doesn't work as well as it does on TV, but it can be quite powerful. Volunteer to play the role of a witness at a trial practice court. Feel the rush of combativeness and fear when the judge says, "You may cross-examine." It's only you and the lawyer, and you must answer the questions. Gone are your jokes, your charm, your easy evasions.

"I didn't ask you that. Please answer my question."

Another limitation on witness testimony is that, unless the witness is called as an expert, the witness cannot testify as to her *opinions* or *conclusions*. This is best illustrated by the cartoon showing a rather smug dog on the stand, and the frustrated lawyer shouting, "We're not interested in what you *think*. We are only interested in what you *smelled*."

Rebuttal

Once the defense finishes its case, it rests. Certain things may come out during that case that plaintiff feels he can prove wrong. Rebuttal is his opportunity. Suppose defendant calls a witness who testifies he saw the accident. Plaintiff, during rebuttal, can call a witness who will put the defendant's witness, at the time of the accident, in Nova Scotia. Then there is rebuttal of rebuttal, and, as they say, we didn't start the fire.

Closing Argument

Once the evidence is in, and after (or in some jurisdictions, before) the judge instructs the jurors as to the law and their role as fact-finders, lawyers make closing arguments. Here they "marshal" the evidence, wax poetic, and strut. We'll see this in the next chapter.

One criminal defense lawyer of the Civil War era used to call, as his only witnesses, his own small children.

"What would happen if Daddy were to die?"

They would mourn, cry, and ultimately have to be helped off the stand.

The lawyer's closing was short, focused, and effective.

"Ladies and Gentlemen of the Jury. If you convict my client, I am going to kill myself."

This is no longer considered good form.

Who argues first? The party with the overall burden of proof (the plaintiff in a civil action, the prosecution in a criminal action). Then it is the defense's turn. Finally, the opening party gets to rebut the defendant's argument. In theory, this can only be for rebuttal, and a lawyer should not bring up new matter; to do so would be unfair because her opponent would not have the opportunity to respond.

The two most common mistakes lawyers make in closing arguments is putting *their own credibility in issue* and *arguing evidence that is not in the record.* You put your credibility in issue by arguing, *"I know my client is telling the truth."* It is fine to argue, *"The evidence shows my client is telling the truth."* Subtle but important distinction.

Good lawyers will make a list of the evidence they want to argue and, as the trial goes on, check off items that have been covered. If they forget to introduce the evidence, they can't argue it, even if it is true, even if it is not contested.

Finally what about the tree falling in the forest?

It's a question of *habit* evidence. Can you introduce evidence that someone has a "habit" of doing a particular thing as evidence that he probably did it at a particular time? In some jurisdictions you can; in others, you can't. Thus, as trees habitually make a noise when they fall, if they fall in a jurisdiction that admits habit evidence, they will make a noise even if no one is there to hear.

Come to think of it, it may be that falling trees habitually make noise *only* when there is someone there to hear. When profs can't figure things out, they turn them into exam questions:

A tree, standing in a jurisdiction that admits habit evidence, falls into one that does not. It is in that jurisdiction the person who wasn't there would have been.

Discuss.

CHAPTER 29

K v. LANDLORD, **GREATEST HITS**

Here we take a closer look at trial dynamics. Years away from your first trial, now is *not* the time to take notes. Just sit back and observe what a trial looks like. It ain't *Law and Order* but it's funnier (a rather low bar) *and* you will learn the secret identity of Ms. K.

Ms. K tripped. She claims that Larry Landlord failed in his duty to provide a safe place to live by failing to repair a defective step. Ms. K is represented by Ms. C. Darrow and Larry by Mr. Quibble Weaver. In the last chapters, we went through their pretrial haggling.

Plaintiff has the *burden of proof* and goes first. Darrow plans to call Ms. K to testify as to her fall and injuries. She plans to call Dr. Dread to establish the extent of those injuries and also a carpenter, with the unlikely name of Woody Nails. He inspected the stairs shortly after the accident and concluded that they had been in a dangerous condition for at least two months. To establish Larry Landlord's negligence, she will call Joe Ham, a tenant of the apartment house, who will testify:

324

"A couple of weeks before the accident, I told Larry that the steps were dangerous and needed repairs before someone got hurt."

Quibble Weaver, for the defense, will call Larry Landlord who will testify he had no idea the stairs were in bad repair. To rebut the seriousness of Ms. K's injuries, Quibble will call Dr. Polly Anna, a doctor who usually testifies for insurance companies. Pursuant to a discovery order, Dr. Anna, hired by Quibble, gave Ms. K a complete physical. She thinks Ms. K is a malingerer. Even worse!

Waiting in the wings, for the defense, is Billy Knowles. When Quibble deposed plaintiff's witness Joe Ham, he learned just how devastating his testimony would be. He decided he needed an *impeachment witness* and his investigator found Billy Knowles. Billy will testify that Ham hates Larry Landlord because he has called the police on his parties. Ham told Billy, "I'll get even with that jerk!" When Quibble gets to cross-examine Joe, he will ask about this. If Ham denies them, then Quibble, with great fanfare, will call Billy Knowles as a *rebuttal witness*.

Darrow can call her witnesses in any order she pleases. Trial lawyers advise to open and close with strong witnesses, putting the weaker ones in the middle. People tend to remember the first and last thing they hear. Darrow decides to put Dr. Dread on first and to put on Ms. K last. She wants to begin and end with a powerful presentation of her client's suffering. The weak part of her case, that of

Larry's negligence, she plans to sandwich in between high points.

One reason she puts Ms. K last, rather than first, is that this will allow Ms. K to hear of the evidence before she testifies. It's bad to have your client testify and then be contradicted by her own witnesses who testify afterwards. Witnesses, *except* for parties, are prohibited from listening to other witnesses testify before they testify.

Darrow knows she can develop the *testimony* in any order she selects. Chronological order is often the easiest to follow but, frankly, lacks flair. Take the testimony of Ms. K. The chronology of it is:

1. She trips.
2. She goes to the hospital.
3. She misses some work and loses some wages.
4. The mail arrives, with the doctor bills.

To have Ms. K testify in this order would put even me to sleep, and I'm doing this for love. Darrow first sits down and lists what points she wants to make.

First, she plans to use Ms. K to prove up medical bills and loss of earnings. These matters are not controversial and lack emotional impact; they go in the middle of the testimony. Second, Darrow wants Ms. K to testify as to the terror of the fall. She also wants to establish that Ms. K was careful at the time. Even if the defendant doesn't raise the issue, Darrow is concerned that during deliberations, a juror might remark, ''If she had been looking where

she was going, this never would have happened."
Darrow wants to shut this down. Third, Darrow
wants to have Ms. K testify as to the pain and
suffering she has experienced and continues to experience.

1. Description of the accident and the fact that
   Ms. K was being careful.

2. The amount of her medical bills and the
   extent of her loss of earnings.

3. The pain and suffering; the fear she would
   never walk again.

There is no magical order, but a good trial lawyer
should be able to answer the question, "Why did
you present the testimony in the order you did?"

Of course, the first problem Darrow faces is getting Ms. K on the stand, making her comfortable,
and, if possible, bringing in some interesting tidbits
which will make her more human and compelling.
Most judges will allow such tidbits although they
are technically irrelevant. You wouldn't be allowed
to go on and on about things: "OK, those are all the
good and kind things you did in the third grade;
now, turning your attention to the fourth...." It
would be nice if Ms. K coached Little League or
chaired the United Way Campaign at her job. Alas,
you play the hand you get.

Q: State your name and address for the record.

A: Ms. K, 1601 E. Kleindale.

Q: Are you nervous?

A: *Yes. After what the judiciary did to my broth-er, you'd be nervous, too. He woke up one morning and found himself turned into a giant roach.*

Q: *(by Quibble): Objection! Wrong novel!*

Court: *Sustained.*

A: *Oh yes, that was my other brother. We're a hard luck family. My brother K was accused of a heinous crime. No one ever told him what the crime was. It really grated on him. He ended up, like, you know, killing himself.*

Q: *(by Quibble): Objection! Metaphor! Literary license!*

Court: *I've given you a lot of leeway, Darrow. Move on.*

Q: *(by C. Darrow). Now, Ms. K, you weren't at fault in this, were you?*

Q: *(by Q. Weaver). Objection. Leading. You can't lead on direct. You know better!*

Q: *(by C. Darrow). Of course I do. This is an instructional book, and the author keeps mak-ing me do things that are wrong. Then he can come in and be a big hero. Sometimes I wish I were real!*

Cut.

Q: *(by C. Darrow) The afternoon of the accident, had you been drinking?*

A: *No.*

Q: *Were you tired or sick?*

A: *No, I was feeling fine.*

Q: *Now, prior to the accident, did you know the step was loose?*

A: *No, I seldom use the back stairs. I hadn't used them before my fall for at least two months.*

Q: *Now, as you approached the top of the stairs, were you distracted in any way?*

A: *No, I was looking where I was going.*

Q: *Then why did you step on a step that was loose?*

A: *Well, I did look down and nothing seemed out of the ordinary. I had no idea that the step was going to give way like it did.*

Note how Darrow develops the facts. It is far more effective to develop a conclusion than it is to simply come to it:

Q: *Were you careful?*

A: *Yes.*

Details convince.

Q: *After the accident, did you have occasion to inspect the top step?*

A: *Yes.*

Q: *Is it your opinion that Larry Landlord was negligent?*

Q: *(by Q. Weaver) Objection! That question is clearly improper as it calls for an opinion of a lay witness. Darrow knows better than that.*

Court: Sustained.

Yes, Darrow does know better than that. She knows that the question is improper. She also knows that it is *unethical* to ask an improper question in order to sneak impermissible material before the jury. You can't ask, *"When did you stop beating your spouse?"* unless you have a good faith belief that the witness once did.

Enter, stage left, "the hero." I forced Darrow to ask the impermissible question to tell you about the *opinion evidence rule*. One statement of the rule is found in the Federal Rules of Evidence:

Opinion Testimony By Lay Witnesses

If the witness is not testifying as an expert, his testimony in the form of opinions or inferences is limited to those opinions or inferences which are (a) rationally based on the perception of the witness and (b) helpful to a clear understanding of his testimony or the determination of a fact in issue.

The rule forces witnesses to testify about the raw data of experience: what they saw, heard, smelled, tasted, and felt, not what they concluded from those experiences. Drawing conclusions is the job of the jury. A witness cannot testify, "Landlord was negligent." That opinion is neither "rationally based on perception" (the witness didn't *see* the landlord being negligent) nor is it helpful to a "clear understanding of his testimony." A witness can testify:

I stepped on the stair and <u>felt</u> *it give. I* <u>looked</u> *at the stair and found a crack about 6 inches long*

and a quarter of an inch wide. I told Landlord
about it and <u>heard</u> *him say, "That sounds dan-*
gerous. I will fix it immediately." A week later I
<u>looked</u> *at the stair and* <u>saw</u> *nothing had been*
done.

From the facts witnesses testify to, the jury concludes whether the landlord was negligent.

Some witnesses can testify as to their opinions:
experts. For example, the Federal Rules provide:

Testimony by Experts

If scientific, technical, or other specialized knowl-
edge will assist the trier of fact to understand the
evidence or to determine a fact in issue, a witness
qualified as an expert by knowledge, skill, experi-
ence, training, or education may testify thereto in
the form of an opinion or otherwise.

Darrow plans to call two experts. Dr. Dread, based
on his training in medical school and his experiences as a physician, will testify as to the extent of
Ms. K's injuries and prognosis. Woody Nails, carpenter, will be the other expert. He will testify
about the condition of the stairs. Let's pick up the
trial with him.

Court: Call your next witness.

Darrow: Plaintiff calls Woody Nails.

Witness is sworn.

Q: (by C. Darrow) State your name and address
for the record.

A: Woody Nails.

Q: And you live at 5010 Randlett Drive? (A leading question, but it is okay as it goes to preliminary matters.)

A: Yes, that's right.

Q: What is your occupation?

A: Carpenter. I have been a carpenter for thirty years.

Q: Have you ever built staircases?

A: More than I can count.

Q: Do you ever have occasion to inspect staircases for safety?

A: Quite often. Several insurance agents ask me to inspect buildings before they insure them. I pay particular attention to stairways, because, if they're not built proper, folks can get hurt real bad.

Q: What happens if you find a staircase that is dangerous?

Q: (by Q. Weaver) I object, Your Honor. This line of questioning isn't relevant to the issues of this case. What happens when this witness inspects other staircases is beside the point.

Q: (by C. Darrow) Your Honor, this line of questioning is relevant to show this man's expertise. That insurance agents rely on him is evidence that he knows what he is talking about.

Court: Objection overruled.

Q: *Again, what happens when you find a stair-case that you think is unsafe?*

A: *I'll tell the owner or the agent. They have me repair it.*

Q: *Do they ever go ahead and insure the building without insisting on having the stairs repaired?*

A: *Not that I know of. It would be real dumb.*

Q: *Did you have occasion to inspect the back staircase at the Owl Apartments?*

A: *Yes. I went over there about two days after Ms. K fell.*

Q: *What was the result of your inspection?*

A: *The top stair was unsafe. It was loose and gave when you stepped on it. The problem was that it had a big crack in it, about 6 inches long and a quarter of an inch wide.*

Q: *Could you determine how long the crack had been there?*

Q: *(by Quibble Weaver) Objection, Your Honor. There is nothing about this witness that would make him an expert in this matter. I let his testimony about "unsafe" pass but not this. Without some showing that this witness has some expertise in knowing how long conditions have existed, I object to the testimony.*

Court: I'm going to allow the question. I think carpenters can make these decisions. You can cross-examine Mr. Nails about how he came to his conclusion. How much weight to give his testimony will be up to the jury, but I will admit it.

Note here the very important distinction between *admissibility* of evidence and its *weight*. The judge decides whether to *admit* the evidence; once it is admitted, the jury decides whether or not to *believe* it. The fact that Nails' conclusion will be admitted into evidence does not mean the jury will believe it. Weaver will still argue that carpenters really can't make that determination; this time he will argue to the jury rather than to the judge. On the other hand, if the judge refused to admit the testimony, the jury would never hear Nails' conclusion.

To exclude evidence on the basis that it is untrustworthy strikes me as problematic. For example, if Woody Nails really doesn't have the expertise to offer an opinion, why shouldn't the jury be allowed to hear his opinion and then, after cross-examination, reject it? A lot of rules of law you will study seem to come from a deep suspicion that jurors are, not to put too fine a point on it, dunces.

But I digress. Here the judge let the evidence in.

Q: *(Darrow, continuing) How long would you say the stair had been in that condition?*

A: *Well, from the dirt and grime embedded in the crack, I'd say a fairly long time.*

Q: *Could you be more specific?*

A: *At least a couple of months.*

Q: *Thank you, no further questions. You may cross-examine.*

Cross–Examination.

Q: *(by Q. Weaver) Now, isn't it a fact that life's a stage and we're but actors?*

A: *(nervously) Well ... er ... I guess you can say that.*

Q: *And isn't it true that your testimony has been sound and fury, signifying nothing?*

A: *(looking desperately at C. Darrow) I ... I ... just don't know.*

Q: *Well, you know this, **Mister** Woody Nails. That isn't even your real name, is it!? And not even a very clever one, at that!?*

Note that leading questions are *not* questions. They are statements of fact disguised as questions. Note, too, that when you ask a question, your voice goes up at the end and this encourages an answer. When you make a statement of fact, your voice stays flat and does not invite long responses but, at most, an agreeing grunt. Try it! Cross-examining a witness, you don't want answers, you want agreeing grunts.

A: *(beginning to sob) I ... I don't have a real name.*

Q: *Of course you don't. That's because you don't exist. You are not Prince Hamlet, nor were you meant to be. You're a bit player in an instructional manual. Your Honor, I move to strike his entire testimony! Your Honor? Where's the judge? What's happening in here?*

The rest is silence. Exeunt.

To illustrate something of *cross-examination*, let's take the testimony of Joe Ham who, on *direct*, stated that two weeks before the accident he told Larry Landlord of the bad condition of the stair. Larry claims that the conversation never happened. As this is not something Ham could merely be mistaken about (like an eyewitness identification), it must be that Ham is lying (or Larry is). The purpose of cross-examination in such cases is to suggest possible motives for perjury. Note, however, that Weaver realizes that even hostile witnesses can be used to make needed points, here to throw doubt on the testimony of Woody Nails. Note, too, that the questions on cross are leading.

Cross-Examination of Joe Ham

Q: *(by Q. Weaver) It's true that you used those stairs on several occasions both before and after Ms. K's fall.* (Ed. note: the period, not a question mark, is correct. You want an agreeing grunt.)

A: (Grunting) *Yes.*

Q: *And you never noticed the defective condition before the time you reported it to Larry Landlord.*

A: *That's right.*

Q: *So, as far as you know, the condition was of fairly recent origin; isn't that right.*

A: *Well, I didn't notice it before.*

Q: So as far as you know, the stairway was not cracked before the time you reported it?

A: Yes.

Q: And that was two weeks before Ms. K's fall, and not a couple of months.

A: Yes.

Q: Thank you. Now you never fell on those stairs, did you?

A: No.

Q: And you never heard of anyone else tripping on those stairs, isn't that right.

Q: (by C. Darrow) Objection, Your Honor. The question is not relevant.

Q: (by Quibble) Your Honor, the lack of other accidents is relevant to the issue of whether the stairs were safe.

Court: Objection overruled. You may answer the question.

This ruling might be error. Maybe, under the law, the lack of other accidents cannot be used to show that the stairs were safe. If Ms. K loses, she can appeal and base her appeal on judicial error. But good luck if this is all she has. Appellate courts don't like to reverse cases and make the parties start all over again. Despite what you may have read in the local press, appellate judges are not vultures looking with sharp eyes for mere technicalities to reverse convictions and thus thwart justice. Appellate courts reverse only when the judge below really screws up. There is what is known as "the harmless error rule." (One particularly flamboyant trial court judge used to brag, "I've overruled the Supreme Court many more times than it has overruled me.")

    A: No, I never heard of anyone else falling.

    Q: Thank you. Now, you are a very good friend of Ms. K's, isn't that right.

    A: Yes.

    Q: And you want her to win this lawsuit, don't you?

    A: I think she should.

    Q: Please answer the question. Do you want her to win this lawsuit or don't you?

    A: I guess I do.

    Q: Do you guess or do you?

    A: I do.

Note how Weaver pursues the witness. Most witnesses will try to deflect the lawyer's questions; you must become something of a bulldog.

    Q: And isn't it a fact that you don't like Larry Landlord?

    A: Well, maybe not.

    Q: Maybe not? Isn't it a fact that he has called the police on your wild parties?

    A: Well. They weren't wild, but yes.

    Q: And didn't you tell Billy Knowles that you would get even with Landlord?

A: No, I didn't say that.

Bingo! Now, as part of his case, Quibble can call Billy Knowles to testify as to that conversation. It is admissible as a *prior inconsistent statement*.

During trial, lawyers make points to use in closing argument. Weaver's closing argument, as it relates to Joe, will run something like this:

Ladies and Gentlemen, there is one glaring contradiction in this case. You remember Joe Ham, the tenant who testified that he told Larry of the faulty condition of the stairs a good two weeks before the accident. Not only did he tell him, but he told you Larry said, "That sounds dangerous. I'll get it fixed immediately."

Now it's quite convenient Larry said that. Note how well it fits into the plaintiff's theory. It shows not only that Larry knew of the condition, but also, that Larry knew it was quite dangerous. What better evidence could you ask for?

Larry testified he never had that conversation with Joe. You must decide who to believe. Someone is lying to you. How can you decide who is telling the truth? His Honor will instruct you that you can consider the "character and quality of the testimony" and the existence of any bias or interest.

Does Joe's testimony make sense? To believe that that conversation actually took place, you must believe that Larry knew that there was a very dangerous condition on the stairway but simply failed to do anything about it. Joe would have you believe that Larry was content to wait until someone tripped and fell, to wait until someone sued. Joe's story doesn't make sense. Further, Joe continued to use the stairs. Does it make sense to go on using a staircase after you have reported its dangerous condition to the landlord?

Joe's story just doesn't hold together. Had he told Larry of the condition, it is reasonable to assume Larry would have acted, not only to prevent someone's injury but also to avoid a lawsuit. Does Joe have a motive to make up his testimony? A motive to lie to you? You bet. He is a good friend of the plaintiff. He admitted that he wants her to win this case and obviously he knows his testimony is essential for her victory. And he dislikes Larry. He threatened to get even with Larry. Sure, he denies that, but Billy Knowles, who has no interest in this case, came in here, raised his right hand, and swore that he did.

No, Joe is not to be believed. He was simply lying about his conversation with Larry. Larry told you it never happened because it never did.

Closing Argument: Weaving Law and Fact

Effective closing argument relies on the primary lawyering skill, the ability to bring law and fact together. The witnesses and the documents and the exhibits have put before the jury bits of information: that Joe was threatened with eviction, that the carpenter believes that the stairs had been in a state of bad repair for a long time, that Ms. K fell.

At closing, the lawyer *marshals these bits of information into factual conclusions that have legal relevance*. To illustrate this, let's pick up part of Darrow's closing argument.

Closing Argument: C. Darrow

From the fact that Joe told Larry of the condition of the stairs and from the fact that they had been in disrepair for a long time, we can conclude that Larry knew or should have known that the stair was dangerous.

Next Darrow shows the jury what these factual conclusions mean in terms of law.

That Larry Landlord knew of the dangerous condition and yet did nothing about it means that he was not acting as would an ordinarily careful person under the circumstances. An ordinarily careful person would have done something to prevent the accident. As the judge will instruct, if you find that Larry did not do as would an ordinarily careful person, you are to find him negligent.

This mode of analysis is quite familiar. You have been doing it, if not since your cradle, at least since your first law exam, where you turned the bits of information into factual conclusions which you then turned into legal conclusions.

Closing arguments are, however, more, much more, than logic. They are emotion and power. In the hands of a good criminal defense lawyer, "reasonable doubt" becomes the finest and most delicate flower of Western Civilization, a flower about to be ground under the shiny black boot of the State. Listening to a good personal injury lawyer, you experience the victim's anguish as he lies sleepless in a hospital bed thinking of what might have been.

When it comes your time to make a closing argument, there are few experiences so intense and immediate. When you start, there will be distractions. You will be nervous, you will be aware of the spectators, of the judge, and of your trembling hands.

Soon, however, you soar. Forgotten are your notes and gone is the judge; for awhile it is just you, your argument, and the jurors.

Just once makes three years of law school worthwhile.

Most law schools offer Trial Advocacy courses. I urge you to take one. As one of my students told me, "Now I know I don't want to be a trial lawyer." There are several excellent books on trial advocacy. One of my favorites, by the way, is Hegland, *Trial and Clinical Skills in a Nutshell.* (Has this man no shame?)

Finally, of course, the jury is instructed, goes out and, eventually, returns.

"Ladies and Gentlemen of the Jury, have your reached a verdict?"

"Yes, Your Honor, we have."

Okay. It's not debuting at Carnegie Hall nor is it returning the opening kickoff at the SuperBowl. But, for most of us, damn near!

PART SIX

FINISHING SCHOOL AND BEGINNING A CAREER

There are accidental law students; those who, hearing and fearing the rush of oncoming reality, have scurried back for another three years of academic safety. As to what lawyers do, and as to what they want to do when they graduate, they don't have a clue. Then there are those who come to law school with specific career goals in mind. More than often, however, career goals will change in the rough and tumble of law school.

Read this part at your leisure but read it in your first year. Critical choices lie ahead. I will give you a lot to think about in terms of the kind of career you want to pursue. You have vastly more choices than you might think and there are variables that you might not appreciate. Choosing a career is much more than choosing a job; in some ways, you will be choosing the kind of person you will become.

Of course, before you get to your career, you have to finish law school. The first chapter in this part is about the courses and activities in your second and third years. My main point is that law school offers rich opportunities that will not pass your way again: a talented faculty, interested and interesting classmates, and issues that matter. My advice is somewhat biblical: time to put away childish things. For a long time you studied hard to advance yourself, to get into a good college, to get into a good law school. From now on, it is no longer about you; it's about your clients.

CHAPTER 30

THE SECOND AND
THIRD YEARS

So, what's next?

I'll talk about course selection and extra-curricular activities, such as law review, clerking, and *pro bono* work. Along the way I'll tell you something of the history of American Legal Education. I'll close with some of the distortions legal education can cause.

My main point: *continue to push yourself.* I'll tell a story that, well, frankly, makes me look pretty good. But that's okay; I'll close the chapter with one that makes me look rather foolish.

On Theoretical Legal Education

It was the 1960s in the small town of Americus, Georgia. Congress had recently passed the Voting Rights Act, and it was to have an immediate impact. Americus was holding an election for Justice of the Peace and, for the first time since Reconstruction, black citizens were going to vote. In fact, a black woman had decided to run for the office herself.

On the momentous day, when she arrived at the voting place, there were two lines, one marked "Colored." She stood in the "White" line. The deputy sheriff who arrested her was later incredulous at being asked why he had done so. He testified, "I ain't completely color blind, you know." I'll never forget that; sitting in the courtroom, I remembered reading in a Supreme Court case, "Our Constitution is color blind."

Between my second and third year, I worked as an intern for C.B. King of Albany, Georgia, who was then one of the two black lawyers in the state. C.B. wanted me to research the law to see if we could get a court to throw out the election and make them do it over; make them do it right. I looked up the cases on election irregularities (mostly from Chicago).

"C.B., we've had it. You can't challenge the election. The law is clear. Unless the illegalities affected the result, it stands. Given the fact that the incumbent got 83 of the 95 votes, we can't allege that."

C.B. simply sat and stared. Didn't say a word.

I went back to my desk and went into a funk. Why had I gone to law school? A monkey could have looked up those cases and reported the bad news to C.B. Why had I sat in class for two years, struggling, if I couldn't even try to use the law to do the right thing?

I went back to the cases. Maybe they could be distinguished. Indeed, maybe I could find language in those cases suggesting that, if the controversy wasn't simply about dead people voting, the rule might be different.

I sat and thought and read and reread. And yes, eventually I was able to distinguish those cases and, yes, I even found *language*.

I went back to C.B. This time he smiled.

A year later, under federal court order, the small town of Americus had another election. The same guy won, but this time: one line.

––––––––––

Sitting where you are sitting, I thought I was learning the law. I was often confused and resentful. But I now know I wasn't sitting there to learn the law; I was there to get ready for that hot summer in Georgia.

Push yourself. Take hard courses. Enjoy the challenge. Don't run away from tough professors, and don't tune out those "nice" theoretical discussions. They won't be easy, and you won't understand them all. Stay awake. Down the road you'll have your own hot summers.

Course Selection

So many courses; so little time.

After a rigid first-year curriculum, most law schools throw up their hands and leave the second and third years up to you. You will have a dazzling menu. First, realize that your legal education does not end with law school. After graduation, there will be Continuing Legal Education (CLE) courses and scads and scads of on-the-job training. Ask yourself: *"What can I get in law school that I can't in practice?"* I think it comes down to great professors, challenging courses, and meaningful clinical work.

Professors

Every school has a group of truly remarkable teachers. Make them your first choice, not only for their knowledge but also for their style. Some stick closely to the "black letter," while others spin off into the realms of philosophy, economics, and social theory. With some, classes are like boot camp, and, with others, encounter groups. Sitting there, you are learning more than "Federal Jurisdiction" or "UCC." You are learning how one lawyer approaches and solves problems, uses and communicates knowledge, treats and reacts to people. You'll need models.

Take professors you *disagree* with, the fascists or bleeding hearts on your faculty. You know who they are. If you take only professors you agree with, you won't be prepared for the ill winds that will surely blow.

Courses

Don't forfeit the riches of law school by focusing on "bar" courses or those you "know" you will need in practice. There are *bar review courses* after graduation that cover the required subjects and it is foolish to over-specialize during law school. Career interests can and often do change.

There are substantive courses that every "well-rounded" law student should take, if for no other reason than to hold your own at cocktail parties (if there are such things anymore). Friends read the newspaper and will ask basic questions dealing with *Evidence, Corporations, Federal Tax,* and *Constitutional Law.*

Writing courses are important. The more you write, the better you will write. Take at least one course requiring *extensive research and writing,* even if (particularly if) you dread it. *Seminars and problem courses* are a refreshing break from the traditional three-cases-and-you're-out courses. They also give you a real sense of lawyering: lawyers don't *learn* the law, they *use* the law. *Skills courses,* such as trial advocacy, client interviewing, and negotiation are helpful. Trial advocacy is almost a must. Trying a lawsuit gives you a different and more profound understanding of law, an understanding particularly important if you have vowed never to enter a courtroom as a lawyer.

Clinics

Many states have "student practice rules" that allow students to represent clients in court under the supervision of a practicing lawyer. Most law schools have clinical programs. There is no better opportunity to learn ethics and problem-solving than in the clinical setting.

If you take a clinic, consider the role of an anthropologist living with the natives. During the day, do your job, work the pots. At night, sneak off to your tent and get out your pencil:

Are lawyers happy? Are they bitterly adverse or is law practice something of a country club affair? Why are some witnesses more credible than others? Some legal arguments more compelling? What are the most important skills for a lawyer to have?

In practice, you won't have time to *study* practice.

In addition to class work, there are a host of activities in the second and third years. If your law school is part of a university, there will be a variety of cultural events to remind you that the question of life's meaning is as important as who gets the decedent's stuff.

Some will write for the law review, others will earn money clerking for law firms, and still others will do *pro bono* work, perhaps helping out at legal aid, teaching law-related courses in high schools, or delivering Meals-on-Wheels to the elderly.

The Curious Institution of Law Review

It is an honor to be asked to write for law review. Membership is based on good grades or on a writing competition. It is hard, but worthwhile. As a second-year student, you will write on a recent case or on recent legal trends. You will be involved in the law's development. Lawyers and judges read student notes, and your work may influence actual decisions. Your work will be extensively edited (by a student editor), and you will come away with a feeling of how hard it is (and how satisfying) to produce good work. And, of course, having written for the review helps come interview time.

Law reviews, however, present a mind-boggling affront. Law students write articles criticizing (or praising) judges. Do second-year medical students crowd around operation tables and then fault the procedures of heart-transplant teams? Do budding young scientists trash Einstein? That beginners can play on the same field as veterans is one of the curious facts about the law. Whether this is a good or bad thing I'll leave to you. It does, however, tend to put the lie to Holmes' famous dictum:

The life of the law is not logic; it is experience.

Law reviews do play an important institutional role. Confronted with the argument that judges can do whatever they like, some have answered that they must justify their decisions in writing and this keeps them intellectually honest. Law reviews are the only institution that routinely critiques the work of courts.

There is another institutional role that law reviews play that is more problematic. We all know (alas, some of us better than others) that in the academic world, it's publish or perish. While most academics (English profs) publish in journals refereed by experts in their field (other English profs), law professors publish mostly in law reviews. Student editors decide what gets published. Are these editors qualified to pass on the quality and importance of legal scholarship (and hence decide, at least

in some measure, who gets tenure and who
doesn't)? Absolutely! They did well in Contracts!

The style of law reviews deserves comment. In
1936, Yale Law Professor Fred Rodell wrote a de-
lightful essay, *"Goodbye to Law Reviews."*

> *There are two things wrong with almost all legal
> writing. One is style. The other is content. It seems
> to be a cardinal principle of law review writing
> and editing that nothing may be said forcefully
> and nothing may be said amusingly. . . . Even in
> the comparatively rare instances when people read
> to be informed, they like a dash of pepper or a
> dash of salt along with their information. They
> won't get any seasoning if the law reviews can
> help it. The law reviews would rather be dignified
> and ignored.*

If you ever get to be a law review editor, first, my
congratulations. Second, lighten up. Otherwise, I'll
never get published. (One of my early mentors once
advised me, "Never change your style, even if it
means getting published.")

But I digress.

Don't make too much about law review. If you
don't make it, realize that *most* famous lawyers
didn't. Once you get out, you will find that lawyers
will judge you by your ethics and hard work, not by
whether you made law review (or where you went
to law school, for that matter).

That said, it is always good to hone your writing
skills. You will find a plethora of opportunities;

there are many legal writing "contests"—dealing with such topics as environmental law, elder law, family law, and criminal law.

Pro Bono Activities

Every lawyer, regardless of professional prominence or workload, has a responsibility to provide legal services to those unable to pay, and personal involvement in the problems of the disadvantaged can be one of the most rewarding experiences in the life of a lawyer.

— American Bar Association, Model Rules of Professional Conduct

The American Bar Association urges, but does not require, lawyers to devote *fifty hours* per year to providing free legal services to the disadvantaged. Should it be mandatory? Why lawyers and not, say, plumbers?

Lawyers have a monopoly and the notion is that those with monopoly power have special public service obligations. This is not to say that *pro bono* activities should be mandatory. Indeed, most lawyers probably devote more that fifty hours a year to such activities. Making those activities mandatory tends to diminish their value.

Consider *pro bono* activities. They are a terrific way to experience your own uniqueness, recognize your own competence, and give something back to a community that has given you so much.

Often volunteer work is legal work, at Legal Aid, women's shelters, AIDS clinics, or public interest firms. But a lot of law students volunteer in non-legal capacities. In Washington D.C., law students help prisoners learn to read by tutoring them as they read storybooks to their children. Elsewhere, law students tutor elementary students as part of "Lawyers for Literacy" programs. Still others deliver "Meals-on-Wheels" to the elderly.

Most law schools have *pro bono* programs. If yours doesn't, don't curse the darkness. Light a candle. *www.probono.net; www.pslawnet.org; www. aals.org.*

One of my favorite *pro bono* activities is teaching in local high schools. Lawyers spend a lot of time addressing groups and a lot of time explaining the law to non-lawyers. High school teaching programs allow you to do both. We have had a program here for years and years, and almost every student who has taken part has said that it was one of his or her best law school experiences. The experience can be rewarding and moving.

Two students once presented the program in a custodial institution for juvenile delinquents. At first the law students were greeted with,"Pigs!" They stayed with it. Ten weeks later, I got letters from the "inmates": "I always thought all the police and lawyers were pigs, out to get me. Now I know that some might actually understand me and help me."

One sociologist studied attitudes toward the law. He found that a major predictor of whether people respected the law and its various institutions was whether their first contacts with the law were positive or negative. Growing up next door to a loud and drunken lawyer tends to poison one's attitude toward the Supreme Court. Teaching in high schools, particularly inner city high schools, you may be the first "lawyer" your students will ever meet. In a very real sense, you become a "drum major" for law.

One great aspect of these programs is that you get to discuss law with people other than law students, law teachers, and bored and resentful companions at cocktail parties.

If you want information on starting such a program, contact "Street Law" at (www.streetlaw.org). It can provide you with materials and information on how to set up a program.

But what if you need money?

Clerking

Many students clerk during school. Generally this involves legal research. Some professors advise against clerking, as it will surely compete with class work. I think it's fine. Many students need the money, and a good clerkship, just like a good clinical experience, can be quite educational.

If you are going to clerk, consider negotiating a meaningful clerking experience. Most lawyers like spunk. Ideally you get feedback, and tasks that are varied: not *always* memos, sometimes interviewing witnesses and observing trials and depositions.

So what else is there to say about clerking? Not much, except to say that the debate about its propriety reflects a very important division in thinking about legal education: is it better to learn law from *books* or from *working*? This debate continues today over the role of clinical legal education. The remainder of this section puts that debate in its historical context.

A Short History of Legal Education

In the old days, there was *only* clerking. There were no law schools, no LSAT, no teacher's dirty looks. See, generally, Milton, *Paradise Lost*.

After working several years as an apprentice, the novice took the bar and that was that. When law schools started, they *supplemented* apprenticeship. Apprentices worked in law offices in the daytime and gathered at night to hear lectures on law. Slowly law schools took over more turf. Eventually they became *alternatives* to apprenticeship, and novices became eligible to take the bar by *either* route.

The key year in legal education is 1870. Christopher Columbus Langdell became dean of the Harvard Law School. Langdell faced a real problem: how to make law school academically respectable. A lot of traditional academics (English professors) thought that law school did not belong in a university. It was a trade school devoted to *practical* knowledge (*yuck!*). It merely prepared people to make a living (*double yuck!*). The economist Thorston Veblen once remarked something to the effect,

"Law schools belong in the university no more than schools of dance."

That hurt.

How to make law academically respectable? Lawyers may be crude, but they're bright. Call law a science and you're in! Langdell wrote:

[L]aw is a science [and] all the available materials of that science are contained in books.... [T]he library is the proper workshop of professors and students alike; it is to us all that the laboratories of the university are to the chemists and physicists, all that the museum of natural history is to the geologists, all that the botanical garden is to the botanists.

The Harvard model became the rage. Casebooks replaced lectures (Langdell wrote the very first one). Why is your law school *three* years? The correct answer is "c"—because Christopher Columbus Langdell set his up that way.

With law schools safely established in universities and recognized as an alternative to apprenticeship, two more steps had to be taken to establish today's law school. The first was to kill off the competition: apprenticeship. After years of struggle, in a vast majority of states, law school, not apprenticeship, became the *only* way to become a lawyer. The second step was to raise law school admission standards. At first, some college was required, then college graduation, and now, as you are painfully aware, very good grades and a high LSAT score.

Consider the result. Without good academic credentials, you can't attend law school; without graduating from law school, you can't take the bar. The circle closes.

Law professors, in their assault on apprenticeships, marched under the banner of the "public good" (as do all budding monopolists). Learning law by reading cases, they argued, make for better lawyers than learning law by working with lawyers. Well, perhaps.

In any event, the "practical training" of law students was routed. Law school became almost entirely academic. Very few professors even practiced law. They were hired because they had excelled in law schools (usually Harvard) and then clerked for an appellate court for a year or two.

Beginning in the 1970s, the "practical wing" of legal education counter attacked, marching under the banner of "clinical education." Clinicians today have a solid place in the hollowed halls: clinical education is an accepted part of modern legal education, although just how big a part remains open to dispute.

The Distortions of Legal Education

Admittedly I have been something of a drum major for legal education. Realize, however, that it can distort your view of people and rob you of your common sense.

I gave my contracts students a hypothetical. *Seller* is continually late in making his deliveries. *Buy-*

er, after pleas and much patience, finally cancels the contract. After stating the problem, I asked:

"If you were *Seller*, what would you say?"

I was looking for a discussion of the various legal theories that throw *Buyer* into breach for canceling the contract, legal arguments that would allow *Seller* to *crush Buyer*.

I looked around the room. As is so often the case with first-year students, they were all inspecting their shoes. There was, however, one eager face: that of the eight-year-old son of one of my students. He had been biding his time, drawing pictures. Suddenly he raised his hand. Such behavior, even from an eight-year old, must be rewarded.

"Okay," I said, "What would you say if you were *Seller*?"

"I'd say I'm sorry."

———

Professor William Simon cautions that legal education presents a caricature of human existence. Plaintiffs always want *more* money and prosecutors always want *more* time; civil defendants want to escape all liability, and criminal defendants simply want to escape. In the hundreds and hundreds of cases you will read, there are very few heroes.

Holmes once wrote that law students should study the law from the perspective of the "bad man"—the class bully who has no regard for morality and is only interested in what he can get away with. No doubt this is a great learning strategy. *But don't confuse either the caricature or the bad man with life.*

One of my first clients came to me with a consumer problem. After some research, I triumphantly advised: "You don't have to pay any more on this bill! I have found several legal violations. We can get your money back, you can keep what you bought, and we can sue for punitive damages! We will *crush* the store!"

My client looked at me. "But I bought it and I owe the money. I just want you to help work out a payment schedule."

One of our chores is to help people say, "I'm sorry."

————————

Don't check your common sense at the door; life is more (or less) than clever legal argument.

My first job was with a state-wide program that provided free legal services for the poor. I worked in the Los Angeles office, where my first assignment was to find out whether a business license would be required if the program opened an office in Delano, California. Of course, my pricey and demanding legal education gave me no clue about how to even begin to answer that question. Fortunately, a friendly librarian in the county law library got a copy of the City Code of Delano and found the applicable section.

"Yes," he told me, "You'll need a license and it costs $20."

Did I simply report back? No! It was suddenly an exam question, a law review topic. After three or four days of intense research, I wrote, "Yes, a license is required and it costs $20. However, that City Ordinance is *unconstitutional* as a violation of *Free Speech*, *Equal Protection*, and *Due Process* because...." and I continued for about twenty pages. Pretty spiffy stuff.

Expecting high praise, and perhaps an early promotion, I gave it to my boss, Gary Bellow. "Do this again, Hegland, you're fired."

CHAPTER 31

CAREER CHOICES

I distrust plots for two reasons: first, because our lives are largely plotless, even when you add in all our reasonable precautions and careful planning; and second, because I believe plotting and the spontaneity of real creation aren't compatible.

Stephen King, *On Writing*

So you're gonna be a public defender? Do Intellectual Property work? Work on Wall Street? Start your own firm? Your own business? Things change, despite our careful planning. If you are too set on your goals, you will lack the spontaneity to create a wonderful career. Perhaps TV legal analysis would be best for you or perhaps, just perhaps, writing novels.

You'll hear disturbing rumors: "You won't get a job unless you are in the top 10% of your class." Not so. Let's turn to some little known facts:

Of 100 lawyers, about 50 were in the bottom half of their class.

About 90% of law school grads get jobs within their first year out.

Except during a job interview, the chances that anyone (clients, judges, lawyers, friends, plumb-

ers), will ask you how well you did in Contracts are about the same as winning PowerBall (which are the same whether you play it or not).

In practice, success is not measured by grade point; it is measured the old-fashioned way: hard work, honesty, and common sense.

55% of lawyers are in private practice, the vast majority in firms of five or less or on their own. Only 5% are in large firms. (By way of comparison, 8.3% of Hollywood actors play lawyers on TV.)

Only 5% of lawyers defend and prosecute criminals.

Many lawyers, about one-third within three years, change jobs; some leave law altogether: to govern nations, to make revolutions, or to broadcast the Dodgers.

Studies *suggest* an inverse relationship between money and job satisfaction.

Very few "hired guns" exist. Most lawyers are convinced they are doing "the Lord's work," be they personal injury lawyers or insurance defense lawyers, prosecutors or criminal defenders, business lawyers or public interest lawyers.

This chapter will not offer any tips on resume preparation (except don't come off too pompous, as in "Why your firm needs me") nor tips on interview technique (except to *really want* the job: enthusiasm sells). Rather, I will first discuss influences that can distort your quest; then discuss job attributes that you may want to consider; and, finally, offer some ideas as to what you can do in law school to test your alternatives. But first, you need a goal.

Once I asked a college basketball coach, "Are basketball coaches happy?"

"I don't know about all coaches," he told me. "All I know is that I wake up at 4 o'clock in the morning and realize, 'Great, I get to go to work today.'"

Frankly, I don't know a whole lot of lawyers (or law professors) that feel that way. But why not? Shoot for the National Championship.

Don't Panic

Getting a job is more than getting a job—more than resumes, dressing up, and handling difficult interview questions with aplomb.

Choosing a job is a <u>very</u> serious matter; you are choosing what kind of person you will become.

I went to school in Berkeley. One of my radical friends was hired by a commercial firm in Santa Barbara. They told him he would be a Republican in a year. I saw him about a year later.

"They couldn't have been more wrong. It took six months."

George Orwell had a marvelous insight. When we get a job, we want to conform and hence put on a professional mask. As time wears on, however, *our face grows to fit the mask.* After twenty years prosecuting criminals, what world view will you have? After a career of advising business, defending insurance companies, or teaching law, whom will you know? What books will you read? Who will you be?

Around "interview time," classmates will begin getting jobs. You will feel an incredible amount of pressure to land one. It doesn't help when friends and family ask, "Well?"

The danger is that you might take a job simply because "it's there."

Take an hour or so *now* to write about the kind of job you want. Rereading later might help you remain calm until the ideal job—the one that wakes you at four o'clock in the morning—comes along.

Of course, it is always possible to take one job for a while and then switch to something else. Many, probably most, lawyers do just that.

Distorting Influences

A brilliant law school career might not be all it's cracked up to be.

Many students (maybe you) come to law school for idealistic reasons: to work with business in improving the environment, to work with abused children, or to return to their community to help those less fortunate. Many of these end up with Blah, Blah, and Blah, fighting traffic in Gotham City.

Why?

Many change goals for good reasons: learning more about themselves and about their options, they realize that they will be happier doing something they hadn't previously considered. Some of my best friends work for Blah, Blah, and Blah and love it. More power to them.

However, some change goals because they get caught up in law school hype.

Tom Wolfe, in *The Right Stuff*, writes that America's astronauts were not motivated by money, fame, or challenge; they just wanted to win the competition; they just wanted to prove they were the "right stuff."

There is nothing wrong with this, as long as the "right stuff" is *your* stuff.

In law school, the "right stuff" is working with *ideas* rather than with *people*. This is the implicit lesson. Law school goodies are passed out on the basis of academic performance. Compassion, common sense, and, alas, humor can't be graded ... and hence don't count for much.

To prove that they are the "right stuff," the "best" students go to large firms. This career path rests on two assumptions; first, that all the "smart lawyers" end up in such firms and, second, that all the interesting legal work is done by them. Both assumptions are false. The two smartest lawyers I have known worked for poor people at Legal Aid. As to engaging legal work, when I was a trial lawyer, doing misdemeanors, I woke up at night to jot notes to myself. When I was an appellate lawyer, arguing cases of great moment, I slept soundly.

Law school hype is one danger to avoid; another is selling yourself too short. We fear success as well as failure. The psychologist Abraham Maslow calls it "fear of one's own greatness" and "running away from one's own best talents." He asks his students:

"Which of you in this class hopes to write the great American novel, or to be a Senator, or Governor, or President? Or a great composer? Or a Saint?"

His students giggle, blush, and squirm, until he asks, "If not you, who else?"

"Mind-forged manacles"—a phrase of William Blake. "I could *never* do trial work." "I could *never* make a living in Hicksville representing kids." "I could *never* be Senator." If not you, who else?

Career Choices

It is okay to be indecisive. At least, I think it is. After law school, you can take a job that lasts, by definition, only a year or two. This is a good option. You will have time to mull things over before making the big leap. These jobs are exciting "once in a lifetime" variety. They provide valuable training and effectively silence those who, with the biggest of smiles, ask, "Now that you are done with law school, what?"

A *judicial clerkship* is a good choice. Most appellate judges and many trial court judges hire recent graduates as clerks. You get to sit, do legal research, discuss legal matters, and maybe even get to write an opinion or two. Employers think a clerkship is a real plus.

Additionally, there are numerous *post-graduate clerkships and fellowships* offered by governmental agencies, public interest groups, and even some law schools.

Clerkships are highly competitive, and the race starts second year. See your Career Services office. Recommendations from professors help, so get to know them now.

Of course, you can *stay* in school. Some law schools offer advanced law degrees in such things as tax. Or you may wish to get another degree in a field that you plan to use in conjunction with law, such as business, finance, real estate, counseling, or ventriloquism. The hardest part of the "stay-in-school" option is: "You mean, like next year? I think, with your continuing emotional and financial support, I'll stay in school a tad longer."

Non-Legal Careers

Kafka went to law school. He hated it. In fact, it has recently come to light that the first line of his classic, *The Metamorphosis*, has been incorrectly translated. The inaccurate translation reads:

Gregor Samsa awoke one morning and found that he had turned into a gigantic cockroach.

The correct translation reads:

Gregor Samsa awoke one morning and found that he had turned into a rather rotund tax lawyer.

A surprising number of disgruntled lawyers become novelists (and, no doubt, disgruntled novelists swell our ranks). Others go into business, teaching, politics, and the media. A good friend of mine went into "development" (fundraising), using his legal knowledge of wills and tax law. Another wanted to get into producing movies. She went to Hollywood, rented an apartment and hung out at the studios. After several months, she got a law job, and now, after several years, is producing her own movies.

Routine want ads can help. "Would this job involve the use of legal skills?" Many jobs do (such as risk management and compliance work), but traditionally have been filled with non-lawyers.

Show up and surprise everyone.

Of course, it is *easier* to get a traditional law job. However, the rest of your life is worth a little effort, a little imagination, a little gumption.

Traditional Law Jobs

Your choices are vastly more than big firms versus small firms, prosecuting versus defending.

Public Interest Law, Legal Aid

Law reporting (print or TV)

Teaching (law school, college, community college)

Risk management; contract compliance

In-house legal counsel

Legislative counsel, lobbying

Government work

Law librarian (law schools and large firms)

Law publishing (writing ALR articles)

Law enforcement (FBI)

Military justice

Jungle, law of

Your Career Service office has tons and tons of information.http://Www.nalp.org. In weighing your alternatives, what factors should you consider?

Some Variables to Consider

Ideas versus people. Do you like ideas or people? Some practices involve mostly research and drafting. These jobs offer "nice" theoretical problems, the luxury of extended research and reflection, and the satisfaction that comes in drafting a well-written and thorough legal document. Large firms traditionally offer this kind of employment, but so, too, do many smaller "specialized" law firms, public interest firms, and "appellate departments" of the public defender and of the district attorney.

At the other end of the continuum are *people* practices. Great satisfaction can come in solving real-life problems: helping work out a sensible child custody arrangement, helping two friends set up a partnership, helping a client understand a bureaucratic maze. As a general matter, smaller firms and some government agencies offer greater opportunities to work with people. These practices do not usually involve thorny legal problems: you will quickly become expert in the areas you need to know.

Responsibility. The larger the firm or agency, the less responsibility you will have. Your work will be constantly reviewed. Other jobs throw you directly into the heat of battle. In some small firms and legal aid offices, you interview clients the first day; in some district attorney and defender offices, you try cases your first week.

Responsibility can be exhilarating; after all those years of studying about the real world, you are suddenly *in* it, but perhaps over your head. Responsibility can be terrifying. Law is quite complex, and, as a beginner, you know so little. Add to that the elusive criteria of good practice: "Have I worked hard enough?" "Have I raised all the points?" "Has my client been well represented?"

Training. It is essential to develop your professional skills. Larger firms and agencies generally offer good training. This is the other side of "lack of responsibility." Generally you will be given time to "do it right," and the standards of the practice will be quite high.

Many smaller firms and smaller public agencies also insist on the highest professional standards. Don't take a job that allows for sloppy work habits.

An aside on solo practice. Some "hang out their own shingle" upon graduation. But times, since Lincoln, have changed.

Without someone to show you the ropes and discuss your cases with, you will teeter on the edge of malpractice. The most common cause of legal malpractice is missing deadlines. Once you get three or four cases, it gets very difficult to keep track of things. Working with an established firm or lawyer, you will learn the various retrieval systems. Going out on your own, you may not.

Two pieces of advice, assuming you ignore the implicit advice in the last paragraph. First, keep your overhead low. Second, don't take "dog cases," even if it is just to put some short-term bones on the table. If you are the "Third lawyer they've seen," chances are that their case is hopeless or that they are very difficult clients.

Contentiousness. Even if you restrict your practice to "happy law" (adoption, business planning, elder law), there will be some days when another lawyer will be yelling at you. In other law jobs, such as trying lawsuits, it is pretty constant.

What about clients? It is said that, in criminal practice, you deal with bad people at their best and, in family practice, with good people at their worst. Interviewing for a job, ask lawyers not only about how they get along with adverse lawyers but with their own clients.

Income and security. Larger firms start associates at higher salaries; partners in large firms do exceedingly, embarrassingly well. Some lawyers in smaller firms undoubtedly overtake their fat-cat brethren and occasionally make "megabucks" by getting into business ventures with their clients.

Governmental lawyers often do nicely. Gone, of course, the dream of vast wealth, but some earn more than many lawyers in their area, with better benefits and job security.

Travel and adventure. It's possible. Think International Law.

Esprit de corps. Some jobs involve a strong sense of shared purpose. One of the things I most value about my own days in practice was my relationship with the other lawyers in the office. We knew about each others' cases, we talked about them, argued about them, and shared the moments of joy and despair.

I found this sense of shared purpose and involvement in both legal aid and public defending. I am sure it exists in most prosecuting offices, in most government jobs, and, I am told, in most small law offices. The larger the firm or agency, the less likely the feeling. This lack of *esprit de corps* will not bother some; those who prefer to work alone (perhaps writing Nutshells) and those who simply want a job and will look for a sense of community elsewhere.

Weighing Careers During Law School

A sports agent was discussing how difficult it is for players to readjust after their playing days are over. "I tell them to keep a diary when they are still playing. What do they enjoy doing in their off

*hours? What are they good at? That way, when
the time comes, they will have some idea of what
kind of job they may like."*

Do you enjoy the conflict of Moot Court or Trial
Practice? Do you find the verbal encounter in the
classroom exciting? Do you love research? Do you
rush to your computer to get your thoughts on
paper? Do you like close supervision? Do you like
working with classmates?

Although law practice is much different from law
school, many facets are the same: reading cases and
statutes, making arguments, advising on how the
law would play out in a given situation. Once you
have given law school a fair run, at least a year, and
you find you don't like the law, find it too nit-picky,
too confining, too boring, consider getting out.
Kafka went on to achieve modest success. So did
Harry Truman, who had a year of law school. So too
Vince Lombardi, who had a semester.

Course Selection

Considering a legal specialty, in addition to law
school courses, check out whether there are courses
in other departments of the university. For example, if you are considering something in the media,
go to the Journalism Department and chat. Another
obvious example is Business School. However, *as
career goals often change*, it is a *mistake* to focus too
exclusively in the area of law you think you'll
practice.

Most law schools offer courses in *trial practice* and have *clinics*. Clinics involve representing real clients either in a law school clinic or in a field placement. These courses are very important, particularly if you are shying away from them. It may be a matter of breaking out of "mind-forged manacles." You may find that you enjoy the hurly-burly of trial and that you find deep satisfaction in helping people solve real-life problems. Or you may conclude, "Never again." Either way, you win.

Clinical courses are needed by those students planning to work for small firms or on their own. There is the danger of developing sloppy work habits. Law school courses will instill a sense of excellence in practice.

Work for Lawyers

Doing the research, hanging out at the office, and talking to attorneys and staff can give you a good feel for that particular kind of law practice.

If you are to work for a lawyer, what kind of lawyer? Should you take a job with the kind of firm or agency you "think" you would like to eventually work for? Or should you take a job with one of those "I-could-never-work-with-them" firms? There are pros and cons for each. Some students find permanent employment through their clerking. On the other hand, much can be said for testing as many alternatives as possible. Even if you confirm your suspicion that you could never do insurance defense, having clerked with such a firm will make you a better personal injury lawyer.

Ask Lawyers and Professors

Most of us like to give advice (I, apparently, more than others). If you are considering prosecuting, why not go to the prosecutor's office and ask to see one of the attorneys?

I'm not here looking for a job. I'm here because I want some advice. I am thinking about prosecuting when I graduate, but I really don't know much about it. Perhaps you can tell me about it; perhaps I could sit in and watch what you do.

Note: This can be turned into a very clever job-getting ploy.

Now, Ms. Banker, I'm not looking for a job working in your legal department. I realize you are probably full. What I would like is some advice on how to go about getting a job in the legal department of a bank.

Of course *I* would never be bold enough simply to show up at a law office, unannounced. The problem is meeting lawyers. One possibility is to get together with some classmates, ask a friendly professor for some names of recent graduates, and throw a party.

We're first-year students, and we want to meet some lawyers so we can get some feel for what it's like. Want to come to a party?

You can also infiltrate sections of your local Bar Association; many have student memberships. Another way to meet lawyers is to attend Continuing Legal Education (CLE) programs and go to Bar conventions.

Try to get your professors talking about their practice experiences. Most likely that will be more interesting than the Rule in Shelley's Case.

Go to Court

It takes absolutely no courage to walk quietly into the back of a courtroom and sit through a trial. Again, this experience is probably most needed by those who will "never" step into a courtroom. Who knows, perhaps they'll never leave.

Read Books

There are several books about law practice. I recommend, as openers:

The Associates, Jay Osborne (author of *Paper Chase*), deals with life in a Wall Street firm.

Trial and Error, D. Michael Tomkins, is the story of a young lawyer starting off in solo practice.

Confessions of a Criminal Lawyer, Seymour Wishman, presents a criminal defense lawyer reflecting on several years of practice.

These books are relatively short, quite candid, and at places, humorous. They are excellent introductions to various kinds of practice. Ask your professors for other titles.

A Final Word

What does your future hold? Perhaps you will argue cases that shape your times, or perhaps you will be the trusted advisor of powerful groups, huge corporations, or even Presidents. Or perhaps you will never make the front page and will be simply another lawyer in the yellow pages, helping people with everyday problems. There is greatness in that as well.

Don't make too much of your ambition. It's okay if you don't get your fifteen minutes of fame. In Robert Bolt's play, *A Man for All Seasons*, Sir Thomas More is discussing careers with the politically ambitious Richard Rich.

More: Why not be a teacher? You'd be a fine teacher. Perhaps even a great one.

Rich: And if I was, who would know of it?

More: You, your pupils, your friends, God. Not a bad public that.

CHAPTER 32

LAWYERS ON LAWYERING

The lawyers you will meet here are friends, not statistics. I selected them because they are reflective and insightful. They do different jobs. I made no attempt to balance type of practice nor did I prescribe a format. "I'm writing a book for first-year law students; what you think might prove useful."

Coleen Thoene: Law Clerk

The most exciting and terrifying day of my life was the day I got my bar results. I felt vindicated. That little piece of paper confirmed that, at least in the eyes of some nameless essay grader—who I continue to bless on occasion—the last three years had taught me *something* about how to practice law. As of that moment, I could conquer the legal world.

Then that wonderfully giddy euphoria started to fade away, and it hit me: I knew squat about how to be a lawyer. Law school will teach you a lot of very important things: how to research and brief an issue, how to argue a case, and how to pick the most appropriate Rule. But: I knew how to write a motion, but not where or how to file it; I knew how to figure out what sentence a client faced, but not how

379

to tell that client or his family that he was probably going to go to prison. Suddenly, that little piece of paper seemed to stare coldly back at me and say, "You're *so* not ready."

To bridge the gap between law school and practice, I took a job as a law clerk for a judge sitting on the criminal bench. She has always treated me as an equal and includes me in different aspects of her job. I've observed dozens of trials and meetings she has with probation officers and attorneys before sentencings. She has always been very open to answering any questions about legal issues and tactics. I will be a more effective attorney.

Reputation really is everything. Attorneys who are on time, professionally attired, well prepared, and ethical have much more credibility than attorneys who aren't. On close issues, judges tend to rule in their favor—something to keep in mind if you ever want to ask for a mitigated sentence and your client isn't exactly Pollyanna. Bad reputations are easy to earn and very, very hard to lose. I have seen attorneys misstate crucial facts. Judges do not like to be misled, and a misstatement—whether intentional or not—can make a judge distrust your word in other cases even if you're being completely forthright. And judges talk to each other, especially about attorneys they dislike.

All of that being said, mistakes are different. If you make an honest mistake, admit it immediately (or sooner, if at all possible). Your clients will thank you.

Court staff can make your job hell or heaven. If you treat court staff like second-rate citizens, they may not be as sympathetic or helpful as they might have been. Treat a court reporter poorly, and you may not get those transcripts you need until the absolute last minute. Be rude to court security, and your in-custody clients could be brought up near the end of a calendar, regardless of whether you have been sitting in the courtroom for an hour or more. Treat them well, and they will give your client preference even if they are horrendously short-staffed.

Staff go out of their way to help the attorneys they like. If you are a new attorney, court staff can be a great resource when it comes to figuring out local filing procedures, or who to call when something unexpected comes up in one of your cases. It is worth the effort to act professional and like a human being.

My judge presides over the Drug Court program in our county. It is based on the idea that drug addiction is a disease that can be very difficult to treat due a complex interaction of various personal, medical, and social factors. Simple incarceration often has no long-lasting effect because, even though it may give a person a period of forced sobriety, it does nothing to address the causes of addiction. As a result, defendants who receive little to no treatment often find themselves incarcerated repeatedly, and for longer periods each time. The Drug Court program, instead, uses a mixture of intense treatment coupled with positive and negative reinforcement to try to treat the root causes of a person's addiction. I have seen many people come into the program, literally, on Death's door after decades of heavy drug use. Some have lost custody of their children or been alienated by their relatives. Many have histories of being abused, are under educated, and unemployed. By the time they graduate from the program, they have jobs, some are enrolled in college, some even get their children back. Being able to watch these individuals regain control over their lives has been the most rewarding part of my job.

Being a law clerk and watching court proceedings is a good way to make all those things you learned in basic trial advocacy make sense. I learned the rules of evidence almost by osmosis simply by listening to attorneys introduce exhibits during trial. I have also gotten to watch attorneys that are so well prepared and passionate that one would think they only represented one client at a time. I have also seen attorneys that have left me feeling very sorry for their clients because the attorneys were so obviously unprepared, burnt out, or unprofessional that the clients wound up suffering. I have gotten to interact with jurors during both the voir dire process and their actual service. On more than one occasion, I have seen jurors completely ignore some fact that an attorney considered to be the lynchpin of their case and decide the case on something that both sides threw away as a non-issue during their closing arguments. I have seen attorneys pick certain jurors because they believe they know how that juror will vote based on his or her background, only to later wonder why the juror voted a different way. I have seen jurors that have left me wondering whether they had any common sense whatsoever.

I see the human element. Obviously, clients are effected the most by a court's decision. My judge sits on the criminal bench, and we always seem to have at least one person in the courtroom crying when she hands down a sentence or ruling. I get to see how the law effects people who are not directly involved in the case itself, like a defendant's or victim's family, or that person who was simply standing on a street corner and is called as a witness. I have seen attorneys and probation officers lose sleep trying to figure out how to help a person turn their life around and avoid going to prison. I have seen victim and defendant families get into fights in the hallway, and I have watched those same people hug one another once a case was concluded. I have heard people yell at and threaten attorneys who were unable to get them the exact result they wanted, and I have heard others bless them. I have seen my boss wrestle with her rulings, and wrestled myself over whether something I was writing was the right decision to make. This part of the legal system cannot be taught in law school. My job is one of the few that lets you experience all of it.

Robert Fleming: Elder Law

It seemed to me that most of the students in my law school class were unsure of their ultimate goals.

I was different. I knew with absolute certainty why I was in law school, what I would do with my degree and my professional future. As it happened, I was wrong.

Although my plans drifted from environmental law to the more prosaic water and mining law practice, I knew that I would want to utilize my undergraduate degree (chemistry) and my scientific orientation. Two years out of law school I had learned the hard truth: a new lawyer has little control over what cases or clients might appear. There was a softer truth as well: I surprised myself when I found that I enjoyed working with individual clients, and particularly those with mental or physical limitations.

In one regard, my law school predictions were correct. I doubted that I would "fit in" in a corporate or large firm practice, and the passage of time has proven that my doubts were well founded. I have practiced alone, with a single associate, in partnerships of up to four lawyers and in government settings. Each arrangement has had its attractions.

One other thing I correctly predicted in law school was that I would not be drawn to a litigation-based practice. An office practice filled with appointments with real clients is very rewarding and professionally satisfying.

Our firm practices "elder law." We prepare estate plans, advise clients about long-term care costs, and counsel family members on end-of-life issues. The common thread is that our clients tend to be elderly or disabled, or to be the children or parents of elderly or disabled individuals.

Recently I went through an extraordinary personal experience related to the law practice. A young woman had been a long-time client. I had handled the proceeds of a personal injury settlement while she was a minor, and she left the money in trust with our firm after reaching her majority. She was physically disabled and had a shortened life expectancy, but she exhibited personal strength. A few years ago she decided to name me as her agent for health care decisions—not because she distrusted her family, but because she wanted to remove her mother from the agony of making the ultimate decision.

When I received the call from the hospital, I expected to be told that she had become non-communicative. Instead she remained articulate, and was demanding the removal of the breathing machine which kept her alive. Her father objected, hoping for a miracle. Her mother agreed with her decision, but was in agony. Her siblings represented several different views on how she should proceed. Her physician was sure that if he could get her through her current treatment, she could live several more years—though, he acknowledged, she would never be weaned from the breathing machines.

At her bedside I asked her how she felt about the decision. She clearly mouthed the words "I'm tired– let me go." I went to a room filled with the well-intentioned individuals in her life, each of whom was grappling with her wishes in a different way, and argued for her personal autonomy.

The legal principle was never at issue. She was competent, and had the absolute right to direct the removal of the treatment, and the hospital staff knew it without having to hear it from me. I left the hospital with the certain knowledge that by the time of my arrival at the office she would have died—and she did. In a strict sense, I did not practice law that day—but I accomplished something terribly important to me personally, and my faith in the law and the practice of law was reinforced.

Law school was at least an adequate preparation for the legal aspects of the practice of law. It did not, however, prepare us for the medical, social work, financial, personal or emotional components of the practice. It may be that those components are more easily learned in the on-the-job training of the real world. Still, it would have been nice to have some sense of the application of legal principles to real people's lives.

Amy Wilkins: Small Firm/Big Firm

I never thought I would go to a small firm. I started at a large, 800–lawyer national firm in a big city, then went to a smaller, but still large national firm, and then went to a mid-size regional firm. I understood big firms, I thought. I knew how to keep track of my time, how to make sure I had a presence on firm committees, which firm events to show up to, and, most importantly, which partners to work for and which partners to avoid. I had it down.

Until I started to wonder what my life was all about. Did I want to be a partner? Why were most partners divorced? Did I have the drive it took to commit to being a partner, or working to be named a partner? I had a sneaking suspicion I didn't want it. I fantasized about opening a Starbucks franchise in Payson, or perhaps being a children's librarian (the good kind, the kind who wouldn't ban Harry Potter or Catcher in the Rye, if that is still banned somewhere). I considered signing up for interior design classes. I went to happy hour a lot.

After a good friend convinced me the good life was to be had at his firm, I made the leap. And after three different big firms in six years, I reckoned making a move to another big firm didn't make much sense. It is a plaintiff's firm, which I thought would be a nice change. Now I'm at a firm with four other attorneys in the office, and thirty more at other offices. One perk is that I know all the other lawyers, where that would never have been possible at the other firms. It has more of a family feel. We have a newsletter where we poke fun at each other as well as announce big life events like weddings and sports triumphs, and some people actually have sports triumphs. The pressure to bill millions of hours as well as somehow participate in the bar and pro bono and develop clients at large corporations is off. As a plaintiff's firm, we don't need to develop clients like GM or Citibank. And now I can say things like, "I'm on the side of the right. The little guy. You represent an insurance company."

But putting aside things like newsletters and fun jabs at my defense lawyer friends, the work has improved. I learned a heck of a lot working at the firms I worked at, and I worked for top quality, smart lawyers. I am glad I had that experience. But now, since there is no one else to do certain work, I am doing a lot more advanced lawyering. I get to write the appellate briefs instead of that senior lawyer down the hall who clerked for Justice Stevens. I get to argue motions instead of the partner. I am scheduled to take witnesses at trial shortly, including an expert witness. I've never even been to trial before—I thought I was the defense firm's secret weapon, as every single case I worked on settled—and now I'll get to try out my Clarence Darrow skills. Part of the problem at a bigger firm is that the client doesn't want the risk of having an associate argue the big motion or take the deposition or the witness, so partners end up doing it and associates don't necessarily get the experience they need. I'm not saying this is every firm or every case, but it can definitely be a problem.

So my day is different now. It used to be I'd get in, listen to my voicemail, and return calls from anxious clients and partners. I'd figure out an action plan for my day—what had to be done today, what should be done today, and what would have to wait. And then I'd try to get it done. Now I have fewer cases and more time to work them up. If your case is based on contingency rather than billable hours, you can spend time chasing down research angles that you may have been reluctant to pursue before. I'm finding my stress level is less, because I feel I have more time to get my cases right. After all, we all want to do a good job for our clients, and there's no stress worse than realizing you made a mistake or missed something. I'm excited about my practice now, instead of dreading the road to partnership and what I might find there.

What I used to tell summer associates at big firms was, "Stop stressing so much about your decision where to work. You can always lateral to another firm." This was probably not a firm-sanctioned recruiting technique. But you can. You can always make a move, and where you want to be when you graduate probably isn't where you'll want to be after five or ten years of practice, or even one year of practice. The important thing is to be open to change. You'll find a fit for yourself in the law eventually. Or there's always that Starbucks franchise.

Dan Cooper: Criminal Defense

The most satisfying part of being a criminal defense lawyer is representing people who are despised by the public, the press and the prosecutors. Most cases remain obscure and create no reaction. On occasion, however, a defendant comes along who stirs the conscience of the community into moral outrage. It is defending this person that makes me proud to be a lawyer.

I recently represented a man who, along with his wife, was charged with child abuse. The facts were grisly. When I first met my client I was somewhat taken aback by his absolute and total lack of guilt. I try not to prejudge my cases. I was, however, aware when I received this case that the evidence was overwhelming against my client. I was perplexed at his total lack of emotion. Throughout the duration of the case he remained stoic in the face of constant hostility. The prosecutor called my client "a monster." The newspapers covered the case extensively and without objectivity. Even some close friends of mine asked how I could represent this man. The trial lasted nearly two weeks and, although I could not honestly say that I had fun, it was an experience I would not trade. The victim in the case, a nine-year-old girl, was found hog-tied in a motel room. She weighed thirty-two pounds and had been beaten. She had a chipped front tooth, bruises on her face and at least twenty scars on the top of her head which, the State alleged, came from a blunt object. A psychiatrist testified that she had never seen a worse case of psychological and emotional child abuse. A pediatrician testified that the child had been systematically starved for at least four years. A radiologist testified that the child's growth would, in all likelihood, be permanently stunted. And the most damaging witness of all was the little girl—tiny, charming, precocious. She broke down in tears as she turned to look at her mother and stepfather. My client stared at her impassively.

Against the advice of some very skilled trial lawyers, I put my client on the stand. The other lawyers felt that my client's testimony would only enrage an already upset jury. But I wanted the jury to see how narrow and rigid was my client's view of the world. His testimony was stilted, rigid, unsmiling and, I felt, demonstrated a myopic, inadequate personality perfectly capable of being unaware that his nine-year-old stepdaughter had been systematically starved and abused. Certainly his testimony would not prove his innocence. But there was an outside chance that the jury would convict of the lesser, non-intentional child abuse charge if they felt my client was rigid, myopic and pathetic. It was a slim chance in an unpopular, highly publicized case. My closing argument to the jury was emotional. I had convinced myself, if no one else, that the lesser offense would be the appropriate verdict. That the jury convicted my client of the greater offense has not changed my mind. But perhaps my feelings today about that child abuse case typify the nature of this job. I am proud that, in the face of overwhelming adverse publicity, against insurmountable evidence, while not able to convince a jury of my client's innocence, that jury knew that the defendant had a lawyer who fought for him.

Grace McIlvain: Mid–Size Firm

When I decided to become a lawyer, it was not because I thought the law would be exciting. I thought it would be boring. I did not expect to like the law, let alone love it the way one is supposed to.

I wanted a job that would give me responsibility, a chance to use my brain, a good salary, and a chance to advance, none of which I had as a secretary. Those were my sole reasons for applying to law school.

It is amusing to recall what I expected the practice of law to be like when I was in law school. I expected it to be boring and tedious, so tedious that the hours in the office would drag by. Nothing could be further from the truth. I enjoy at least 90% of the things I must do. Filling out time sheets and preparing bills to send to clients are no fun at all, but litigation is very interesting. I think about my cases all my waking hours and often most of the night. I even dream about them.

The responsibilities and time pressures are, however, very stressful. The matters one handles are extremely important to the clients, and they place a great deal of trust in you. Because of that, and for many other more selfish reasons, there is great pressure to achieve an excellent result in every single case which is, of course, impossible. There is never enough time to be as thoroughly prepared as you would like to be. No matter how well organized and self-disciplined you are, every day is a struggle against time. There are never enough hours in the day. In that respect, law school is good preparation for the practice. But the time pressures in practicing law are much greater than time pressures in law school.

There is so much emphasis on legal theories in law school that you begin to believe that legal knowledge and analytical skill are all you need to be a good attorney. Law school doesn't prepare you for the psychological aspects of practicing law. You must build a good relationship with your client and make him or her have confidence in you. You must make the opposing attorney at least respect you, and it is to your advantage to convince him that you are tough, that you know the law, and that you will persevere no matter what. It is to your advantage to make him afraid of you. Yet sometimes you need his cooperation, so you must know when to be nice to him and when to apply pressure. (I use "him" when referring to the opposing attorney because, in litigation, usually your opponent is male. If you are a woman, the difficulties of dealing with him are multiplied because even before he meets you, he may have decided that you are either a pushover or a bitch, and that whichever you are, you are not a good lawyer.)

You need to convince the judges before whom you appear that you know the law, that there is a good reason behind every statement you make, and that you would never ever mislead them. You must convince juries that you are credible and that your client deserves their verdict.

There is always room to grow. There are always ways you could have handled a case better, which is one of the reasons you are never bored.

Theresa Gabaldon: Large
Firm; Law Teaching

My sister, who is a romance novelist, has the best job in the world. This is largely because she has self-defined it to involve working at night, getting up very late, and eating chocolates for breakfast.

I, a law professor, have the second best job in the world; if eating chocolates were a necessary part of the job description, it would clearly rival my sister's. As it is, I have enormous flexibility about what I do and, within reasonable bounds, when I do it. The highlights, and only strictly scheduled events of the week are, of course, classroom appearances. I currently teach to an average class size of around 120 students; put a microphone in my hand and I become Oprah Winfrey. Coming up with different ways to cover the material is part of the fun, and if I choose to play a game of "Jeopardy" with corporate law topics, none of my teaching colleagues will object (at least not to my face.) My students are good-natured and appreciate whatever effort is expended in their behalf.

Performing scholarly research and writing is another important part of my task, and it is here that the possibilities for marching to one's own drumbeat are most unlimited. I choose my own topics for inquiry, and simply work on them until I have said what I have to say. My most productive "thinking" time starts at 4:00 a.m. and I try to take advantage of it. This may lead to a lull later in the day, but a quick trip to aerobics class recharges my batteries.

Although the description thus far may suggest that the law professor leads a life that is somewhat distanced from others, this is only true if he or she decrees it. If you display any disposition to listen, as well as to impart, students will be by to chat about a truly breath-taking assortment of subjects. Your colleagues can, if you choose, be your sounding boards, your confidantes, your matchmakers, and, every now and then, your bowling partners.

My immediately prior incarnation was as a partner in a large law firm. As such, I had the third best job in the world. In all honesty, flexibility was not one of the things that commended it. Rather, it was the technical challenge—present also in law teaching—and the sense of command. Frankly, the money wasn't bad, either; in ten years of teaching I have yet to achieve my salary in my last year of practice.

I specialized in corporate and securities law, and these are the areas that have carried over into my teaching and my scholarship. It was, at the time, something of a "glamour" practice. The deals were huge, the pace was fast, and the travel arrangements were luxurious. The pressure, however, was intense, and I can remember the feeling in my chest as I realized that a deadline was approaching and that the legal judgment being brought to bear on a multi-million dollar deal was mine. I have no regrets about having lived that life or about having left it, simply because I have found something I like more.

Because I have truly enjoyed both of my law-related professions, I have to believe that there is something about the law that has "worked" for me. I know that it has not, and does not, "work" for everybody. I enjoy the solving-the-maze aspects and the challenges of communicating my solutions to others. I suspect, however, that I lack the passion for justice, fairness, etc., that motivates some—and that's probably just as well for a corporate lawyer. In fact, from my observations, it is passion of this sort, combined with some type of corporate law-practice, that frequently leads to dissatisfaction with the law. There is fulfillment in serving particular clients well, in teaching, and in being an upstanding citizen and contributing member of society, but it will still leave some people feeling that there should be something more.

Bryce Alstead: Mid-sized firm

I am a transactional real estate lawyer. Some people feel that the term quasi-lawyer is the best descriptor of my job. No less 95% of what I learned in law school is completely irrelevant to my workplace life, but, strangely, Sallie Mae did not give me a discount on my student loans. Bastards. I have never been in the local courthouse, have never signed my name to a pleading, and have absolutely no idea what my Westlaw password is. I did write a demand letter once; it was scary.

Most of my days are spent drafting documents like contracts, leases, and easements, primarily for land developers. While this may not hold the popular appeal of storming into a courtroom and yelling at people, which I assume litigators do at least three times daily, I like to think that my job is just as important. I create the documents that allow developers to construct and improve subdivisions, resorts, and stores. Without real property attorneys, most development in this country would quickly stall; to be blunt, the environmental movement is not too fond of people like me.

One of the primary benefits of working in transactional real property law is that my stress level stays reasonably low. This is not to say that my job is stress free, but there is much less pressure to abide by sometimes arbitrary client-imposed deadlines than those set by a court. Maybe a client will send me an angry e-mail if he does not receive an easement inside his requested period, but no one will go to jail or lose a pile of money because of it. There is also much less yelling on my side of the building. Most of my battles are fought over things like whether there is a material difference between stating "included, but not limited to..." and "including, without limitation...". Obviously, working in transactional law lacks some of the visceral thrills of litigation, but I think the corresponding trade-off in stress is more than worth it.

Two things, above all others, are crucial to succeeding as a transactional lawyer. The first is being able to write—not being able to write particularly interesting things, but being able to write in an efficient and grammatically correct manner. The billable hour ensures efficiency. If a client gets billed nine hours for my work on a basic lease, the first questions that jump into a partner's mind are whether I was drinking on the job or whether too many years of fantasy sports have irrevocably dulled my mind. Not good. I would love to spend more time on my documents, but this simply isn't possible in private practice.

The second key skill is responsiveness. The ability and willingness to promptly return calls is more important to my career than the quality of my documents. Many attorneys are capable of producing effective documents; amazingly, far less are willing to return phone calls. My clients really have no idea what sets a good easement apart from a bad one—this is for the firm's malpractice carrier to decide—however, they are absolutely aware that I receive emails within minutes of when they send them. If I respond quickly, they will generally sing my praises to potential future clients; if I wait more than a day or two, there is a substantial chance that they will take their work elsewhere. Though pure legal skills are obviously necessary, the somewhat surprising truth is that the ability to communicate is far more important in building a client base.

I am sometimes asked whether I would rather work in litigation, or, more pejoratively, as a "real lawyer". The answer is always no. Though I don't amass too many war stories in my line of work, I am actually a happy attorney. I can't say this for many of many colleagues.

Randy Stevens: Prosecutor

It took just a little more than a year after my graduation from law school for me to realize that private practice wasn't for me—at least not at that time in my life. I wanted more variety, more action, more excitement. I also wanted to be handling cases that had greater significance than just importance to the client. Having watched several excellent trial attorneys perform in court, I knew that courtroom practice was something I had to try, but I also realized it would take years to get any meaningful experience if I stayed in private practice. Telling the people I worked with that I'd be back in a year or two, I left and joined the local prosecutor's office. That was fourteen years ago.

From my perspective, the *total* experience available in prosecution cannot be duplicated elsewhere, especially for an attorney in the first four or five years. It isn't just the legal experience; it is the broader awareness of life, people and society, awareness of aspects of our society that most of us never dreamed existed. While at the same time, prosecution is an accelerated course in all aspects of trial practice.

Prosecution is the perfect opportunity for you to find out if you really want to be a trial attorney. Almost every young attorney experiences some degree of trial resistance—a hesitancy to try a case in front of a jury. There is a fear of making mistakes, of embarrassing oneself, of "freezing up" and not knowing what to do next. In a busy prosecutor's office, this resistance is usually overcome simply because there isn't time to dwell upon it. A heavy caseload doesn't allow for it. It isn't unusual for new prosecutors to find themselves trying several cases a week. If they begin to enjoy what they are doing, and are comfortable in court, it is only a matter of time before they want to begin trying more complicated and more serious cases. But not all attorneys experience this. After six months to a year, and sometimes even sooner, some realize that they aren't enjoying courtroom work, that they don't like the pressure and the demands of trial work, something no one can really know before they've given it a try. Most prosecutor's offices expect this to happen with a percentage of the young attorneys they hire.

It is usually during the fourth and fifth years when trial skills begin to reach a plateau, which means the attorney can try any type of criminal case with a high level of competency. Most trial attorneys will agree: if a person can competently prosecute a lengthy, difficult criminal case, that person can probably try almost any type of civil case. Law firms recruit heavily from prosecuting offices.

Most attorneys who prosecute do so for five to ten years, then they move on to something else. Looking back, asking myself why I've stayed so long in prosecution, the answer really isn't that hard to determine: I've thoroughly enjoyed myself. I've actually looked forward to going to work each morning. The constant flow of different types of cases, the interchange with victims and witnesses; working with every level of law enforcement: all go together to constitute a level of excitement that makes the job more than just enjoyable. It's experiencing life three or four times more than the average person. Along with this is the additional feeling that in some small way, you are doing something positive for society.

Zelda B. Harris: Representing Victims of Domestic Violence

The most amazing part is that people trust you with their most intimate, painful and difficult secrets. I remember the first time that someone, other than my family and friends, put their trust in me. The weight of that experience was overwhelming. As a young attorney practicing poverty law I frequently violated the age old principle of "never take your work home." But to me, it was more than work, it was livelihoods, homes, children, safety and dignity. I must admit that I also engaged in quite a bit of social work practice by helping clients move from one home to the next, purchasing groceries, holiday gifts for children, the endless rides to and from court and the occasional cash that I could spare. The only thing I would trade is the fifty pounds of stress, oddly and strategically located on my hips, that I gained trying to "cure" my client's poverty.

I am a witness to the truth of violence, violence survived by victims of domestic abuse. I am in debt to the scores of clients who have risked their personal safety, privacy and the unknown to reveal the horrors of their lives to me. To the attorney considering embarking on this venture, I'd like to outline some of the very harsh realities of this practice, but also let you know that the benefits are life changing and shape your humanity.

I have stood witness with "Karen T." when her daughter, still nursing, was physically removed from her breast by court security officers when I lost the temporary custody hearing. I also remember the day when the three of us stood strong before the same juvenile court judge, who had to publicly and openly admit that Lisa should be returned to the nurture and protection of Karen.

I am a witness for a 22 year-old woman, "Tammy E.," who was raped by her father for seven years, disbelieved by her mother and sisters, removed from her home, abused by two partners, yet was able to bear two beautiful, healthy children only to have them taken from her by the state in their best interests. My photo album today still holds the picture of the day that Tammy's third daughter that was successfully, openly and with Tammy's consent adopted by a loving family that would never erase the reality of Tammy from the child's life.

I bore witness to a mother addicted to drugs, "Deborah P.," beat her addiction, stay clean, gain housing, employment and custody of her children, only to be found dead in her apartment, stabbed to death by a never-caught killer. My heart will not forget the warm embrace that I received from Deborah's children the last time I saw them in court; they knew and I knew that Deborah loved them.

A lawyer is a witness, but not a passive witness. We have voice and power. We can give credibility to the indignities that our clients have suffered. And, more than that, we have an absolute obligation to demand that the legal system, with all of its insensitivity and unfairness, listen and act.

You will not win every case or argument. But if you pursue each case with rigor and integrity, then you have earned the privilege to hold your client's trust. That is an absolute victory.

Hector Campoy: Judge of Juvenile Court

Never in my wildest dreams did I envision myself becoming a Juvenile Court Judge. In my mind's eye, before, during and for many years after law school, I was going to become the consummate trial lawyer. One day however, the Presiding Judge of our Juvenile Court invited me to become a part time judicial officer at our Juvenile Court. It took me very little time before the process enraptured me.

While issues of public safety and the safety of children are always foremost in our consideration, Juvenile Court Judges are constantly monitoring the development of relationships. When we take a child into our legal custody through a child abuse action, we hope to provide services to parents in order to rehabilitate the family and reconstitute it- in the event that those efforts fail we attempt to develop new, permanent relationships for these children through adoptions or other permanent legal arrangement. When we take a child into our fold through a delinquency process, we again aim to provide services and a corrective action plan, if you will, to rehabilitate children's behaviors.

Having done this for in excess of 18 years, I can honestly state that I am still surprised at the response of children and parents in our venue. Children, very many times, overcome incredible obstacles in order to correct the direction of their lives. This is wonderful to witness. Parents on the other hand, all too often, fail to seize the opportunity that the relationship with their child brings to them. This is not so wonderful.

The work is gut wrenching. The future of children and the future of families, in the face of societal pressures and trends, can provide some joy and exhilaration–it can also provide some extremely sobering moments.

All in all, our review of relationships at Juvenile Court is much more stimulating than how other courts review transactional events. Other courts determine whether a crime was committed, whether a person ran a red light or whether a contract was breached. These occurrences relate to events that in turn prescribe a remedy or response. The subject matter at Juvenile Court focuses on relationships that are dynamic and unpredictable.

Captain Vicki Marcus: U.S. Air Force Judge Advocate (JAG)

The first question I'm always asked when I tell people what I do is: "Like in *A Few Good Men*?" Not even close.

I work at an Air Force base legal office and am excited to come to work. One of the main reasons is the variety of opportunities. I am the Chief of Legal Assistance and Preventive Law. We provide free legal services to military members, retirees, and their families. Interacting, face-to-face, with clients, I write wills, advise on domestic matters, such as divorce, child custody, and paternity, and deal with issues involving debt, landlord/tenant, and the Service Members Civil Relief Act. I know the work I do makes a big difference in the lives of those I advise.

The Preventive Law aspect of my job is a little different in that I am trying to prevent legal problems for both individuals and my main client, the United States Air Force. I write articles for our base newspaper on topics that have the potential of being legal minefields and run the ethics program for the installation where I'm stationed. There is a multi-layered web of ethics rules and standards of conduct applicable to all who operate in the government sector, and especially the military. It is my job to make them aware so they can seek legal advice before mistakes are made.

I have prosecuted numerous criminal cases, and in each instance I was lead trial counsel. The responsibilities given to a new JAG can seem overwhelming at first. I was given my first case within a week of arriving at my base. Within three weeks I was in a courtroom, in front of a judge, arguing my case.

The military law environment also offers opportunities in contract law, labor law, environmental law, and a whole host of other issues most civilian attorneys do not get the chance to address.

For all the advantages, what I do is hard work. I put in long hours, especially leading up to trials. I have to be able to multi-task, compartmentalize the various parts of my job, and keep everything running smoothly on a tight schedule. A new attorney is expected to get up to speed quickly, and while allowances are made for the learning curve, I was not entrusted with fewer responsibilities because of my lack of experience.

Law school did not fully prepare me for this career. However, one thing has served me well. I was involved in many projects and organizations in school, and the ability to juggle all of them successfully put me in good stead for the demands of military law.

Remember that the military, by its very nature, is different from the private sector. The life of a JAG is different than that of a civilian attorney. I am not just a lawyer. I am also an Air Force officer, and that position also has responsibilities attached to it. I am subject to recall, I will deploy like the rest of our military members, I must be physically fit, and many of the lesser duties I perform at my base are unrelated to the law. They are part and parcel with the commitment to the military I made when I took my oath. I can say, though, that there is a sense of pride that comes with having chosen this profession that cannot be underestimated. I know that the work I do has value. Not just on a small scale, either. I put on my uniform everyday and serve my country.

As my career progresses, more doors will be open to me. I can apply for the Master of Laws (LL.M.) program and go back to school to further my legal education. I can be selected as an Area Defense Counsel and serve as a defense attorney for military members in criminal cases. I may even have the opportunity in the future to be a military judge. There are JAGs at every Air Force base world-wide and at every level of the Air Force, so the sky is the limit on what challenges I can pursue.

Whether I make this a four-year commitment or a lifetime one, I will have continued opportunities to grow as an attorney and as a person. The military has tested me in ways I had not imagined before joining.

DISCLAIMER: The views expressed in this article as those of the author and do not necessarily reflect the official policy or position of the Air Force, Department of Defense, or the U.S. Government.

Rita A. Meiser: Large Firm

I write as a person whose initial perception envisioned a happier legal life in a small firm, and who has been pleasantly surprised at where I have ended up. My primary orientation in becoming an attorney was to maximize my involvement with people. The areas of law in which I am mostly involved reflect this goal. Mostly I practice hospital law. This is one of those areas that you do not know exists when you are in law school. It encompasses: removing from a hospital staff a physician who does not perform at the proper standard of care; determining what procedures must be followed when a physician decides to remove life support, and working through the administrative procedures necessary to have a hospital add a department or beds. The work appeals to me because it involves effecting positive, tangible change in a way that is often lacking in the practice of law.

My second area of practice is employment discrimination, primarily from a defense perspective. This work is intriguing. I learn the business operations of the client, as well as meet and work with people involved in the world of business. It has not been my experience that practice from the defense posture necessarily mandates advocacy of personally offensive legal positions. Business people are generally fairly practical. If they recognize that a policy or practice is unlawful and will cause them continuing economic harm, they are generally receptive to changing it. The lawyer plays a role in advancing this recognition.

Finally, I represent two adoption agencies on a pro bono basis. The gratifications are obvious and the ability to participate in this type of activity is often a luxury less easily available in a small firm.

A large firm offers a new lawyer diversity, not only in terms of the type of legal practice offered, but in the people themselves. I initially perceived this to be an advantage of a small firm, but I now find it to be one of the greatest attributes of a large firm. I assumed that I would have closer personal relationships and find the working atmosphere more pleasant and intimate in a small firm. I now believe that a large law firm incorporates numerous types of personalities, and its size permits this diversification not to generate conflict. To the extent one specializes, the pool of working relationships narrows, thereby promoting the more intimate working relationships.

There are advantages and disadvantages to large firm practice, and what those factors are is the function of the given firm. The emphasis upon time commitments, responsibility, and client contact are all variables which must be assessed in evaluating the personality of any firm. In my particular firm, client responsibility and contact came quickly; however, this is not true in every large firm. If you are considering work in a large firm, interview carefully, particularly for second year clerkships, and try to select the firm which you think has the personality with which you are most compatible. Use your second year clerkship at that firm not only to verify whether your perceptions were correct, but to develop your ability to analyze the makeup of other firms, so that if you interview at another firm, you will more quickly be able to assess whether it's for you.

Margaret McIntyre: Representing Workers

When I went to law school I knew I wanted to practice public interest law. Many think that to do so one must work for federally funded legal services program or for a non-profit agency. I now know that you can also represent low income clients in private practice and still make a living. I have been doing so for five years.

Most of my clients have been fired from their jobs for discriminatory reasons, although some of them are still employed and are being subjected to a hostile work environment, such as sexual harassment or harassment based on another discriminatory motive. Others have been denied wages or benefits owed to them by their employers.

Some of those who come to see me may not have legal claims and some may have arguable claims, but weak evidence. For those it is better to accept early that the law cannot redress all wrongs, rather than go through the painful process of litigation, only to have the case dismissed for insufficient evidence. It can be very difficult to persuade some people of that, but it's my job as a lawyer to give them the best advice I can, not to tell them what they want to hear. Others are visibly relieved when I tell them that I don't think they have a case, and they realize that they can just put their losses behind them and move on.

Listen to a client's goals. Some want to feel vindicated, to hear a jury say that their employer violated the law. Others are willing to settle for money, whether to compensate them for lost wages, or to soften the hurt of whatever humiliation they have suffered. Most people want something in between, and are unsure about their goals until they learn the strength of their case and what will be involved in pursuing their goals, in terms of time, expense and the psychological toll litigation will take on themselves and their family. For each client, the answers to those questions are different. But in every case, I need to know a potential client's goals, because I must believe I can accomplish those goals before I offer representation.

One of the hardest goals to accomplish for employees is to get them back to the jobs they have lost. This is difficult to achieve because in these cases the emotions run high, and relationships have become strained. Some clients don't even want to go back to a bad situation. But when they do want to go back, and you help make it happen, that is tremendously rewarding.

Most cases settle before going to trial, usually for close to what the person lost in wages and benefits, although some will recover payment for emotional distress damages as well. Sometimes a client is able achieve other goals apart from a monetary settlement. For example, an employer may agree to undergo anti-harassment training, or agree to adopt comprehensive medical leave policies. Such agreements will give a client the sense of accomplishing something beyond his or her own case, and that brings a great deal of satisfaction.

One of my biggest challenges as a sole practitioner is figuring out a fair price to charge my clients for my services. Fortunately, the civil rights stat-

utes provide for fee shifting, meaning that if an
employee prevails in his or her claim against her
employer, the employer must pay the plaintiff's
attorney's fees. Even so, with each client, I must
figure out whether to charge by the hour (at my
regular or reduced rate), charge on a contingency
basis, where my fee is a third of the employee's
recovery, or charge some combination of the two,
where I charge a reduced hourly rate and also a
small percentage of any recovery. The right fee
arrangement will depend on the economic value of
the case, the client's ability to pay and the forum
where the case is being litigated, i.e. at an administrative agency or in court. In a lawsuit, expenses
alone can run from $2,000 to $5,000, depending on
how many witnesses must be deposed. The financial
decisions involved in commencing a lawsuit are
difficult, but when the risks are shared by the
attorney and the client, all decisions in the case are
made with great care. In the long run, that's the
best strategy for maintaining a successful practice.

If you are thinking of going it alone, know where
to get help. It's important to link up with other
lawyers through bar associations and other professional groups. I have learned a great deal about
employment law through activities and seminars
sponsored by the National Employment Lawyers
Association. In addition, I remain connected to my
law school, CUNY, the City University of New York.
It has created the Community Legal Resource Network (CLRN), which provides technical and research support to alumni in small or solo practices

who are trying to keep legal services affordable. For more information about the Community Legal Resource Network, contact www.lawschool51fconsortium.net.

Richard Davis: Mid–Size Firm

I arrive in my office at 7:30 a.m. I look at my calendar and realize that I have to travel to a hospital which our firm represents to meet with the Administrator and Risk Manager. Others will be present. A few days ago a 20–day-old premature baby died at the hospital while on a ventilator. The original account suggests that the machine malfunctioned, preventing the baby from breathing normally.

Immediately after the accident, the Director of the Medical Lab at the hospital wanted to test the ventilator. I advised a delay long enough to notify each of the interested parties and to give them an opportunity to be present. The manufacturer of the ventilator and the parents of the baby were notified.

The test is scheduled to begin at 9:00, but I get there early. This will allow me to become familiar with the machine and interview the hospital's personnel who were on duty when the incident occurred. Arriving at 8:15, I talk to the respiratory technician, the nurse on duty and the medical lab technician who will do the testing. By 8:45 I have a general idea of how the machine works, of the suspected problem and of what happened the day in question. I also learn that the hospital coffee gets old after the second cup.

The first person to arrive for the meeting is an investigator from the County Medical Examiner's Office. The family asked that office to be present and to determine the cause of the baby's death. We exchange pleasantries. I am a little anxious and apprehensive because I really do not know what the tests will reveal. My hidden hope is that the tests will prove my client blameless.

The manufacturer is sending someone from its national headquarters in Texas. It is now 9:00, and we receive a call advising us that the manufacturer's rep will be late. The small talk and anxiousness continue. At 9:30, the manufacturer's representative arrives. There is an immediate disagreement over the tests that should be run and who should run them. After discussion, ground rules are laid and pictures are taken to verify and preserve settings on dowels and pressure gauges. Each test is run carefully and meticulously. The pressure gauge is saved for last because it is the suspected culprit. It proves faulty.

Further tests are necessary to determine why the system failed but that necessitates a breakdown of the unit. Moreover, the necessary equipment is not available. The manufacturer's representative wants to take the machine back to the factory for further testing. I disagree. I feel that the machine should be stored in a place where no one can get to it without my knowledge and prior approval. Besides, there should be no destructive testing without giving every interested party an opportunity to be present along with an expert. I suggest that since the Medical Examiner's Office is involved, it should store the machine at its facility. The Medical Examiner's investigator nixes that idea but recommends that it be placed in the Police Department's storage room. We agree and the police are called.

When I arrive in my office around 3:30, I find thirteen telephone messages, most of which require a return call. I learn that two cases were settled and a person with a 2:30 appointment showed up and left after waiting about one-half hour. My secretary says that she was very angry.

I dictate a memo to the file concerning the test because I am certain that a lawsuit will be filed. I sort through the telephone messages and mail so I can arrange them according to some priority.

At 4:30 I receive a telephone call from a friend who is being investigated by the FBI. He wants my advice. I make an appointment for the next day. Next I receive a call from a representative of Farmers Insurance Group. He has a question concerning the value of a case and what should be paid to settle it. I recommend a figure. I answer a few letters and review tomorrow's schedule. I realize that I have a deposition scheduled at the same time that I set the appointment for my friend. I call him back but there is no answer. My calendar indicates that I have a trial next week and there are some things that I must do to be ready for it. I make a list. It is now 6:10 and it is dark outside. There is still a lot of work to be done but it will have to wait until tomorrow.

Leslie Cohen: Disability Law

When I decided to go to law school, it was always to become a "peoples" lawyer. I always wanted to fight for individuals' civil rights. However, when I went to law school, I perceived that fight to involve struggling against racism and sexism, and encroachments on first amendment rights. At that time, little did I know that 12 years later I would actually be fighting discrimination, but for a different group of people—one of the last groups to gain civil rights in our society—persons with serious disabilities or mental illness.

For the last three years, I have been working for a public interest law firm which is the recipient of several federal grants to represent persons with disabilities to be free from abuse and neglect, free from discrimination and to promote access to adequate services and programs. No day is a typical day, but any day could include part of the following:

I discuss with an advocate on how to approach a school district's failure to provide a child with traumatic brain injury appropriate services. Under the federal Individuals with Disabilities Education Act, all school districts are required to provide children with special needs a free and appropriate education including any related services they may need. Should we request a hearing to get the school district to pay for the services of a cognitive trainer to help the child? We decide to submit our expert's report and let the school district respond.

I next speak with an attorney in our office about a pending Americans with Disabilities Act case. Her client, who is deaf, has not been provided interpreter services during required training and in-service meetings at his job. The client is frustrated and feels he can't learn how to do his job better or advance because he is not receiving the technical assistance other workers are. We are in negotiations with the employer and discuss whether providing the client with interpreter services in the future will be enough, or should he receive remedial training and/or compensation for being denied an interpreter for so long.

I receive a phone call that a former client, who had been inappropriately institutionalized at the state hospital for many years. Now he might be returned. Evidently, through lack of appropriate care at a local mental health agency, the client has deteriorated and is in need of hospitalization. I dash off a letter to the local mental health agency telling them of the situation and demanding that they stabilize our client's care so that he can be returned to his community placement.

I then rush off to a meeting of persons discussing proposed legislative changes to the criminal rules concerning the competency to stand trial law. I am concerned that proposed changes may result in incarceration of individuals with mental disability for long periods of time unnecessarily and in contravention of constitutional principles.

There are just a few of the issues I will address on any given day. Representing persons with disabilities involves important civil rights issues. As our jurisprudence begins to address the rights of persons in the United States who have been previously ignored, such as persons with disabilities, gays and lesbians, immigrants, and children, there should be lots of exciting opportunities available for law students to enter public interest law.

Mike Chiorazzi: Law Librarian/Legal Information Specialist

To quote a famous 20th century philosopher poet, "Lately it occurs to me, what a long, strange trip it's been."

I entered law school with no real idea exactly what an attorney did, let alone what kind of law I would like to practice. Then, one day in my first year, a light bulb went on. I was being trained in this newfangled thing called Westlaw. I had, what was for me, a profound insight—this computer stuff is going to be big! That was the extent of my vision. I never claimed to be particularly deep.

Talking with law school librarians, I found that several of them had law degrees. As I learned more about what they did, an idea took hold; after law school I would go to library school. At worst, I could delay adulthood for a year; at best, I could find a career. My decision was not well received by my family. They had hoped for another F. Lee Bailey Jr.; they were getting Marian the Librarian.

What do law librarians do? Work in law firms, corporations, legislative libraries, administrative agencies, court libraries, law book publishing houses and law school libraries. The field also offers opportunities to specialize, in areas such as foreign, comparative and international law, collection development (what to buy to meet an institution's needs), special collections (rare books), and web design. There are more law librarians out there than you might think—the American Association of Law Libraries boasts over 5000 members.

I work in an academic setting and have found the work always interesting, varied and challenging. Starting as a reference librarian, I assisted and trained library patrons in the use of library materials. One moment it might be members of the public researching their own legal problems (from barking dogs to Living Wills), the next a professor interested in a comprehensive listing of 19th century contract treatises. I also taught a class on computer assisted legal research.

Best of all, I get to work for and with law students—an eager and intelligent group, and always interesting.

More and more law firms are hiring librarians to supervise their information technology infrastructure and to provide highly specialized expertise in in a wide array of areas of practice (some examples: complex litigation, securities law, environmental law, government contracts and intellectual property).

With the Internet becoming increasing more important, the demand for librarians, and their knowledge of cutting edge technologies, will surely increase. What the Internet needs is a good librarian.

Beginning law school, I never in my wildest dreams imagined a career as a law librarian. It's not for everyone, but since I have thoroughly enjoyed the long, strange trip I've never looked back.And, after a while, even my family came to agree that I made a great decision.

William C. Canby, Jr.:
Federal Appeals Judge

My work cycle is monthly, not daily. One week a month I travel to another city to hear appellate arguments. The other three weeks I am home in chambers dealing with the results of those arguments.

An Argument Day. I arrive at the courthouse where I am supplied with a desk. I have read the briefs for today's arguments during the past week, and now review bench memos prepared by my law clerks. The bench memos summarize the facts and analyze the legal issues.

After half an hour I leave for the robing room, where I meet the other two judges assigned to hear cases with me that day. We enter the courtroom and the presiding judge calls the calendar. The first case is a criminal appeal. Was there probable cause for the search that revealed the cocaine? That determination is highly factual, and all three of us ask questions about the evidence presented at the suppression hearing.

The next case came from the National Labor Relations Board. Was there substantial evidence to support the Board's determination that a union steward was fired for union activity? He had been guilty of some unrelated discipline infractions. When there are mixed motives for firing, what is the test to determine whether the firing was permissible?

We continue through the calendar, hearing either 15 or 30 minute arguments per side in each case. I find that I am on edge during the arguments, both because I find arguments exciting and because I don't want to miss what is said or pass up the opportunity to inject my own questions. We continue through the calendar, without stopping to rule or recess. We hear an admiralty case (man overboard), a diversity case (breach of contract), and an antitrust case (vertical conspiracy).

We return to the robing room to discuss the cases. Because I have least seniority, I give my views first. Some cases are quickly disposed of; the search was legal and the conviction can be affirmed in a short memorandum. We disagree about the antitrust case; that one will take a long time, require an opinion, and I may dissent. The presiding judge makes the writing assignments and we all go to lunch. As I relax I am reminded that arguments are the most satisfying but tiring part of my job. I will spend the rest of the afternoon dictating notes of this morning's cases and getting ready for tomorrow's calendar.

A Day in Chambers. I begin by going through the morning mail, good and bad. Some are memos from other judges concurring in opinions I have drafted and circulated, almost invariably with minor suggestions or corrections. One memo from another judge suggests that one of my proposed opinions is seriously off track. I will have to go back through the opinion, read the cases the other judge cites, and either make changes or risk his dissent. Next I review two proposed opinions by judges in cases where I was a member of the panel; they were heard six weeks ago. I assign each to one of my three law clerks for review. Each will come back to me with a memorandum commenting on the draft.

I next work on the pile of proposed opinions that have come back from my clerks with such memoranda. I go through each opinion, read a case or two if crucial, and check my notes from argument against the opinion. I review my clerks' comments. I then draft a memorandum to the other judge, perhaps concurring, including suggestions for change and noting possible problems.

I meet with my secretary and law clerks together to go over the work in the office. How many opinions are in the mill, and how late they are? Clerks are making initial drafts of almost all of them; I am working on one or two from scratch. We review assignments of bench memos for next month's arguments, and set deadlines for them.

Finally, I get to work on an opinion I am writing: Indian law. I have been working on it off and on for six weeks, and find it difficult and challenging. Ideas for it keep coming up when I am doing other things, and I use some of them. Soon I will float it to my colleagues; eventually it will come down, I hope the way I want it to. *The result matters to a lot of people.* Sometimes it is hard to see that fact behind all the paper in the office, but it comes to the surface every so often. And that makes all the matter to me.

Barbara Sattler: Criminal Defense, Solo Practice

I used to watch Perry Mason and think about how great it must be to be a criminal defense attorney. At the time it was only a dream because I didn't know any lawyers, no one in my family had ever graduated from college, and all the lawyers I saw on TV were men. By the mid–70's the world had changed considerably. After living through the 60's and earning a BA and MA, I found myself working as a counselor in a state agency feeling extremely frustrated because my efforts to help people seemed fruitless due to bureaucracy and regulations.

At the old age of 29, I revived the long-dormant idea to going to law school. Now fifteen years later, after trying over a hundred cases including murder, terrorism, and dog abuse, I am a sole-practitioner doing criminal defense, and trying to raise a child. To my surprise I often do more counseling than legal work and still butt my head against a system that seems unresponsive, hostile and unconcerned with individual justice. Often my most valuable service to a client is listening or hand-holding, rather than giving legal services.

With all its frustrations, I wouldn't give up criminal defense or private practice.

Criminal defense work is fast-paced and exhilarating. People ask me all the time, "How can you represent those people and sleep at night?" Although sometimes the people I represent are stupid, uneducated, and may have committed a heinous act, the system is so badly skewed, to punish and to expedite, that the majority of the time the punishment so outweighs the crime that representation is easy. Someone once said a criminal defense lawyer sees "bad" people at their best; a divorce lawyer sees "good" people at their worst. What is difficult for me is dealing with prosecutors who seem more concerned with statistics, and judges who seem more concerned with expediting their calendar than with finding what justice is, or trying to solve a real social problem.

At the end of a trial which didn't go well, I may question my performance (perhaps I could have been better, but I never question that my client deserves my best).

On a typical day, before going to the office, I have to figure out with my husband who will take and pick up our son at daycare and arrange for his other daily activities. Because I run a business (and employ a full-time secretary, part-time attorney, and other support staff), often many hours in the day are filled with administrative matters such as paying bills, deciding what books and supplies are needed or can be put off, fighting with the IRS, and my version of billable hours. These are problems neither law school nor my five years as a public defender ever prepared me for.

I usually handle around twenty active cases (not including inactive appeals or cases which are in other stages of waiting) which typically include DUI's, drug cases, child molestation and rape, domestic violence, and murder. On a typical day I talk to clients (this is where the counseling comes in), write motions, write letters begging for, or explaining, why a certain deal or plea bargain should be given, go to court hearings, interview witnesses, do research and speak with other lawyers, probation officers, or police officers. Sometimes I don't have time to eat lunch or make a personal call.

I will never forget the first time I head the words "not guilty," nor the first time I heard "not guilty," in a murder case. I still feel a thrill seeing my name in print or my picture on TV (at least on a good hair day) and, of course, winning a case. However, over time what has provided the most satisfaction and pride is receiving cards from clients who are writing to thank me, not because of the result (which sometimes is not good), but because they know I fought hard, did my best, and, most importantly, cared.

Jane Anon: Holiday Letter from Second–
Year Associate in Large Firm

Dear Friends & Family:

I am writing you my First Annual Holiday Letter. I apologize that it is emailed to you and not in a letter but I haven't had time to buy a) cards b) stamps or c) to address envelopes. Frankly I'm not sure where my address book is. It may well be buried underneath a pile of laundry. Or leftover take-out. Considering how rarely I am home, you would think my apartment would be cleaner, but quite the opposite: I tend to think when I do have time off, I deserve to spend it resting, not tidying.

This has been a year of ups and downs for the family. I should point out that the family consists of me, my five plants, my possible rodent problem (see take-out containers, supra), and all the motions I have given birth to this year. The motion family has been a mixed bag. Back at the beginning of the year I was able to really nurture them and they turned into fine upstanding citizens with a command of the facts, attention to deal, and real persuasive skills. They were winners. But then, I don't know, people wanted me to write more and more of them, and their gestation periods grew very short. Now people seem to want me to write a motion in about a day, or perhaps six hours. All I can say is they're just asking for crack babies.

I know what you're thinking, that this is a pretty pathetic holiday letter. It doesn't have any PEO-PLE in it, you're saying. Why is she talking about her motions like they are her children? Let me explain. You see, here at the Firm, we learn you don't need to have people in your life to be happy! In fact, the people you deal with—opposing counsel—make you want to have even less contact with people, unless it's contact between them and the grille of your car. The only people you need in your life are those on your Team. If you have others in your life, they might not understand why you need to work on Christmas Day. And your birthday. For example, the Firm fed-exed work to me at my parents' house the day after Thanksgiving last year. Perhaps Fed Ex doesn't deliver on Thanksgiving itself.

Nevertheless, this year I learned a great deal. I made three court appearances, took two depositions, and wrote seven hundred motions. I have learned that Receiving a Fax is almost always a bad thing. I have learned that if you manage to stay awake past 3am or so, you get a second wind and feel like you've slept. I have learned that it is better to work on Sunday because you are less distracted. I have learned that if you stop exercising altogether you don't get fat right away but one day you wonder what happened to your butt.

And I learned that while practicing for a big firm can sometimes be very hard, it can also be great. Winning is great. I have written some motions that have had big impacts, and the partners here are very good about giving credit where credit is due. It is a fantastic feeling to know that your work and ideas and writing and research convinced a judge to rule for you. It is good to work with people who are extremely smart; I am learning a lot from them and feel like my writing has improved immensely. I like having responsibility and figuring out hard-to-solve problems. I like having clients that people have heard of. On the other hand, I worry I should be using my law degree to help people more, not corporations. I know there are pro bono opportunities, but I never seem to have enough time. Overall, I enjoy the intellectual challenge of the work and think my cases pose interesting challenges.

And I learned that my friends and family are pretty patient with me, even though I never see them. I keep promising I'll call soon. When things slow down. Soon, I promise. Right after I finish this motion.

Andy Silverman: Legal Aid

It is 9 a.m. I arrived at work awhile ago. The waiting room is filling up and it is my day to be "on."

Being "on" in the legal services parlance signifies your day to do intake interviews. It is the first time the client talks to a lawyer. Such days generally amount to 10 to 15 of these encounters ... the real guts of a legal services practice. I know it is a day that I will get no other work done but seeing clients.

The phone rings ... it is the intake worker informing me that my first client is ready. I am now officially "on" and the stream of clients may go on all day, one right after another.

A young woman with a three-year-old tagging along walks into my office. After the introductions, I go for the extra legal pad and colored pens I always have ready and hand them to the child. I know that if the interview is going to be at all meaningful I have to keep the child happy and busy.

The woman tells me that she is two months behind in rent and the landlord has sent her an eviction notice. She has been out-of-work for the past four months and her ex-husband who she cannot find has not paid child support for the past year. Her problems sound overwhelming. Where do I start? Is there anything legally I can do?

Well, being a lawyer, my initial reaction is to think of legal remedies, the law school approach to the problem. Is there a violation of the landlord-tenant law? Is the eviction notice proper? Will she have any defenses to a possible unlawful detainer action? I start going down this road and quickly realize she can no longer afford this apartment and all she wants is time to find suitable but cheaper housing for her and her child. A phone call to the landlord from me, the lawyer, might do it. She tried the day before and failed. I call and the landlord reluctantly agrees. And another call to a friend in the public housing office helps her cut through the bureaucratic maze to find new housing. She leaves a bit relieved.

Before my next client I think about whether I am a lawyer or a social worker. Did my last client need a lawyer? Or did I do for her just what a corporate attorney does for the corporation president: identify the true problem and find the easiest and fastest way to resolve it. Well, it does not matter, I helped someone and that's all that really counts.

No more time to reflect, the next client is standing at the door. He is a man in his 50's who works part-time as a laborer. He had purchased an insurance policy because of a newspaper advertisement that had made generous promises. But when he became ill, the company said his claim was not covered. Sounds like a legal problem and one that another lawyer in the office may be interested in pursuing. She has handled similar problems and is looking for "the" case to litigate. This may be the one. I get the facts and tell the client we will be in contact. I will talk to the other lawyer tomorrow when I am "off" intake.

Legal problems keep flowing in all day. Food stamp cutoffs, car repossessions, housing foreclosures, there is no end. They have one common ingredient: a person in trouble that needs help. That personal side of legal services keeps me going. It is frustrating; it is gratifying; it is being a legal services attorney.

At the end of the day an older woman walks into my office as my final intake of the day. She does not speak English well but gets across that her son is in the county jail. My first reaction is that she has a criminal problem which legal aid lawyers do not handle. In my tired state I think that I may be able to get rid of this problem quickly. But I hear her out and become fascinated. I remain after closing hours talking to her about her son's complaints about the conditions in the jail. I have heard about that "awful jail" for years but now may have a real, live client that wants to do something about it. She tells me that her son and others in the jail would like to talk to a lawyer about such a suit. I promise her I will see her son tomorrow. It all seems worth it.

Jamie Ratner: Government Attorney

When I was in law school, I did not have any definitive plan for what I was going to do when I got out. I ended up taking a job with the Transportation Section of the Antitrust Division of the U.S. Department of Justice. I did not have a lifelong dream to prosecute, and in fact philosophically I was not inclined to be a prosecutor. But the job was wonderful. It gave me an opportunity to see from the inside how the U.S. government behaves, it gave me a chance to live and work in Washington, D.C. (which is a fascinating place to live for awhile, although not necessarily a place to ultimately settle down), and it gave me a chance to practice law in a setting where the client was only good analysis and the right thing to do.

Practicing law for the government is a unique thing, but in many ways I consider it the only way to practice law. Money is not the issue: getting it right is the issue. If you think something should be done, you do something. If you think something should not be pursued, you recommend dropping it. Sure, it is a little hard on your stomach lining when you are asked to cross-examine a well-known econo- mist during an airline merger hearing at the Civil Aeronautics Board before you have found out whether you passed the bar. True, you spend a lot of nights at the office when a merger of the South- ern Pacific and Santa Fe Railroads is dropped in your lap and you and another lawyer are told that the two of you are the two people in the country responsible for making sure that the railroad indus- try in the western United States remains competi- tive.

But one great thing about practicing law for the government is that very early on, you get responsi- bility and great work. If you accept that responsibil- ity and do your work properly, you can accomplish a lot. Your job makes you the adult in charge. You investigate and prosecute price fixers who are tak- ing money from ordinary consumers. You make sure mergers don't give a firm so much power that there will be significant harm to the economy. You help to develop coherent policies concerning deregu- lation of the airline industry. You write Senators explaining the economic and legal implications of proposed legislation and you may even help negoti- ate treaties.

I will never forget the people. Most of us, non- lawyer and lawyer alike, were there because they liked the work and cared about it, and we were all in it together rather than competitors for some mythical status on some hierarchy. Usually we worked in staffs of two or three. We traveled together, investigated together, threw frisbees down the hall shattering everyone's name plates, jointly wrote briefs and memos and stuck our own brand of humor in the footnotes, played softball, fought with the front office and opposing counsel, and spent a lot of time in that strange state which is relaxation and intensity and humor and frustration all combined in the same space at the same time. Some of my colleagues even married each other. Some of the smartest, most capable, and funniest people I have met in my life I had the opportunity to work with at Justice, and some of them remain my closest friends.

I don't want to lie to you—while I treasured my time in Washington, working for the government in Washington, D.C. can also drive you to the brink. The tourist traffic around the White House gets on your nerves when you are running a grand jury at the federal courthouse and you are a little late. Or you may not have the same political bent as the people in charge. Political appointees who do not have much of a clue can be your supervisors. (What you learn to do in such a situation is to explain everything fully in an effective and persuasive way; I used to feel confident that if I had managed to explain the matter to some of the people in our front office, persuading a commission of experts or a judge would be quite easy by comparison.)

Practicing law for the government offers a large reward. It isn't monetary; it is something more lasting. You can get training, you can get experience, you can make it a career if you want, you can get things done, and you have an opportunity to accomplish things that improve the quality of life for others in the world, which is what being a lawyer is really all about.

Deborah Bernini: Judge—Trial Court

I have only been on the bench for six months, so I begin each morning by asking myself, "Is this the morning I will succumb to 'Black Robe Disease'?" I spent a good deal of my fourteen years as a litigator criticizing the boneheaded, biased, and cowardly decisions of the judges I appeared before. I had no trouble challenging their authority. Now I feel as if I have stepped through the Looking Glass.

I am amazed at how difficult it can be to "do the right thing" and how unclear the answers often are. I often feel like a first year law student, wanting to yell at the professor, "So what's the damn answer?" Evidentiary rulings are easy, as are most legal rulings. It is the questions of fact that make me pause. Decisions regarding credibility, intent, sincerity, remorse, motivation, fear, and anger are what make the courtroom one of my favorite places to be, but are also what make this job so difficult. I realize that decisiveness is one of the most appreciated qualities in a judge, but I am less quick to judge other human beings in my formal role as judge, than I ever have been in my personal life.

My biggest problem is bad lawyers. I do not mean inexperienced, but rather those who are unprepared, ignorant of the law, or some combination of the two. I have lost my patience with three lawyers in my brief tenure, and all three were criminal defense lawyers whose unpreparedness resulted in costly prices paid by their clients. Having spent most of my lawyer years as a public defender, I struggle with my desire to interrupt or intervene when a defense lawyer appears to be blowing it. Perhaps I am simply not aware of what the lawyer's tactics; perhaps my "help" is not welcome. But there are times when I know major mistakes are being made. If I feel that an accused's rights are going down the toilet, I get involved. No lawyer's ego, theory of the case, or reputation is more important to me than the right of a Defendant to get a fair trial.

I wish that lawyers talked less and said more. I cannot believe how many attorneys can talk for over thirty minutes before they tell you why they are there and what they want. I also now understand why judges fall asleep during trials. I have actually drawn blood digging my nails into the palms of my hands in an attempt to appear alert while trial lawyers waxed eloquent to a jury. Everyone in the courtroom appreciates a lawyer who can get to the point: the clerk, the court reporter, the judge, and especially the jury.

Get to the point and watch your reputation. A trial lawyer's reputation is everything. It means more than ability or talent. The best reputation is that you are honest, you quote the law correctly, and you don't play disclosure games with your opponents. Judges talk among themselves and messing up with one judge will quickly be held against you by others. That doesn't mean that you should never challenge a judge. But pick your fights carefully, find some law that backs you up, and always start with the comment: "With all due respect, your honor." It will at least give you limited immunity for any carefully disguised insults you plan.

I have the greatest job in the world. I get to spend my days in the courtroom, my favorite place to be. My goal is to see that justice is done, and sometimes I see that goal reached. I get to work hard, meet interesting people, watch talented lawyers practice their craft (sometimes), and explain to the public how important our system of justice is—and at the end of each day I go home without the worries and burdens of the trial attorney who constantly wonders if some issue was missed, if some deadline was forgotten.

I hope I always remember how hard it is to be a trial attorney. Maybe I don't have to succumb to the Disease.

Paul Bennett: Representing Children

I represent children in Juvenile Court who have been removed from their homes by Child Protective

Services. Their parents may have been neglectful, abusive, or too indisposed to care for them. Many parents have a drug or alcohol problem. Some have mental health problems. Some just need a little help to get through bad times. When the children cannot safely stay with their parents, they become wards of the Court. The Court then makes many significant decisions affecting their lives: where they live, with whom, how often they see their parents, when they can return safely home.

When I am asked what I do when I represent children, I am reminded of two lines from the Cat Stevens' song, *Father and Son*. In the first line, the Father says to his son: "You're still young, that's your fault, there's so much you have to learn." In the other, the Son replies: "It's always been the same old story. From the moment that I could talk, I was ordered to listen."

The adults in the child welfare system often exhibit a point of view like that of the Father. "What do they know? They are just kids!" And there is some truth to that. Kids have a remarkable capacity to behave like children. They can be stubborn, irrational, impulsive, self-destructive, succumb to peer acceptance, and think only of themselves. Sometimes. (What is the old adage? One teenager, one brain. Two teenagers, half a brain. Three teenagers, no brain.)

On the other hand, sometimes children can have remarkable insights into their situations, their own behaviors and even their parents' behaviors. Kids can know a whole lot more than we think they know. They have important things to say and the adults in the system need to hear what they have to say. So, on behalf of the child in the song, our job is to get others to listen (and I mean really listen) to what these children have to say.

To get others to listen to our child-clients, we have to understand them ourselves. So we spend time with them and listen to what is going on in their lives. Sometimes we are all business. Sometimes we just hang out. But in all cases, we try to pay attention and build trust. We let them know that we work for them—not the other way around. We give them our best advice to help them to make good choices. But they are their choices, not ours. So, in the end, we have to be careful to express their voices, not ours.

It is not always easy. It can be frustrating to figure out what a child is really saying. Sometimes what a child wants makes no sense or is even dangerous. It can be frustrating when we are not effective in getting others to pay attention–especially when a child has something very meaningful to offer. Sometimes, it can be frustrating because the situation is bigger than any of us and all of the choices are second best.

But when it works, when we do our job well, it can be tremendously rewarding to represent a child. We know that we can make a difference in a child's life in a very positive way when we persuade a Judge or a child protective worker to see the situation through the child's perspective. At the very least, we can make the adults in the system pay attention. When we are more effective, we can help the adult decision-makers to make better decisions because they have heard the child's point of view. At our very best, we can help a child weather a most difficult time in their lives.

Charles Ares: Law Professor

Teaching law is hard work. I've been at it a long time and keeping up with movements in the law and getting prepared for class seem to take me about as long now as when I started.

But there is another way in which law teaching is hard. The longer I'm in the academic world the more I worry about just what it is that we teach our students. I don't mean "the law" and "the legal method"—we do that better and better all the time. I mean what we teach, mostly implicitly, about the role lawyers are supposed to play. We teach students from the very outset, as we should, that they are to be highly skilled partisans, that they are to be analytical and very skeptical of factual and legal propositions. They learn under our prodding to state the case as strongly in their clients' favor as the credulity of their audience will permit. They may, in fact, learn not only that truth takes many elusive forms but that sometimes it doesn't really exist. Only zealous representation of our client really counts.

I wonder how many students think that the "legal method" involves lying, or at least "massaging" the truth. Many of us who have been in the profession a while don't realize that we may, at least unconsciously, convey the wrong message to neophytes. One of the most heart warming and yet depressing statements I've heard from a law student was recently uttered at the end of my course in Professional Responsibility. On the way out of the classroom, this good and conscientious student said, "I had almost decided I didn't want to be a lawyer because I don't want to lie for people. But now that I've learned we're not supposed to lie for clients, I feel a lot better."

Good people can be good lawyers. It isn't easy, but then preserving one's integrity never is.

INDEX

References are to Pages

Acting
See Oral Argument

Admissibility/Weight
See Evidence

Affirmative Defense
See Pleadings

Analytical Ploys
"Yes ... but ... " 5
"So what?" 245–246
Arguments that eat Pittsburgh, 69, 226
Hypotheticals and analogies, 51
Law as Ping Pong, 24–26
Over and under-inclusive, 79
Reading cases: who argued what? 29–31
Relationship between issues, 22–23

Answers
See Pleadings

Anxieties
Flunking out, 158–159
Getting a job, 364–365
Making oral argument, 263
Sitting in class, 147, 156–157

Arguments that Eat Pittsburgh, 69, 226

441

Argument
    See Oral Argument:
Closing argument (trials), 321–323
Opening statements (trials), 314

Authority
Dealing with adverse authority, 225
Need to question, 125, 224–225
Primary/secondary; controlling/persuasive, 47–48

Bad Jokes, passim

Bar Review Courses, 348

Bright line rules, 77–81

Briefing cases
See Study Methods

Burdens of Proof and Their Politics
See Juries

Candor, 265–267

Canned Briefs
See Study Methods

Career Choices
    See also Lawyers Talk About Their Jobs
In general, 362–378
Distorting influences, 365
Factors to consider, 370–373
Non-legal careers, 368–369
Traditional law jobs, 369–370
What to do in law school, 373–375

Case Briefs
In general, 111–128

Casebooks
The very first one, 357

Case-in-Chief
See Trials

Cases
    See also Pretrial Process; Trials
Analyzing and distinguishing cases, 19–21
Cases of first impression, 21–22
Case synthesis, 38–40
Dicta, 122

Cases—Cont'd
Holding, 116, 122–124
How to brief cases, 111–128
How to read cases, 98–111
Overruling prior cases, 31–32

Cases of First Impression, 21–22

Circular arguments
See Loops

Classes
   See also Course Selection
In general, 129–137
Warming up, 131
Taking notes, 134–135
Terror and confusion, 152–158
Volunteering, 132, 157
Use of laptops 135

CLE
Continuing legal education, 347

Clerking
For lawyers, 355, 375
For judges, 367–368

Clinical Education, 349–350, 358

Closing Argument
In general, 321–322

Complaints
See Pleadings

Competitiveness, 151–152

Contract Cases
Lucy, Lady–Duff Gordon, 114–116
Williams v. Walker Thomas, 99–104

Controlling Authority
Two meanings of, 47–49

Course Selection,
Second and Third Years, 347–350

Cramming,
See Study Methods

Creativity
In general, 53–55

CRITS,
See Jurisprudence

Cross-Examination
See Trials

Decision Making
How judges decide, 211–229
Checks on judges, 68, 82
Deciding on grounds not argued, 28–29

Depositions
See Discovery

Dicta, 122–124

Directed Verdict
See Motions

Discovery
Generally, 302–306

Distinguishing cases
See Cases

Drafting
Dangers of precision, 67–68

Drawing the sting, 218

Dumbest One Here
Not necessarily, 150

Eats Pittsburgh, 69, 226

Editing
Cut 10%, 251
Murdering your darlings, 247–252
Practice, 253–259

Ethics
Approaches to Ethical Issues, 86–89
Candor to Court, 265–267
Closing argument, 321–322
Dealing with unfavorable material, 217–229, 265–267
Cross-examination, 319–320
Improper questions, 330

Evidence
Admission/weight, 334
Opinion evidence, lay and expert, 330–331
Hearsay, 315–317

Exams
  Generally, 161–174
    Practice test, with analysis, 175–197
Goals, 164–165
Checklists and mnemonics, 206
Common mistakes, 166–169, 183
Conclusions, importance of, 170
IRAC, 169–172
Gameday, 205–208
Multiple Choice exams, 198–204
Psyching out the prof, 206–207
Spotting Issues, 172–173
Zen and Exams, 205–208

Expert Testimony, 331

Explicitness
See "So what?"

Facts
  See Oral Argument
Factual uncertainty, 283
Operative facts in case briefs, 118–120
Statement of Facts, 212–220

Fear and Loathing, 147–160

Fees and Retainers, 285–287

Floodgates
  See Slippery Slopes

Flunking Out
It Won't Happen

Grades, 158–159

Hearsay, 315–317

High School Teaching Programs, 354

History of Legal Education, 356–358

Holding/Dicta, 122–124

Hypotheticals and analogies, 51–52

Inconvenient truths
Inconvenient authorities, 225–226
Inconvenient facts, 217–229
To test positions, 155–156

Interpretation, 60–66

Intuition, 53–55

IRAC, 169–172

IRS transitions,
Explained, 189–190, 242–244
Practice writing, 259

Journals, 145–146

Judicial Clerkships, 367–368, 379

Judicial Discretion
See Decision Making

Juries
Burden of proof, 290–291
Jury Instructions and their politics, 287–291
Jury nullification, 291
Peremptory challenges, 314
Selection (Voir Dire) 312–314

Jurisprudence
General concerns, 70–85
How judges decide, 211–229
Bright line rules, 77–81
Deciding cases on issues not argued, 28–29
Easy cases, 75–77
Fact-finding, 283
Jury Nullification, 291
Law as Science, 39, 357
Natural law, 83–85
Overruling cases, 31–32
Stare decisis—costs and benefits, 70–82
Retroactivity, 107
Theory building in law, 38–47

Jurisprudence—Cont'd
Schools of
    Critical Legal Studies, 75
    Law and Economics, 76
    Legal Formalism, 77
    Legal Realism, 77

Language
Power of, 221

Laptops, 135

Law as Science, 39, 357

Law Review
    In general, 350–353
Danger of pomposity, 159

Lawyers Talk About Their Jobs
Law Clerk, Colleen Thoene, 379
Elder Law, Robert Fleming, 383
Small firm/big firm, Amy Wilkins, 386
Criminal Defense, Dan Cooper, 389
Mid–Size Firm, Grace McIlvain, 391
Large Firm, Law Teaching, Theresa Gabaldon, 394
Mid-size firm, Bryce Alstead, 396
Criminal Prosecution, Randy Stevens, 399
Domestic Violence, Zelda B. Harris, 401
Judge of Juvenile Court, Hector Campoy, 403
JAG, Vicki Marcus, 404
Large Firm, Rita A Meiser, 407
Representing Workers, Margaret McIntyre, 409
Mid–Size Firm, Richard Davis 413
Disability Law, Leslie Cohen, 416
Law Librarian, Mike Chiorazzi 418
Federal Appeals Judge, William C. Canby , Jr., 420
Criminal Defense, Solo Practice, Barbara Sattler, 423
Large Firm, Jane Anon, 426
Legal Aid, Andy Silverman, 428
Government Lawyer, Jamie Ratner, 431
Trial Court Judge, Deborah Bernini, 434
Representing Children, Paul Bennett, 436
Law Professor, Charles Ares, 439

Leading Questions
See Trials

Legal Education
A brief history, 356–358
Compared to undergraduate, 1–6
Distortions,
    On stereotyping clients, 358–360
    On career choices, 365–367
    On common sense, 360–361
    On stressing law over fact, 213
Theoretical approach cheered, 345–347
The depressing (or refreshing) uniformity of, 6

Legal Writing
        See also, Case Briefs, Exams, Editing, Transitions
    Generally, 230–246
Editing, 247–252
How judges decide, 211–229
Goal, 230–231
Hallmarks of good writing, 238–246
Getting better and getting started, 233–236
Quotes, 238
Stating facts, 212–224
Stating law, 224–226
Writing Exercises, 253–261

Loops
See Circular arguments

Memorization,
Retention and retrieval, 7–8

Motions
Pretrial motions designed to avoid trial, 306–310

Moot Court, 262–282

Natural Law, 83–85

Negligence
Pleadings, 296–298
Investigation, 291–295
Jury Instructions 288–289

Note-taking
See Classes

Operative Facts, 118–120

Opening lines
Importance of, 220–221

Opening Statements
See Trials

Opinion Evidence
See Evidence

Oral Argument
    Generally, 262–277
Goal, 263
Illustrated, 278–282
Acting insights, 275–277
Arguing facts and telling stories, 212–220
Arguing precedent and policy, 224–229
Arguing what you don't believe, 266–267
Argument as ping-pong 24–26
As conversation, 264
Reversibility of legal arguments, 107
Themes and exit lines, 271
Use of hypotheticals and analogies, 51

Over and Under-inclusiveness, 79

Overruling Cases, 31–32

Outlines, 138–140

Peremptory Challenges
See Juries

Persuasive Authority, 47

Ping-Pong and the law, 24–26

Pleadings
    See generally, Pretrial Process
Answer, with affirmative defense, 300–301
Complaint, with alternative theories, 296–298
Demurrer, 309
Motion for summary judgment, 306–309
Motion to dismiss, 308
Notice Pleading, 299

Points and Authorities, 310

Policy Arguments, 55–56, 227–229

Practice Opportunities
Briefing Cases, 111–116

Practice Opportunities—Cont'd
Distinguishing cases, 13–18
Critiquing an Office Memo, 253–259
Reading Cases, 98–105
Synthesizing cases, 38–47
Taking a law exam, 175–182
        Short practice tests, 33–37
Writing transitions, 259
Writing a statement of facts, 213–215

Precedent
Arguing precedent, 224–227
Following and distinguishing cases, 16–17
Rationale of stare decisis, 70–82

Predictability, 73–81

Pretrial Process
        See also Pleadings, Discovery
        Generally, 296–310
Case planning, 285–295

Primary Authority, 47–48

Prior Inconsistent Statements, 317

Pro Bono Activities, 353–356

Psychological Aspects
        Generally, 147–160
Class participation, 156–158
Competitiveness, 151–152
Fear of greatness, 367
Fear of failure, 158–159
Self-doubt, 150–151

Quandaries, Solved
Chicken/egg, 53
Trees falling in forests, 322–323

Relativism 153–154

Restatements 78

Retroactivity of statutes and cases, 106–107

Rules versus Standards, 79

Secondary Authority, 48

Silence
Importance of, 275–276

Slippery Slopes
Responses, 57–58, 228–229

So what? 245–246

Solo Practice, 371–372

Socratic Method, 152–158

Sources
Abraham Maslow, 367
A Man for All Seasons, 60, 378
Alessandro Manzoni, 295
Anna Quindlen, 135
Benjamin Cardozo, 79–80
Carl Rogers, 150
C.B. King, 346
Christopher Columbus Langdell, 39, 356
Dan Dobbs, 188
Elihu Root, 89
Emmanuel Kant, 73, 87
Francis Wellman, 320
Fred Rodell, 352
Gary Bellow, passim
George Orwell, 267, 364
Grant Gilmore, 94, 96
Ian McEwan, p. vii
Irving Younger, 316
Jeremy Paul, 172
Jerome Frank, 222, 283
John W. Davis, 212, 264
Kay Kavanagh, 144
Karl Llwellyn, 77
Max Weber, 155–156
Maurice Sendak, 129
Ms. Fizzle, 97
Norman Mailer, 236
Oliver Wendell Holmes, 44, 125, 224, 351
Plato, 153
Paul Bergman, 319
Paul Freund, 5
Paula Nailor, 144
Porgy and Bess, 242
Richard Fischi, 172

Sources—Cont'd
Richard Pryor, 85
Rogelio Lasso, 187
Robert Bolt, 60, 378
Robert Browning, 235
Scott Turow, 147–148
Shakespeare, 159, 198, 222, 276
Shylock, 222–223
Sir Oracle, 159
Sir Toby, 276
Stanislavsky, 277
Stephen King, 83, 234, 237, 251, 362
Thomas Kuhn, 44
Tom Shaffer, 88
Tom Wolfe, 366
Wendell Berry, 94
William Blake 341
William James, 7, 38, 94
William Simon, 359

Split Brain Research, 53

Spotting issues, 172–173

Stare Decisis
Pros and Cons, 70–82

Status Quo
Need to question, 17, 125

Statutes
Method of Interpretation, 60–66
Relationship to case law, 60

Story telling 212–224

Student Practice Rules, 349

Study Methods
Briefing cases, 111–113
Cramming, 8
Outlining and old exams, 140
Reading cases, 98–111
Study Aids, 138
Study Groups, 141
Time, 143–144
Trees and Forests, 145
Writing, importance of, 138

Study Groups, 141

Summary Judgment
See Pleadings

Teaching Yourself
    See Practice Opportunities, Journals
After taking exams, 207–208

Transitions
IRS transitions, 189–190, 242–244
Practice writing, 259

Trees and Forests, 145

Trials
    See Evidence
Overview, 311–312
A trial illustrated, 324–342
Case-in-Chief, 315
Closing argument, 321–322
Cross-examination, 319–321
Impeachment with prior statements, 317
Jury instructions, 287–291
Jury selection, 312–314
Leading questions, 317–319
Opening Statement, 314–315
Rebuttal, 321

Values
See Ethics

Voir Dire
Jury, 312–314

Volunteering in class, 132

Witnesses
    See Evidence, Trials
Expert and lay, 330–331

Writing
    See Legal Writing
Writing down the middle, 27
Virtues of, 138

†